History of Italian Arc

History of Italian Architecture, 1944–1985

Manfredo Tafuri

translated by Jessica Levine

The MIT Press
Cambridge, Massachusetts
London, England

Second Printing, 1990

This work originally appeared in Italy under the title *Storia
dell'architettura italiana, 1944–1985,* © 1982, 1986 Giulio Einaudi
editore s.p.a., Torino.

This book was printed and bound by Halliday Lithograph in the
United States of America.

Library of Congress Cataloging-in-Publication Data
Tafuri, Manfredo.
    [Storia dell'architettura italiana, 1944–1985. English]
    History of Italian architecture, 1944–1985 / Manfredo Tafuri;
translated by
    Jessica Levine.
        p.   cm.
Translation of: Storia dell'architettura italiana, 1944–1985.
    Bibliography: p.
    Includes index.
    ISBN 0-262-20067-8
    1. Architecture, Modern—20th century—Italy. 2. Architec-
ture—Italy.
        I. Title.
    NA1118.T3413 1988
    720'.945—dc19   88-17482
                                                      CIP

Contents

Part One: 1944–1979

Preface   vii

1
The Years of Reconstruction   3

2
Aufklärung I: Adriano Olivetti
and the *Communitas* of the
Intellect   35

3
The Myth of Equilibrium: The
Vanoni Plan and INA-Casa's
Second Seven Years   41

4
Aufklärung II: The Museum,
History, and Metaphor
(1951–1967)   49

5
New Crises and New Strategies
(1968–1975)   97

6
Two "Masters": Carlo Scarpa
and Giuseppe Samonà   111

Part Two: 1980–1985

7
The Fragment and the City:
Research and *Exempla* of the
Seventies   117

8
Architecture as Dialogue
and Architecture as "Civil
Invective"   129

9
The "Case" of Aldo Rossi   135

10
Rigorism and Abstinence:
Toward the 1980s   141

11
Structural Transformations
and New Experiences in
Planning   149

12
The Paradigms of
Pluralism   169

13
Venice 1985: The Architecture
Biennale   185

14
"Gay Errancy": Hypermoderns
(Postmoderns)   189

15
The Threshold and the
Problem   195

Notes   203

Bibliographical Appendix   251

Index   263

Preface

Upon the kind invitation of friends at the Einaudi publishing company, I have agreed to republish in the present volume the essay that originally appeared in 1982 in the series *History of Italian Art (Storia dell'arte italiana)* as part two of the seventh volume *The Twentieth Century (Il novecento)*, edited by Federico Zeri. The reader will find those pages, written between the end of 1979 and 1981, reprinted here with some additions and corrections. The historical perspective that underlies them has not changed, nor do any writings appear to have been published in the meantime that would significantly call into question the general outlines or the particulars of this essay written fours years ago. On the other hand, a second part has been added for reasons more complex than those that might justify a simple updating of the material: above all, the need to adjust the parameters of judgment. Actually, the geographical limits of the area under analysis are not a function of the partial results of the research undertaken, but more a response to editorial criteria: the assumption about the "Italian-ness" of a certain sector of art history could only be questioned in the present context. On the other hand, in studying the develop-ment of twentieth-century architecture, one can readily accept the premise of the specificity of the Italian contribution and debate; what is lost in breadth of plot is recovered in the arena of analysis.

The discourse becomes less linear when one begins to confront the situation of the early eighties, not because one is here dealing with something that has not yet "concluded its cycle"—the

historicist obsession with a *telos* that justifies and explains that
everything is still strong—nor because the "distance" from the
events is small. A historian of the present is always working with
perspectives conditioned by short distances and has at his disposal
methods to construct artificial distances. In the case at hand, it is a
matter of going beyond the symptoms of malaise that characterize
recent architecture, of not lending an ear to jubilant declarations of
faith, of not turning our backs too quickly on the annoying—and
deafening—buzz of opinion, and of immersing what the *res aedifi-
catoria* says about itself in that which it cannot say, or in that which
our language strives to say. In order to deal with the debate on
"modernity," it is necessary to tear away the obfuscating veil that
has been placed over the theme by idle talk, by the disheartening
simplifications of the information makers and of those who
preoccupy themselves with furnishing a continuous stream of
palatable "solutions" to exorcize anxiety.

Given all this, I have outlined a program that is only minimally
respected by the chapters that the reader will find at the end of this
book. Nevertheless, these remarks may help the reader to understand not only the perspective that informs these chapters, but that
of the entire volume. Regarding the latter, a note of explanation is
in order. From the beginning, the essay presented itself as a
historical synthesis and not, therefore, as an occasion for *repêchages*
of a more or less snobbish nature, nor as an illuminating picture
for those who ask themselves every day which disguise is the most
"up to date."

The narrative of the work is nevertheless fragmented, having
adapted itself to events as it confronted them, being composed of
interweavings, isolated paths, and probings into contexts that can
be juxtaposed only with difficulty. Naturally, this is only one
version and, in addition, one conditioned by the need for synthesis, and this obliged the writer to expend much effort in dividing
up and—sometimes polemically—selecting material. In order to
create a frame of reference, it was necessary for a large part of the
narration to suggest, or rather to offer, coordinates for a more
detailed analysis. Extrapolating the essay from the context of the
volume of the Einaudi edition of the *History of Art* dedicated to the

twentieth century had, however, a disadvantage, for which the reader can compensate by heeding the following advice. One of the most significant results to have emerged from recent research—not only in the field of architectural history—regards the strong elements of continuity that link the events, and even some of the structural phenomena, that occurred in Italy in the twenties and thirties with those of an Italy emerging from the Resistance. Naturally, a good sense of balance is necessary to assess those elements of continuity without reducing the change undergone to a negligible *événement*. Still, just by perceiving the dialectic between the two times, many actions taken and choices made during the period of reconstruction—as well as in more recent years—become comprehensible. In the 1982 edition, the break between epochs was bridged by the contiguity of the essay presented here with the one that preceded it, Giorgio Ciucci's "The Debate on Architecture and Fascist Cities"("Il dibattito sull'architettura e le città fasciste"), an essay built on theses generally close to ours and permitting connected and interwoven readings. A reference to that text at this juncture is therefore obligatory.

One last comment to the reader. In this book you will not find terms such as *modern movement, rationalism, neorationalism,* and *tendency;* the term *postmodern* has also been redefined. As our most informed historiography demonstrates, such formulas in fact conceal deep ambiguities and reflect historical considerations that have since become useless.

Bibliographical references covering the years 1944–81 appear in the notes at the end of the book. On the other hand, in order to minimize the use of such notes and for the reader's convenience, texts on various topics published between 1982 and 1985 have been gathered in a bibliographical appendix, though a few of these are also cited in the last chapter.

Finally, the choice of illustrations corresponds not to criteria of personal taste but, as is obvious, to criteria of historical documentation.

Rome-Venice, March 1986

Part One

1944–1979

1
The Years of Reconstruction

After the end of the Second World War, architects who were obliged to respond to the new Italian reality were faced with a difficult dialectic between knowledge and action[1]—difficult because of the contradictory foundations underlying the tradition of the discipline, but also because of the many levels imposed on such knowledge. This was all the more true given that the most competent members of the profession took it for granted that there could be no knowledge divorced from action: an encounter with active politics seemed imperative. In their feverish search for identity, the Italian architects proceeded through a succession of ideologies, continually relying on extradisciplinary themes. It would be almost too simplistic to locate in this "relationship with history" a thread linking the research of the neorealist era to the extreme results of the voyages back in time taken by architects like Carlo Scarpa, Ernesto Rogers, Gabetti and Isola, Aldo Rossi, and Franco Purini. Yet, if Mario Ridolfi, Franco Albini, and Rogers valued the imperative connecting "I am" to "they were thus," the experience of the seventies supported rather the imperative tying the "it is" of architecture to the first sources of its being. The search for the "great house" of architecture was also present in the initial experiments following the war, hidden under terms not as yet suspected of Heideggerian influence.

This is said, however, with an inevitable appeal to schematism. The reexamination of the recent past was characterized by a

Manichean logic, whereas the need for self-criticism did not affect the "discursive units" into which architectural knowledge was disintegrating. This self-criticism was thus limited to questions of "style." The convulsive unrest that agitated Italian architectural culture after 1945—expressed in courageous editorial initiatives, in a new presence in decision making, in the formation of groups and associations—converged on at least one point. Out of the tradition formed by Persico and Pagano—seen quickly as one and the same—were gathered up certain "moral" principles, those that inevitably seemed to lead to the "beyond of architecture." Entire areas of research undertaken in the twenties and thirties were immediately put out of reach. The dismissal was provisional, however, and would eventually be followed by the important "awakening" of more recent years.

The architects who were intent on implementing the values of the Resistance agreed only on the ethical basis of their project: they saw themselves united in the pursuit of "a program of truth." Defining the contents of that truth and the consequent forms of action was more complex. Clearly, they had to create a new cycle. It was equally clear that they had to come to terms with an "idea of reason" that, as Elio Vittorini pointed out at the time, had demonstrated its own bankruptcy.

It was no accident that the development of Italian architecture following the war began with two works conceived as emotional homages to ideals that had constituted, during the preceding twenty years, fragile points of support for an intelligentsia forced to retreat into itself. One was the Monument to the Fosse Ardeatine in Rome erected between 1944 and 1947 by Mario Fiorentino, Giuseppe Perugini, Nello Aprile, Cino Calcaprina, and Aldo Cardelli (figure 1); the other was the BPR's Monument to the Dead in the Concentration Camps in Germany built in 1946 (figure 2). The former is an impenetrable mass in suspension, a mute testimony facing the site of the massacre; the latter a metal lattice on a cross-shaped base of stone, containing at the center an urn filled with earth from the German camps.[2] In one, geometry compromises with matter, reminiscent perhaps of the Albini-Gardella-Minoletti group's project for the Palazzo dell'Acqua e della Luce at the E42: the painful memory of an event that renders all commentary rhetorical contracts into a single sign. In the other, a lyrical homage is paid to the myths of the thirties, expressed in explicit allusions to Persico and Nizzoli's trellis in the Gallery of Milan and to the "captive objects" of Marcel Duchamp, Alberto Giacometti, and Melotti. People have spoken, and rightfully so, of the BPR monument as the "commemoration of an ideal."[3] But this monument, this "too rational" lattice confronting the immensity of the massacre, also constitutes a moment of reflection that gives meaning to the theme of "continuity" later on explored by Rogers.

In the light of subsequent experiences in the Roman context, the monument to the Fosse Ardeatine was a conclusive reflection on the past; in Milan, the monument by the BPR was the focus of a cultural situation still considered to prevail. The lyricism that makes us look backward, that does not let us forget, is, however, accompanied by a commitment to search for specific tools that could contribute to the problem of reconstruction: this culture intent on the new immediately appeared to be tied to discursive practices in use since the twenties and thirties. In December 1945, at the first national convention for reconstruction building, Rogers raised his voice to lament the absence of a national plan, while Bruno Zevi offered the United States' plan for war buildings as a possible model, thereby transferring to the Italian situation an impressionistic interpretation of the New Deal.[4]

It was Giuseppe De Finetti, a former student of Adolf Loos and the spiritual heir of an austere brand of Lombard illuminism—a man completely outside the controversy surrounding the destiny of the "modern" and the author of several hypothetical proposals for a center in Milan, between 1944 and 1951 (figures 4–5)—who manifested a greater realism, interpreting the developments of the Milanese context in the light of the real estate market and promoting a new urban law that would be able to provide adequate state properties as public land.[5] But the political impediment to reconstruction escaped the architects: their petitions had to do with global intervention, and remained evasive with regard to the technical and institutional tools that would have permitted it. Moreover, a document like the one written in 1944–1945 by Della

Rocca, Muratori, Piccinato, Ridolfi, Rossi de Paoli, Tadolini, Tedeschi, and Zocca made clear the ideologies that inspired the assumptions made by Italian culture regarding reconstruction.[6] Priority in the projected intervention went to agriculture. A rural Italy would be restructured and rationalized through urban planning that focused on a "better distribution of population" and on the potential for tourism, which was seen as a secure economic vocation for the country. Italian urban planners, faced with the problem of reconstruction, tenaciously linked the architectural tradition to political and economic choices proposed "on their own." Their work tended toward "simulation" rather than "supply."

It is not, however, correct to see the urban experiments of the years immediately following the war as a real methodological jump, relative to those of the second half of the thirties and to the directives set out in the law of 1942. The enthusiasm and generous illusions that characterized the Ciellenist[*] climate made it possible to capture the still fluid contents of these elaborations in fixed models. The AR plan for a regional capital in Lombardy, begun in 1944 by the Italian CIAM group (figure 3),[7] established an urban system in which new structures would be integrated with a consolidation of the existing fabric: two loaded axes intersect, giving a decentralized office district regional viability.[8] A conservative restoration was planned for the historical center that had just been liberated; regional reorganization called for nuclei combining housing and production facilities, to be located near Gallarate, Como, Varese, Monza, and la Brianza, while actual urban agglomerations would be limited to cities of medium size. The objectives, in Milan as well as Rome, were a struggle against speculation, for the conservation of historical centers, and the development of "alternative cities." In 1946 a commission that included Luigi Piccinato, Mario Ridolfi, Aldo Della Rocca, Franco Sterbini, Ignazio Guidi, Cherubino Malpeli, and Mario De Renzi was asked to elaborate a traffic plan for greater Rome; the result was a complete

---

[*]The Ciellenists were members of the Committee for National Liberation (Comitato di Liberazione Nazionale, or C. L. N.) (translator's note).

urban program, which became the basis for the discussion that eventually generated the 1962 plan.[9]

All this remained, however, within the boundaries of a purely formal exercise. Even when—as in the case of the studies for a regional plan for the Piedmont, which was the fruit of an initiative launched by Giovanni Astengo and Mario Bianco—one encounters a project combining territorial and economic issues,[10] one notices the attempt to condense an indisputable architectural tradition. It is, however, useful to distinguish the various tendencies that characterized the Italian approach to urban planning from 1944 to 1948: the regionalism of the AR plan resembled that which inspired the plan for the Valle d'Aosta, sponsored by Adriano Olivetti in 1936-37, despite the difference in contexts. On the other hand, the plan put forth by Astengo and Bianco for the Piedmont resulted from a statement of principle and analytical research. Because of contingent pressures, Italian urbanism fell prey to dogmatic philosophies linked to ineffectual models of city development. The countryside escaped all planning; the proposals of the AR plan and those that emerged from the 1946 contest for the office district of Milan were destined to end up in a catalogue of utopias, while the gradual crumbling of hopes that followed the struggle for liberation pushed architects—especially those confronting the more dynamic clientele and rapidly growing industrial complex of the north—to articulate in form their aspirations for a new civic order.

The confrontation with history, which in a more or less ambiguous way was to characterize the subsequent course of Italian research, was, on the other hand, triggered by certain events, such as the reconstruction of bridges and of the zone of Por Santa Maria in Florence, which had been destroyed in one of the most gratuitous acts committed by the retreating German troops. In a hurried attempt to contrast the qualities of "civilization" with the ignominy of barbarism, Tuscan architects ventured upon projects and polemics that led to a feeble and greatly compromised reconstruction of the historical fabric: in spite of Giovanni Michelucci's directions—which were also riddled with uncertainty and ambiguity—the Florentine venture resulted in another failure, though it did manage to formulate problems worthy of deeper study (figure 24).[11]

The Italian architectural community soon realized, moreover, that it had to cope with many enemies, not all of them external. There was the battle against "raising the dead," of which Guido Dorso spoke, and also the struggle intellectuals waged against themselves, their own traditions, and the chains tying them to the institutions they wished to subvert.

These issues were confronted by the Association for Organic Architecture (APAO) and by Bruno Zevi, who returned to Italy upon completing his education in the United States. Zevi began his career with a 1945 volume, *Towards an Organic Architecture (Verso un'architettura organica)*, a "manifesto" not only of a historiographical choice, but also of a principle of action. The APAO and the review *Metron* were founded upon ideas put forth in this volume, the methodological lines of which were later made explicit in *Knowing How to See Architecture*.[12] For Zevi, overcoming the legacy of so-called "rationalism" did not include abandoning its notion of a revolution of consciousness. On the contrary, renewal had to complete and deepen the process, even if its ascetic Calvinism was no longer justified, now that the message contained in the terrorism of the avant-gardes had been generalized for the masses. The lessons taught by Frank Lloyd Wright and Alvar Aalto had to be absorbed in order to "liberate" forms, to bend them to a "human" use of space. But Zevi's insistence on spatial values was treated metaphorically. Space is the protagonist whenever there is a dialogue between projection and realization, whenever oscillation between natural and artificial conditions allows a recuperation of "places," and whenever the ambience of a democratic society is made visible. Zevi was unique in attempting to integrate the analytical method of the "Vienna school" with the heritage of Croce and with the desire to intervene in contingent action that was determined by history.[13] The lesson of Francesco De Sanctis, among others, appears in the historiographical method of the young Zevi; the reflection on the past is determined by perspectives made available to the present, while the guiding element is a generous passion directed toward the future. In the stagnant climate of architectural historiography following the war, Zevi's voice decried a methodological renewal whose great historical significance must be acknowledged. Proposing a formal "manner" was undoubtedly far from Zevi's agenda. But his approach catalyzed energies that would otherwise have lacked a center; moreover, it was too mythical not to become adapted to every use. In its ideological program, the APAO affirmed its intention to pursue freedom in urban planning and design as methods for the construction of a struggling democratic society: social freedom would be guaranteed by the socialization of the great industrial, financial, and agrarian complexes.[14] This appeal remained, however, generic and lacked relation to the urgent dilemmas concerning the built environment. Politics were alluded to rather than practiced by the APAO. Its specific objectives were also vague: the formula "organic architecture equals an architecture of democracy" was more useful for self-definition than recognition. The appeals to orthodoxy made by the Movimento Studi di Architettura (MSA) in Milan and the Pagano group in Turin could not compensate for the ambiguities of Roman culture; these formulas concealed a basic uncertainty that historiographical analysis had yet to remove. And yet, reviews like *Metron, Domus* (edited from 1946 to 1947 by Rogers) and *La nuova città* (edited by Giovanni Michelucci from 1945 on), inherited with different orientations the polemical essence of Pagano's *Casabella*. But the fate of the first remained tied to the APAO, the second, presenting itself as aristocratic, barely affected militant architecture,[15] and the third was constrained by its local boundaries. One can, however, credit the writers of this period with broadening the relevance of critical analysis and with revising the historical heritage of the so-called "modern movement" in ways that would soon prove fruitful.

In the meantime, those interested in formulating a new language—one without ambiguous claims on the recent past that might harmonize with hopes for a democratic system and with values expressed by the Resistance—were moving toward neorealism along different paths.[16]

It is almost too easy to sketch an archaeology of architectural neorealism. The exhibition of rural architecture at the sixth Triennale of Milan in 1936, which featured Pagano's debut as a photographer, Quaroni's villa at Porto Santo Stefano of 1938, and

Ridolfi's 1940 project for an agricultural concern at Sant'Elia Fiumerapido, all testify to an antirhetorical stance that resonated, in spite of itself, with the rural visions conjured up by the economic policies of a regime whose desire to respond to the request "just let us live," found its first expression in a myth of "naturalness," and which discovered an ideology of exchange in Le Corbusier's experiments with cheap materials. The dream arose of an archaeology of the future whose artifacts would be neither designed nor constructed, and which was torn by its desire to relate the diverse works mentioned to the complexes planned by Forbat for Karaganda in 1932, to residences built by Püschel at Orsk, to Melnikov's plans for farmhouses of 1918–19, and to folklore in the manner of Norristown, the stronghold of Roosevelt's "conquest" of the Tennessee region. It is impossible to compartmentalize the individuals who were part of this "tradition of the new": avant-gardes, *retours à l'ordre*, and populisms coexisted like the interchangeable masks of an actor.

Let us examine the case of Italian neorealism. Above all, one perceives a traumatic encounter with an unexpected mirror—the convention called "reality"—that reflects disturbing images. One observes emotions experienced when the pride in modesty is exchanged for the immodesty of a frustrated will to power; one traces a voyage to "where the others have been," in the hope of being able to understand the present. Neorealism was characterized by this contamination between individual and collectivity, between part and whole.

The story of the unexpected encounter between intellectuals and the subordinate masses made heroic by the Resistance was in fact autobiographical, as was the revelation of a hope projecting a will for regeneration resembling an expiation of atavistic sins onto the sentimental image of the nation. Equally autobiographical was the structure of works proud of their alienation. This was so much so that one slogan permeated the Quaroni-Ridolfi group's plan for Stazione Termini, the Tiburtino quarter, and La Martella: "I am participating; therefore we are" (figures 6, 8–9, 17–18).

Once these intellectuals had defined their positions, they became politically committed in the manner of Sartre; they chose to

identify the destiny of their technique and language w·
classes that had suddenly come to the fore, and that w
by a "loser's" past that enabled them to emerge as the
new "purities." It mattered little that this identification ᵤ.ₑᵣₒ ₐ
resembled a cathartic bath, that the intellectuals' exploration of
these traditions hid a masochistic need to identify themselves with
the losers, that their search for roots in the peasant hearth assuaged the anxiety of disorientation experienced through contact
with mass society. They could not know that, even though they
thought that they were acting like the Magi and were presenting
their own *engagement* as a gift to the newly elected, their message
was being dictated by the language of a plan whose docile tools
they had become.

But in the years right after the war, this aspect of the situation
could not have been perceived. The pride with which the new
words were spoken was proportional to the desire to erase what
were considered the compromises or errors of the period before
the war. The language of popular experience was invoked to
annul a past founded on an intellectualized or expedient reliance
on constructivist, internationalist, or neoclassical etymons. The
most eloquent work of the "Roman school," a competition project
presented in 1947 by the Quaroni-Ridolfi group for the passenger
terminal of Stazione Termini, was derived from this new program
(figure 6).

It is perhaps overly audacious to read in the project for Stazione
Termini drawn up by the Quaroni, Ridolfi, Fiorentino, Cardelli,
Caré, and Ceradini group as the image of a difficult liberation. It is
a liberation, first of all, of structure from its own materiality. That
does not in the least contradict the expressionist articulation of the
structure's cover, a "big roof" facing a city whose form is solid but
whose destiny remains uncertain. But it is a liberation, also, from
tranquilizing canons and from facile "solutions." Arrival and
departure are problematic in this project that does not relinquish
an allegorical reading—one of swallowing and expulsion—in
order to contaminate the atmosphere, to turn the covered piazza
into a homage to the contradictions of the present.[17] But can one
not see, perhaps, in the attempt to recover a mode of representa-

tion that is willfully ambiguous, and in the bundles of tendons that transmit tension to double-forked supports, a torment that implies an exorcism of technique? In 1947 Quaroni also planned the church at Prenestino in Rome,[18] using an idea he would explore further in the church at Francavilla al Mare of 1948–58: form not only aspires to unite again with technological *inventio*, but also seeks to make the very subject of technical work disappear by levitating that which is represented.[19]

A countermelody is set against the "little technique" of the *Manuale dell'architetto*. By creating a casuistry of "genres" having nothing to do with typology, oblique paths were forged, paths leading to an architecture that would not tolerate being reduced to a simple device, and that was forced, in spite of everything, to denounce its own limitations. The "liberation" of those who were becoming the masters of the "Roman school"—a liberation noted above as the ground of the Stazione Termini project—was in the end an attempt to avoid exploring the project's meaning, while presenting itself as a melancholy question mark interrogating structures of communication.

But the Quaroni-Ridolfi project for Termini says something else as well. In it the object and the *idea of the city* form a unit. In contrast to the severe but exposed structural system of Saverio Muratori's competition project for the new Auditorium di Roma,[20] a language emerging from the pain and hopes of the moment speaks in epic tones. In terms of monumentality, neorealism declaimed in unedited language.

It was not, however, a single event, but rather a general climate that constituted the terrain for neorealism. Quaroni and Ridolfi soon encountered a new class of client. For Ridolfi, the connection between works of the thirties and populist poetics was constituted by the intense research he undertook in writing his reference books.[21] Preparation for his *Contribution to the Study of the Standardization of Construction Elements (Contributo allo studio sulla normalizzazione degli elementi di fabbrica)* and his 1942 *Problems of Unification (Problemi dell'unificazione)* focused on details and the recovery of a secure "craft." Attention to typology and standardization was tied to concrete studies of the fixtures and construction details in the houses on the Via di Villa Massimo and Via San Valentino in Rome; the goal was to isolate specific elements of architectural language. Thus, the way was cleared for the taxonomy of the *Manuale dell'architetto*, published in 1946 under the auspices of the CNR (National Research Council) and URSIS: here was the abacus of a "little technique," intended for an age of reconstruction.[22] It extols the value of "experience"—the building industry of post-Fascist Italy was offered a kind of "shopkeeper's" handbook. In reality, the tradition of construction extolled by the *Manuale* resulted from a cross-section of regional cultures that were not immune to intellectualism: the vernacular Esperanto taking on technological forms celebrates a regionalism in "folk" dress that had been one of the ideological ingredients of the New Deal. The manual, which became a reference text for architecture searching for the "national-popular," served as a conduit for political ideas imported from overseas.

The *Manuale* and the typologies studied by Ridolfi for the regulation booklets of INA-Casa, as typical expressions of the Roman scene, triggered Diotallevi and Marescotti—who had already collaborated with Pagano on the project for a "horizontal city"—to write *The Social, Architectural and Economic Problem of Housing (Problema sociale costruttivo ed economico dell'abitazione)*.[23] This volume, published in Milan in 1948, opposes to the cult of construction detail a sociological and typological analysis, with explicit reference to the models of Weimar Germany, especially in its first series of models. The organization of the entire work, successively interlocking schemas, also characterized its content, which is directly connected with the great tradition of radical architecture and urban planning that developed between the two World Wars. The *Social Problem* deserved attention, but it was destined, unlike Ridolfi's *Manuale*, to become a bibliographic rarity. In context, this unfortunate editorial venture was a necessary intermediary stage in Marescotti's theoretical activity between the exhibition "La città del sole" in Catania in 1945, and his analysis of construction problems for the CGIL work plan.[24] Marescotti's commitment was directly related to demands being made by the labor movement and the cooperative movement; the limited progress of these movements resulted from the leftist defeat of 1948 and the advent of centrist politics, but also from their own internal utopias. For Marescotti, in fact, the social cooperative centers were places where consumers could organize independently, free from government bureaucracy: the cooperative association was depicted as a form of grassroots political action, in opposition to the pyramid of management. It was inevitable that Marescotti should immediately come into conflict with these parties of the left: an impasse opened between Bottoni, who offered his linear technique to the organized labor movement, and the antibureaucratic gestures of Marescotti. Marescotti's ideological populism found expression, however, in ascetic forms: his complexes for the IACP of Milan—Baravalle and Varesina in 1947, Mangiagalli in 1949—conformed faithfully to the studies for the "house of man" that he had elaborated in the thirties, whereas the social and cooperative center "Grandi e Bertacchi" of 1951–53 (figure 10) constituted the swan song of his ideas on participation.[25]

On the other hand, works like the Casa del Viticultore by Ignazio Gardella of 1945–46 and the Rifugio Pirovano in Cervinia by Albini of 1949–51 (figure 11) testify—as would the complex at Cesate later on (figure 27)—to the way in which populist ideologies penetrated even into Milan. However, especially in the refuge by Albini, these ideologies were associated with an aristocratic detachment from material form. The truth is that the volume by Diotallevi and Marescotti, the QT8 complex in Milan, some of the works executed by the BPR in the forties, such as the houses on Via Alcuino of 1945 as well as the loyalty to elementarist syntax of Figini and Pollini (as in the house on Via Broletto of 1947–48), by Ghidini and Mozzoni (the earthy villa at Gallarate of 1948), and by Piero Bottoni (the multipurpose building on the Corso Buenos Aires of 1947–49) and the refined asceticism of Asnago and Vender, whose works include the building for offices and housing in Piazza Velasca of 1950—all of the above express a radically different program for the organization of building production in an age of reconstruction. Nor is it coincidental that such a losing line evolved in an industrial center, whereas Rome maintained the winning strategy: the construction industry would absorb unemployment and remain subordinate to the financial and speculative markets.

From a formal point of view, Lombard "continuity" and Roman populism seemed to agree on at least one point: a bracketing of the problem. A common reductionist line was embraced. One spoke—even in very elaborate works—with "poor" syntaxes, as though reflecting the conditions of a historical reef that was obstructing progress.

Yet in contrast to neorealist work, there was little evidence of continuity with the modern Esperanto. And it is significant that onto the latter was grafted the social practice that had motivated the work of Marescotti and Bottoni: research geared toward mass production and an urbanistic reform of housing was unpretentiously packaged. Furthermore, the problems that Bottoni confronted in planning the experimental QT8 complex for the eighth Triennale of Milan were certainly not formal ones. Bottoni's initiative was undeniably innovative in its attempt to combine a revitalized Triennale with a gathering of the leaders of Italian architectural culture around the theme of public housing. The QT8, whose urban plan became an integral part of the master plan of Milan and of that city's plans for reconstruction, was conceived as a permanent exhibiton of new typologies, of experimental programs in construction and hygiene, and of a technology based on prefabrication and industrialization: special norms were elaborated by Luigi Mattioni in collaboration with the technical office of the Triennale—of which Bottoni was commissioner— while the different types of buildings conformed to a dry elementarism.[26]

Yet in the political and economic climate defined by Luigi Einaudi's strategy, enterprises like the QT8 and formulations like Marescotti's of the social theme of housing assumed utopian features. The monetary stabilization under Einaudi had removed the danger of inflation and had gradually reduced the national deficit. But the cost of this was an increased gap between the northern and southern regions, an unresolved problem of the foreign debt, and above all an enormous increase in unemployment, which went from 1,654,872 in 1946 to a peak of 2,142,474 in 1948. The construction industry was called upon to "resolve" the problem that had been consciously created by free trade policies. The Fanfani plan became law in February 1949, creating the Gestione INA-Casa, with the title *Provisions for increasing worker employment, facilitating the construction of labor housing (Provvedimenti per incrementare l'occupazione operaia, agevolando la costruzione di case per lavoratori).* The aims of the plan were clear: to stem the increasing rate of unemployment; to place housing in a subordinate role relative to sluggish sectors, holding it firm to a preindustrial level and tying it to the development of small business; to keep stable for as long as possible a fluctuating sector of the working class that could be blackmailed but never organized; and to make public intervention a support for private intervention.

It was not clear that the proposals for productive innovation implicit in Marescotti's handbooks or in the QT8 could be used to achieve such objectives. Rather, the elevation of a technology that was both primitive and localized, as it was revealed in the tables of the *Manuale dell'architetto* and by the aspirations of neorealism, enters into a singular consonance with such objectives: the celebration of craftsmanship, of local traditions, and of manual work. Similarly, the insistence on the organicity of installations that would be distant—both ideally and spatially—from the "city of compromise," characterizes neorealist poetics as well as INA-Casa's first seven years.[27]

INA-Casa's urban policy immediately struck the most informed as antithetical to sound urban planning. The INA-Casa complexes, moved to areas far from the urban centers in order to benefit from low-cost land, spawned further planning, stimulating the land and building speculation that, profiting from the infrastructures created by the public sector, progressively reached and encircled them. Not by chance, the program and management of the agency were shaped by Arnaldo Foschini's paternalism: through him, further continuity with the populist unrest of the Fascist era was imposed on the new reality. The Italian architects reunited in the APAO were faced with a "problem of conscience," one that would be resolved by the choice of a Realpolitik, but with important consequences for the organization's solidarity as a pressure group.

A "manifesto" of architectural neorealism, as well as INA-Casa's entire ideology during its first seven years are revealed in the Tiburtino complex in Rome (figures 8–9), which reunited, between 1949 and 1954, the two new "masters," Quaroni and Ridolfi, with young and even younger collaborators, like Carlo Aymonino, Carlo Chiarini, Mario Fiorentino, Federico Gorio, Lanza, Sergio Lenci, Piero Maria Lugli, Carlo Melograni, Giancarlo Menichetti, Rinaldi, and Michele Valori. This was another founding moment for the "Roman school."[28] Exiled from the city, the Tiburtino scornfully turned its back on it. Modeled after places of popular and rural "purity," the new complex was to reproduce the latter's vitality, "spontaneity," and humanity. No longer the rigorous grids or geometrical terrorism of the *neue Sachlichkeit:* here one exalted the craftsmanship that constituted the necessary mode of production of the complex, welcoming it as an antidote for alienation. The result was a vaguely informal plan, only marginally controlled by typology, and an architecture rich in motifs taken from the country's traditions, from the balconies of wrought iron to the traditional roof coverings, from the window designs to the sequences of external stairs and balconies. But it was right here that, involuntarily, the anti-avant-garde polemics of neorealism bit their own tail. The popular lexicon, elevated to a linguistic norm, was assumed as pure "material," especially in the blocks personally controlled by Ridolfi. Communication, sought after with so much sadness, was attained through the *deformation* of this linguistic material, through its *distortion:* the procedure was exactly the same as the one that had been propounded by formalism and the technological avant-gardes. Yet it contained another aspect. The cognitive anxiety of neorealism was revealed, on the basis of such considerations, for what it was: an intellectual group's anxiety to know itself, at worst, through an immersion into the warmth of eternal rural tranquillity; at best, through an expression of anger and of an overflowing will to communicate.

In spite of everything, the Tiburtino remained a slap in the face of petit-bourgeois respectability. Neither a city nor a suburb, the complex, strictly speaking, was also not a "town," but rather an affirmation of both rage and hope, even if the mythologies that sustained it made its rage impotent and its hope ambiguous. It was a "mood" translated into bricks, blocks, and plaster, and, like any mood, it had to be "overcome." The Tiburtino experiment should have been left behind, forgotten between the Sabine mountain, the disconnected industrial zones, the railway, and the San Lorenzo quarter, as evidence of a unilateral encounter between intellectuals and popular unrest.

This is so because it was clear that the whole destructive charge that emanated from the antiformalism of the Tiburtino, from this monument with its uncertain boundary lines belying the illusion of *engagement*, paradoxically pronounces a big "yes" to the forces that turned popular housing into an incentive for speculation and technological backwardness into a means of development for advanced sectors, and made eloquence a force of stabilization. The Tiburtino should have been left alone. Instead, the opposite occurred, and that memorable episode was reduced to a facile formula offering materials for easy use and consumption. Yet Ridofi as well as Quaroni intuited that the experience could not be repeated: their different versions of populist ideology were soon blazing new paths.

Practically in the shadow of the Tiburtino experiment, in fact, Ridolfi produced in the middle of the Roman suburbs one of the greatest testimonies of the intellectual anxiety experienced in the early fifties, and thereby demonstrated the fertility of his own linguistic competence. The nucleus of tall houses on the Viale Etiopia in Rome (figures 12–13), executed by Ridolfi for INA between 1950 and 1954, accepts the building density of what has been called the "African quarter." The continuity of the exposed concrete structure, the volumetric imperiousness of the blunt-angled towers, and the violent chiaroscuro are translated into a popular epic, voicing their own dramatic commentary on the painful participation in a human condition that cannot be assuaged with architectural "certainties." For this reason Ridolfi's proud towers adopted unprecedented solutions. The use of color, of wrought iron, and of enameled majolica was not ironic (figure 12); rather it evoked a "small scale"—in which craftsmanship still had the possibility of expressing itself—that points by contrast to the immense scale of the complex.[29] For Ridolfi, this composition "by contrast" was absolutely new. Without a doubt, the designer found for himself in the Viale Etiopia a situation that pushed him to set aside all sentimentalism and nostalgia; the sensitivity of his treatment of the concrete framework and roofs, which respond in an austere manner to the "shameless" variations of the details, indicates the architect's passage from neorealism to realism.

This was a realism that, in spite of all that has been written to the contrary,[30] was not picked up by Mario Fiorentino in his residential towers built between 1955 and 1962 on the same Viale Etiopia, near the edge of the railway. Graciously agnostic, Fiorentino's towers mitigate the tensions in Ridolfi's work, presenting themselves as "civil" diversions in a violent suburb. Ridolfi's expressive instruments risked being consumed; it is almost too easy to go from *Rome Open City* to *Bread Love and Fantasy*. But Ridolfi's work proceeded obliquely. In 1950 he and his permanent collaborator, Wolfgang Frankl, built an INA complex in Cerignola. The complex resulted from a careful study of the behavior of future residents; its forms were marked by a reduction of typological and material richness.[31] Towers still dominated the Viale Etiopia; but in Cerignola the density of referents taken up in the juxtaposition of materials and in the dryness of volumes did not allow for "copies." The isolation to which fine craftsmanship condemned itself was also a product of realism, albeit involuntary. The poetry accorded and stimulated by backward technology sublimated a transient contingency, and the song that sprang from it expressed guilty happiness. Ridolfi's experience of such "sun" is reflected in a later work of 1950–51, his "palazzina" or apartment building on Via G. B. De Rossi in Rome (figure 14). It was, at the time, a return to building for the middle class, but it was no longer possible for the lyric sensibility of the "other Rome" to confront the theme with the prewar detachment of the buildings nearby on Via di Villa Massimo and of the Parioli. There was no longer a typology to propose for that group, nor a "way of life." The result was an expressionistic clashing of forms, an unmitigated and dodecaphonic series of geometric distortions, epitomized in the tormented concrete plinth with the broken profile that served as its base. The project reiterated the "slap in the face of public taste."

The quarrelsome dignity of the Cerignola complex was replaced on Via De Rossi by a kind of "portrait" of its clients: disintegrated, uselessly anxious, and undeniably vulgar; the latter appears, in Ridolfi's interpretation, singularly close to that given elsewhere by Luchini Visconti. And another comparison comes to mind: the similarity between Ridolfi's building and the towers on Viale Etiopia. They present languages for coexisting realities, the exception and the rule, even if the first one does not graze the surface of the reality from which it is liberating itself, and the second one is limited to simple "commentary."

Ridolfi's poetics moved inexorably toward this drama: the game of manipulating matter became more and more tormented in the buildings on Viale Marco Polo of 1952 and on Via Vetulonia of 1952–53, both in Rome. His designs entered into a dialogue with the urban structure of Terni—a city to which he dedicated a meticulous and ongoing project of "urban care"[32]—the magisterial Middle School on Via Fratti stands out polemically above eclectic edifices, as in the heights of Via Paisiello of 1948–49 and Via Mercadante of 1954–55 in Rome, and obeys a rigorous geometrical imperative in the new prisons of Nuoro, designed in 1953–55.[33] But, on the threshold of the "economic miracle," the gradual disappearance of the conditions that had sustained the emergence of this poetic transformed an encounter between the urgency of a subjective need to communicate and the necessities imposed by the historical situation into a coherence that outlived itself by speaking with inappropriate nostalgia of a "bad" world that had disappeared.

Meanwhile, the complexity of Ridolfi's production contributed to the disruptive polemics at the heart of the APAO. The attention of critics was turned almost exclusively toward the most overt populist motives behind neorealism. But this was certainly not an acceptable situation for anyone who, like Zevi, had developed the "organic" formula as an instrument of enrichment, rather than as a device meant to destroy the "modern" tradition. In 1950, Zevi's *History of Modern Architecture (Storia dell'architettura moderna)* defined and organized definitively the concepts that had been anticipated in *Towards an Organic Architecture* and in *Knowing How to See Architecture.* In a suggestive account, whose omissions owed much to still embryonic historiographical research and whose daring judgments were soon contradicted by facts, Zevi attempted to shift the debate on the "destiny" of architecture to areas not vitiated by folklore or fallen populism. It is no coincidence that in this volume Zevi does not acknowledge neorealism to be the incarnation of "organic" poetics, but identifies as examples of the forming *tendenza* only Samonà's project for the Ospedale Traumatologico of Rome, Claudio Dall'Olio's restaurant in Sabaudi, and the building that he and S. Radiconcini designed for the Via Pisanelli in Rome. Neither Scarpa—who had not yet been "discovered"—nor Carlo Mollino were considered. Yet Mollino himself, with his sled-lift station, his hotel on the Lago Nero in the Val di Susa begun in 1946 (figure 16), and with his product designs, was proceeding toward an integration of skeletal structures and aerodynamic organisms. Thus he furnished, as he had already done in his center for the Società Ippica in Turin of 1935–39, an original and ironic verson of organicism.[34] In reality, a true organic tendency did not take root in Italy, in spite of Zevi's passionate preaching. Works like the Villagio del Fanciullo in Trieste-Opicina designed by Marcello D'Olivo in 1949—one of the most remarkable projects of those years—or Samonà's 1950 villa at Mondello remain, along with Edoardo Gellner's works, Scarpa's genial rereadings of Wright, and a few mannerist exploits, isolated cases.[35] The debate on organic architecture remained on a verbal level. In 1951, Giulio Carlo Argan implicitly responded to the argument of Zevi's *History* with a volume, also published by Einaudi, dedicated to "Walter Gropius and the Bauhaus." It was not a contrast along normative lines. Gropius, as interpreted by Argan, was the heir of a Protestant ethic interpreted by Weber and Troeltsch, the bearer of a European myth of reason "that holds within itself the seeds of doubt and disappointment," and the protagonist of a last-minute rescue "of an idea of civilization from the inevitable collapse of the ruling class." Argan later remarked that Gropius's "rationality," like that of Le Corbusier or Mies, was born of "a last illusion of immunity carried into the midst of the fray," since the modern concept of freedom was no longer identifiable with an "unlimited outpouring into the immense domain of nature."[36] Loyalty to that lesson, already deemed unsuccessful on an ideological level, was considered an inescapable necessity.

It was difficult for Italian culture in the early fifties to interpret Argan. Greeted with as much respect as incomprehension, Argan's work spawned an elite group of young historians. But like Zevi's work, it did not substantially modify architectural practice. The crises of the APAO and the MSA revealed the need for new modes of organizing architectural culture, which had yet to demolish particularly strong academic residues in the universities. Giuseppe Samonà brought to Venice a few of the liveliest protagonists of the Italian debate: Zevi, Albini, Gardella, Belgiojoso, Giancarlo De Carlo, Scarpa, Luigi Piccinato, and Giovanni Astengo. These men helped turn Samonà's school into a stronghold of progressive activity. But Venice was soon isolated from the academic world, and the "happy island" was left to flourish on its own. The INU proceeded, instead, to wave the banner of planning and to seek a dialogue with political forces that were fated differently.

It was as a protagonist in the battle of the INU that Quaroni continued his own course after the Tiburtino. For him, too, that experience was superseded even as it was being completed: without poetics, without "languages," Quaroni was obliged to bathe in Italian reality, to search for instruments of "power." He entered the Gruppo Tecnici Socialisti for a brief period, then committed himself to the south, encountered Adriano Olivetti's Comunità movement, and called for a parliamentary study of poverty.[37] Quaroni questioned not only the techniques of urban planning, but also its methods of analysis. And he further questioned the structures destined to solidify and socialize the demands of the lower class.

The meeting of Quaroni and Olivetti was not fortuitous. Through a kind of capillary action, the *Comunità* movement, an organization that offered its editorial resources to intellectuals in the name of cultural unity, appeared to be a "republic of intellectuals" in direct contact with social reality, and to have unobstructed communication with the new social sciences endorsed by parties of the left. The third force dominating much of the intelligentsia thus found in *Comunità* a natural terrain. *Comunità* became concrete by privileging urban planning, with references—propagandized by the review *Comunità* as well as by the movement's publications—to urban sociology and to Anglo-Saxon models of intervention. The populist tendencies present in the age of reconstruction thus encountered decentralized models and a philosophy of recuperation of communal qualities for settlements conceived as alternatives to "Dinosaur City." The texts of Lewis Mumford, the Greenbelt cities of the Roosevelt era, and the garden city were filtered through Olivetti's idelology and served as the basis for new experiments.[38] Urban planning thus became a language that claimed to synthesize the many languages governing the city; in it, the disturbing plurality of techniques found an abode and a homeland.

For Adriano Olivetti, this work fell in line with the action, undertaken before the war, that had led to the hypothetical projects for the development of the Valle d'Aosta. His ideas were guided by a conception of commerce as the center from which radiates a neohumanistic rationalization of the physical environment. The path that led Olivetti to the presidency of the INU and the vice-presidency of UNRRA-Casas was thus laid, as was the path that led him, along with Quaroni and a group of Roman architects, to act in the heart of the underdeveloped south.

It was as vice-president of UNRRA-Casas that Olivetti, taking advantage of the new funds provided by the ERP (European Recovery Program), directed attention toward southern Italy, proposing industrial decentralization in areas like Campania, Basilicata, and Apulia. He was not only interested in closing the national gap between haves and have-nots. By starting with underdeveloped areas, he could intervene in uncompromised zones, with the goal of establishing a territorial equilibrium more difficult to achieve in developed regions. The models of the New Deal, and that of the Tennessee Valley Authority in particular, had been based on a similar strategy.[39]

The "case" of the Sassi of Matera drew special attention. Carlo Levi's *Christ Stopped in Eboli* had triggered widespread sympathy for this agglomerate of cave dwellings, which Togliatti and De Gasperi had called the "shame of Italy." Matera was envisioned as the capital of the rural world (this being in part due to the popular struggles that broke out in 1945), and was analyzed by both American and Italian sociologists, journalists, economists, and architects.[40] In 1950, a report by Alemanni and Calia to the consortium for land reclamation in the middle valley of the Bradano proposed an agricultural restructuring of territory, including the creation of rural villages and an evacuation of the Sassi. It was at this point that Olivetti intervened. His initiative led to the constitution in 1951 of the Commission for the Study of the City of Matera and Surrounding Countryside, sponsored by INU and UNRRA-Casas. Those employed included Quaroni, Federico Gorio, Tullio Tentori, and Rocco Mazzarone; these men, aided by volunteers, dealt with all manner of difficulties. Law 619 for the reclamation of the Sassi actually used the commission's investigations in a distorted way, preventing the occupation of 2,472 houses out of the 3,374 counted in the census, and barring the creation of rural villages for the evacuated families. In reality, in light of this "land counterreform,"[41] the Matera case exemplified the role that the great industrial capital had assigned to underdevelopment: the underdeveloped area was managed as a pool of reserve labor for industrialized areas. To achieve this the *agricultural vocation* of the south was stressed, the service sector was artificially expanded, and a policy of public works instigated to stimulate consumerism in the south.[42]

The UNRRA village "La Martella" (figures 17–18) and the complexes of Serra Venerdì, Lanera, and Spine Bianche should be evaluated in this context. La Martella was planned by Quaroni, Gorio, Piero Maria Lugli, Michele Valori, and Agati as the model nucleus of territorial intervention and management; several of the planners of the Tiburtino found themselves reunited in "discovering" the reality of the south.[43] The result was a settlement that conformed to geography and that, in its own way, was cast as an emotional homage to that reality. "Neighborhood unity," observed in the Sassi, was reinterpreted in a half-popular, half-abstract language, in houses sited according to the gradation of the land,

and having as a point of reference Quaroni's church, with its prominent tower. But conflicts between the restructured agency and the standards of the UNRRA engineers rendered service inefficient and led to a failure of the village's first objectives. The conservative extremism of the agrarian block was justified regarding projects for economic, social, and land reform.

For Quaroni, it was a double failure. His commitment to the south ran into obstacles created by consolidated interests, and the conflict between powers was poorly resolved because of the ambiguity of the so-called "third force" illusions. Meanwhile, the Sassi were indirectly feeding a community-oriented ideology of decentralization: Matera's new complexes of Serra Venerdí, Spine Bianche, and Borgo Venusio, which reflected the outlines of a plan drawn up between 1952 and 1956 by Luigi Piccinato,[44] emerged as "towns within a town," while the relationship between housing and work in urban development remained uncertain.

The case of Matera, which had so preoccupied Italian culture, was certainly not the most serious in the underdeveloped area of the nation. It was, however, the most "literary," and that justified the concentration of interests. In reality, for southern cities like Naples, Bari, or Palermo, public works and building functioned as a means of containing unemployment and providing training for agricultural groups that would later on be encouraged to migrate to developed areas. There they would form a reserve force, enabling producers to keep wages low.

Architects and urban planners did not have the tools to design such a sustained plan, and the appeal—in any case, generic and diffident—to the parties of the left did not produce them. Wherever architects tried to insert their own technique into the transformation of structures there were major setbacks: the cities and surrounding lands had become sites of the most unbridled speculation, as a side effect of the free-trade policies imposed by the centers of power.

This explains why the building industry that shaped the new Rome of the fifties had nothing to do with Quaroni's experimentalism or with Ridolfi's sad lyricism. The upper and middle bourgeoisie were given the "palazzina" apartment building, a legacy of the master plan of 1931 perfectly adapted to titillate the condominium-hungry ambitions of a substantially static class[45]; the high-density complexes appearing on the outskirts of the city were intended for the working classes; and for the subproletariat, there were the "borgate"—villages—and illegal quarters, which in the seventies still numbered 500,000 and sheltered a fifth of Rome's population. Ugo Luccichenti, Vincenzo Monaco, and Amedeo Luccichenti took it upon themselves to turn the "palazzina" into an object of pleasurable consumption. This typology of compromise politely installed itself in the zones adjacent to the historic center; with its neo-organic balconies "à la Rietveld," its forced and ultimately exhibitionistic play of volumes, and its impeccable materials, it became indeed a status symbol.[46] Nor were "monumental" interpretations of the "palazzina" lacking: Luigi Moretti, in his so-called Sunflower House ("Il Girasole") of 1950 on Viale Bruno Buozzi (figure 20), endowed this building type with the solemn cadences of a temple, its entrance marked by an ascending ramp. A paradoxical situation was thus created. Monaco and Luccichenti's professionalism and Luigi Moretti's rarefied formalism treaded the path of "noncommitment," but exploited a vocabulary rooted in the tradition of the avant-garde. The phenomenon of *engagement*, for its part, seemed to be taking a regressive path. This, too, had its own coherence: the language of the "neues Bauen" demonstrated its availability, but also its nobility. Whoever wished to be "comprehensible" had to distance himself and resort to a less articulate architecture.

Of course, it was easy for a politically "committed" culture to accuse Moretti of formalism. Yet his houses-and-hotel on Via Corridoni of 1948–50 and his complex for apartments and offices on Corso Italia in Milan of 1952–56 (figure 19), even more than the Casa Astrea in Rome of 1949, are articulated in a sure hand, though one tainted by the unrealistic nuances of excess abstraction. Moretti's savvy composition translates classical forms into an abstract language: the eloquent purism of his Milanese buildings is faithful, in substance, to the more "metaphysical" architecture of the thirties, including that of Terragni. But such work was destined to be isolated or rejected in the climate of the fifties.

Moretti's lyricism again reached high levels in the Villa Pignatelli in Santa Marinella of 1952–54 (figure 21) where, as he wrote, he created a space beyond the "great and small adventures" of daily life. Curved and blind volumes, Mediterranean plastering, and Arabic motifs protect a "house that is a jealous Saracen of emotions and thoughts." Moretti's abstractions shifted quite soon, however, toward scripts that were ends in themselves, as in his 1962 Casa San Maurizio in Rome and the new thermal complex of Fiuggi of 1965.[47]

But in the meantime, the Palazzina del Girasole, the Milanese buildings, and the few issues of the review *Spazio* edited by Moretti between 1950 and 1953, appropriated "from the right" the linguistic heritage of the avant-garde, perhaps to try to demonstrate its validity in a culture that had paid its debts to the academy. Though one can read in Moretti's "auras" an unequivocal syntax, as well as a direct response to the whims of his clients, one detects in the works of those architects committed to renewal, rather than to the defense of an "organic" or neorealist line, a cautiousness hidden beneath the timid elegance. Samonà's building for apartments and offices in Treviso of 1949-53 and his Ospedale Inail in Bari of 1948–53 held to sure formulas, while Gardella's houses for employees in Alessandria of 1952, his Galleria d'Arte Moderna in Milan of 1951–54, and his Terme Regina Isabella in Ischia of 1950–53 (figure 22), aimed for subtle dialogues between the vibration of volumes and the texture of materials.[48] The secret convention was always a dialectical overcoming of "rationalism"; without fuss, but with obstinacy, the new quality was pursued in variations based on an exaltation of materials, on polite and indeterminate forms, and on an absorption with craftsmanship that forced all unique works to hide under a cloak of modesty.

Yet it was exactly such a constraint that allowed Albini to attain one of the most remarkable results of this period of research, his building for the Istituto Nazionale delle Assicurazioni (INA) in Parma of 1950 (figure 23). Sewing up the unraveled parts of a loosely defined urban fabric, Albini made use of calibrated measurement: the concrete frame, reduced to a feeble but rhythmic woof, enters into a dialogue with the pure modulation of panels and empty spaces.[49] A design *en plein air*, then, a formal correctness based on technological precision and a taste for the unrealistic—one recalls the internal staircase of the building in Parma—that would be read by Rogers and others as critical interpretations of preexisting surroundings. Albini's work can be compared to the BPR's house on Via Borgonuovo in Milan, to Samonà's building in Treviso, and to Giovanni Michelucci's Borsa Merci in Pistoia of 1947–50.

A dialogue with the "environment" emerges from this group of works and constitutes the originality of the Italian experience in those years. This turning toward the environment, moreover, is nothing but the other side of a turning towards nature. There was a search for "protection," a need to crawl between warm covers and rest. Even here there is a vacillation between two extremes: an exceptional receptivity to the legacy of the avant-gardes and an equally exceptional cautiousness in defining the limits conceded to a dialogue with history. The "environment" was not considered a historical structure in the literal sense; rather, an impressionistic attitude prevailed, exploiting the "essay" as a definitive instrument in the suspension of judgment.

It was Michelucci, in Florence, whose work embodied architecture constantly aspiring to self-negation as a means of resolving its relation to life.[50] After the inhospitable metaphysical figures of his Palazzo del Governo in Arezzo of 1939 and Villa Contini-Bonacossi in Forte dei Marmi of 1941, in which Michelucci seemed to be distancing himself from his achievement at the station of Santa Maria Novella, his sketches for the reconstruction of the area around the Ponte Vecchio in Florence of 1945 (figure 24) pointed in the direction of an urban form that would be modeled by the interwoven fluctuations of existence.[51] A form "that is born with the urgency and evidence of a vital fact": this is the objective Michelucci sought with the delicate equilibrium and clarity of the Borsa Merci in Pistoia, an object that trusts in the elementary notion of a single internal space and in the exposure of structure to attain an Albertian fixity directly related to the typologies of the Tuscan Renaissance. In the church of Collina at Pontelungo, designed from 1947 to 1950 and completed in 1953, architecture tends to immerse itself in the countryside, commenting upon its desolation and indicating human presence solely by variations on the theme of the "cottage." It was a personal variation on a neorealist theme: material like Ridolfi's, but lacking his expressionistic accents. Michelucci, who revealed at times unthinking adherence to contradictory impulses, was, in Italy after the war, among the most intolerant of ciphers or jargons: in spite of everything he aspired to the improbable fusion of language and existence. This led him to assimilate "nonform," or at least to a transient and temporary acceptance, almost in spite of himself, of forms dictated by the *genius loci*. This explains, after the homage to the countryside around Pistoia expressed in his church of Collina, the emphasis on scale in the two embracing skyscrapers planned for San Remo in 1952, the confident simplicity of the church of the Virgin in Pistoia of 1954–56,[52] the clean structure of the Cassa di Risparmio in Florence of 1953–57,[53] and the delicate equilibrium reached in the building for apartments and stores on Via Guicciardini in Florence of 1955–57. That form, for Michelucci, represented an arrest of the flux of life is demonstrated by the obsessive play of vibration on the surfaces of his church of Larderello of 1956–59. His intolerance of the limitations created by all syntax made wild freedom an absolute necessity. Among the results were the restaurant in Collodi known as the Gambero Rosso (figure 25) and the church of the Villaggio Belvedere in Pistoia of 1959–61, both experiments in making space fluid and structure meaningful. This was a prelude to themes that Michelucci would face in the sixties and seventies, starting with the "big tent" of the Chiesa dell'Autostrada.

The "environment" to which the poetics of the fifties had paid homage was, however, an unconscious metaphor for the desire to contemplate a static nature refracted by mirrors in movement. The consolation that could be derived from it was doubtless unsatisfying; nonetheless, the value was pursued. Intervention in rural areas with well-defined characters, or in centers where unity was stressed—leaving vestiges of Giovanni—generated a chorus extolling "sociality" welling up from the historical environment. A classic regressive utopia was being pursued, that of the "community," as opposed to the anonymous metropolis "where one proceeds as though in a foreign land." There was a return to Olivetti's ideologies, to Tönnies's fantasma, to the most romantic Mumford. But one must read such phenomena with a historical vision that penetrates the folds of cultural attitudes, examining their less obvious aspects. Beneath regionalism, humanistic romanticism, and the cult of the uncontaminated and spontaneous, beneath the heavy ideological burden that emanates from the writings and projects of those years, there developed—in an unconscious fashion—an implicit criticism of the futurism animating the very concept of the "project." The hubris that had become second nature to the modern need to "transform" was indicted in a confused way and often from provincial motives. The themes that Francesco Dal Co has recognized as characteristic of the Central European debate in the first years of the twentieth century[54] were reappearing, still unconsciously. Meanwhile a work like Michelucci's church of Collina proposed an architecture of "let it be," in which tradition and countryside, products of long waves of history and of slow collective movements, are removed from the reach of ruthlessly subjective events.

Clearly, not all of Michelucci's designs can be summed up in this way. But for all that is revealed by the formative experiments of the fifties, including the shamelessly nationalistic ones, it was his work that—translated into other cultural spheres—would form a fertile object of reflection for architects like Gabetti and Isola. Moreover, in an era of reconstruction, the ferment implicit in the intolerance of Michelucci's projects (or, on the other hand, of Ridolfi's) remained confined within strict boundaries, even as a general sense of dissatisfaction arose over the results attained. The character of the new "Italian way" was continually exposed to misunderstanding, often by its own apologists.

And it was no coincidence, given the sociological connotations of the "recovery of community," that architects strove, in similar fashion, to redefine their professional techniques to tackle the theme of the neighborhood. Once again, the sociology was imported. The myth of the nuclear city—in which "nuclear" was equivalent to "organic"—found a counterpart in the ideology of the neighborhood unit of standard dimensions, gathered around primary services, such as schools. The neighborhood unit was split into neatly organized subsystems, at least on paper. Small, controllable "communities," designed to educate children and adults, added up to groups that, beneath the search for consolidating values, made "pacts" promoting collaboration between classes.

For Italian architects the mythology of neighborhood unity was only *constituent material*. Rather than attempting to save its soul, sociology defined the neighborhood as an instrument of symbolic control that guaranteed a relationship to reality. On the one hand, the limits imposed by choices from above became the very limits of composition: everything was resolved in the microcosm of the urban subunit, considered to be in possession of its *own* language. On the other hand, the articulation of that language was reticent: once codified, neorealism lost all polemical force and became instead an instrument of dissimulation. One might also add that the syntax of modesty, which had become widespread, allowed even older academicians to reenter the field, although this observation remains marginal relative to the system's requirement that emerged from realizations of INA-Casa's first seven years.

A *mimesis* of manner had replaced autobiographical sadness. One should consider the difference in the formulation of various neighborhoods to be the result of homage paid to a misunderstood *genius loci*. The emphasis on typological distinctions, which is the only element emerging from the disordered palette of the Borgo Panigale quarter in Bologna, finds its equivalent in the San Giuliano quarter in Mestre of 1951–55, by the Samonà-Piccinato group, where environmentalism is so explicit as to approach caricature. It is significant, as symptomatic of a way of thinking, that an architect like Giuseppe Samonà adhered to the language of an all-encompassing domesticity—not only in San Giuliano, but also in the INA complex in Sciacca of 1952–54—when one considers that from the drafting table of the same man came, in 1945, a project for the development of the Lavinaio quarter of Naples, attentive to Corbusierian theses and sure of eternal monumentality.[55] To be "temporal" or "in time" means, on the one hand, to pay one's debts, to make a profession of abstinence, to pretend one is available to the present, even though one's sights "are on the beyond of architecture."

This applies also to the complexes built in Milan and in Turin. In the development at Cesate, begun in 1950 (figure 27), Albini, Albricci, the BPR, and Gardella manipulate with passive linguistic neatness a dialect that had paradoxically become an Esperanto,[56] whereas Figini, Pollini, and Gio Ponti tried to recover elementary relationships in the big blocks pinwheeling around a central green space in the complex of Via Dessié in Milan of 1951–52. It was, however, with singular offhandedness that populism was reduced to an idiolect, then dissolved in complexes that passively accepted typologies defined a priori. Renunciation was concealed behind a shield of "commitment" and morality; contradictions within the intellectual community following the events of 1948 heavily informed public building in Italy. The latter was also influenced, as has been noted, by Scandinavian New Empiricism. It appeared possible, mainly through the example of the complexes of Backström and Reiniusit, which focused on typological and morphological research connected to the single-room dwelling. Nor was the search for identity foreign to such a cultural reference, and it was resolved in a simulation: the image of the small interior of a peasant family home was juxtaposed with that of a rarefied peace attained by the "great family" of social democracy, that temporary and experimental model of a culture that, in the limbo of uncertainty, took its own specific choices for granted.

The UNRRA-Casa complex of San Basilio in Rome of 1949–55, by Mario Fiorentino and S. Boselli, and the Falcera complex in Turin, designed by the Astengo-Renacco group in 1950–51 (figure 29), took their cue from the continuous, experienced aggregations of Swedish New Empiricism and from the polite and obvious facades and details. The most stringent criticism of the first of these complexes derives from the mood experienced during a visit. The complex has become a ghetto for those of marginal social status, its physical deterioration clearly speaking of the conditions of production that surrounded its construction and exposing the hypocrisy of realism's utopian claims. Nor did the more successful results at Falchera, based, like San Basilio, on a succession of open, polygonal courtyards, derive from the reality of Turin, which was becoming more and more of a company town using public intervention to serve its own needs.[57]

Two instances stand out of this definitively mediocre panorama, if only because of their experimental character: the complex of Villa Bernabò Brea in Genoa, designed by Luigi Carlo Daneri from 1950 on, and the horizontal residential unit in Tuscolano, Rome, by Adalberto Libera, of 1950–51 (figure 30), located on the edges of Muratori and De Renzi's dignified complex.[58] Both Daneri and Libera distanced themselves from the fashionable populist sublanguage, conveying through different techniques a potentially anachronistic loyalty to the rigor of prewar Italian experiments. By demonstrating that a building's insertion into nature is more convincing when less mimetic, the Genovese complex introduced into an open but rigorous morphology elements welding formal to productive strategies. Among these were prefabrication in reinforced concrete, piers elevating the building volumes from the ground, typological standardization, and corridors suspended between floors. Even more polemical was the unit by Libera, sullenly turned in upon its own technical and geometric rigor. Here a block of galleries faced a continuous fabric of cells, connected so as to form a slab furrowed by pedestrian paths. Libera's complex recalled Dutch typologies of the thirties and of Pagano's studies for a "horizontal city." Though it was valid as a testimony of an alternative to current formulations, it too looked backward.

It also fit perfectly into the overall intentions of the Fanfani plan—managed with admirable bureaucratic skill by Arnaldo Foschini, a technician certainly not of the avant-garde—that Daneri and Libera's proposals were isolated instances. "Tolerated" guests, and rightfully so, during INA-Casa's first seven years of building, they nonetheless implicitly contained indications incompatible with the objectives of the program that liberally allowed them to operate.

Thus, the encirclement of the "districts" by the speculating city—a predictable and calculated phenomenon—soon revealed that architectural design had not managed to produce even islands of realized utopia. Realism showed itself for what it was, the product of a useless compromise.

2
Aufklärung I:
Adriano Olivetti and
the *Communitas* of
the Intellect

In the meantime, Olivetti focused on the transformation of the work environment at the plant in Ivrea. By concentrating on one city, Olivetti hoped not only to demonstrate the concreteness of his theories on community, but also to offer a "social" image of the firm—which was in full expansion between 1946 and 1954—and to counter the uncertainties of public intervention with the certainties of an entrepreneur's "enlightened intervention."[1]

During the fifties, the alliance between Olivetti's cultural-managerial policies and the image given to them by architects held on the level of manufactured goods, while revealing its faults on the level of planning. The human rationality of the "working community" was obliged to display an Olympian continuity. In the enlargement of the factory that occurred between 1947 and 1949 (figure 31), Figini and Pollini remained, for the most part, faithful to the plan they had drawn up for the factory's nucleus in the late thirties; in the new ICO offices, which they built from1955 to 1957, their language continued to adhere to a monumental asceticism. But the social aspect of industry needed mediating: the *communitas* lived off its own articulations and projected itself into daily life with paternal benevolence. On the one hand, the Olivetti office district of 1955 in Milan, by Bernasconi, Fiocchi, and Nizzoli, once again adopted an International Style vocabulary; on the other hand, the Study and Research Center in Ivrea by Edoardo Vittoria of 1952–55 and even more the zone of social services by Figini and

Pollini of 1954–57 (figures 32–33), the company refectory by Gardella of 1955–59 (figure 46), and the vacation center in Brusson of 1968, executed by Carlo Conte and Leonardo Fiori, employed with cordial offhandedness a geometry based on the rhombus, the hexagon, and irregular broken forms.[2] An"organic" approach characterized these spaces destined for the reproduction of the work force. The smiling reclamation of nature in the restaurant by Gardella, which includes a garden rich in *japonismes*, is the symptomatic testimony of Olivetti's program, and was freely reinterpreted elsewhere .

The "republic of the intellect" had to present itself as comprehensive. Ivrea acquired works of architecture as though they were collector's items, seeking a quality that was less and less tied to prefabricated languages. Among the architects who satisfied this requirement were Gardella, designer of the company refectory and hospital, and Figini and Pollini, with their duplicate version. There was also Quaroni, who in 1955 designed the Neutresque elementary school of Canton Vesco and in 1958 (with Zevi, Adolfo De Carlo, and Sergio Musmeci) the bilevel bridge-dam over the Dora. The bridge-dam, rich in urban implications, was portrayed as a "machine" with complex functions.[3] We should also mention here Ridolfi, who designed the nursery school of Canton Vesco from 1955 to 1963, a dissonant composition in concrete and stone, erected within a quarter dominated by Nizzoli and Fiocchi's residential blocks of 1950–53.[4] Ridolfi's anxieties, severely restrained and ironically expressed (see the aerial cages that culminate on the terraces), comment on the regular grid that shapes the main residential nucleus of Olivetti's "community." On the other hand, the Castellamonte quarter, which was based on Piccinato's 1938 plan, and later modified and executed by Figini and Pollini, was enriched, from 1951 on, by Nizzoli and Oliveri's villas for executives and collective residences. The expansion proceeded first according to international canons, and then with linguistic matrices that seemed to repeat Scharoun's self-satisfied, postwar distortions without conviction.

Olivettti's *appel aux architectes* was rife with pedagogical implications. "Good form" was supposed to settle every difference, to demonstrate that "another life" awaited whoever entered the *koiné* engendered by relations of production in which capital and work had adopted new forms of exchange. The "workshop in glass" sought to pay homage to the transparency of such an exchange by eradicating—as the "organic" service buildings did—the reality of ineradicable differences, the reality of assembly work, and the inscrutable laws governing national and international strategies of enterprise. Already, in the early fifties, these strategies were realizing Adriano's meridional policies by constructing in Pozzuoli a factory by Luigi Cosenza, begun in 1951 (figure 34).[5] The region of Canavese was put forward as an alternative to the metropolitan agglomerations of the north; the plant in the underdeveloped south exemplified a policy different from that imposed by those in power. By intervening directly in Pozzuoli, Olivetti sought to reverse a trend. He hoped to provoke a chain reaction of ruptures and repercussions in the Neapolitan economic system. Not coincidentally, Olivetti's was a model factory, with high technology and high salaries. The social aspects of the project were delegated to a man of letters, Ottiero Ottieri, who in 1955 was charged with selecting future workers for the new factory from the many applicants who had been attracted by Olivetti's firm. The lucid pages of *Donnarumma all'assalto* bear witness to the drama and frustrated hopes of that proletariat, as well as to the isolation to which Olivetti's attempt was condemned.

None of this drama can, however, be detected in Cosenza's terse play of volumes. Cosenza was trying to insert into the Gulf of Naples his "green factory," a building he wanted to appear "anti-industrial," a place where work space and social space would be integrated. The "great house" of the assembly line was articulated in a dialogue with the landscape, with nature, and with sinuously designed small lakes. This catharsis, an antidote to alienation, originated in the private life of the architect and in his forms.

The occasional confluence between the ideologies of the *Comunità* movement and the emerging ones of architects in search of myths to which they could consecrate their extradisciplinary fancies (or their need "to be present") had foundations too fragile to survive the brief season during which Olivetti's utopia compensated for the inaccessibility of the institutions. The collection of architects gathered at Ivrea had, in the fifties, a meaning similar to the one at the Istituto Universitario di Architettura of Venice, under Samonà. Both were golden cages from which it was difficult to escape. But one does not attain a *koiné* simply by being nearby.

Olivetti's aspiration, which failed to become an architectural reality, was to some degree satisfied in the realm of product design. As Fossati has pointedly observed,[6] the American myth—Fordism plus company reorganization—affected the production of Olivetti's objects in a very particular way, beginning with the MP1 typewriter in 1932. Nizzoli and Xanti Schawinsky, with the help of designer Pintori and Sinisgalli, a man of letters, succeeded in incorporating the image into the product, in order to focus on a dialogue, not with a real public and a real society, but rather with a metahistorical image of a public and a society. The "classicism of the new," launched by Nizzoli with the *Lexicon 80* of 1948, the *Lettera 22* of 1950, the *Divisumma* of 1956, and the *Summa Prima* of 1960, did not so much represent the product, as promote a global cultural and political project that grafted itself onto market operation.

This market was, moreover, affected by channels flowing from the multivalent character of the products. As early as the thirties, the existing distribution sites seemed inadequate to Olivetti; Schawinsky and Nizzoli were commissioned to prepare exhibition spaces in Turin and in Venice. What was exhibited more than the object was the "project" of which it formed a fragment.[7] As a consequence, Olivetti's stores, in Italy and abroad, became precious spatial coffers whose character was entrusted to an architectural surrealism that suspended the project in a void that isolates it from its material context in an attempt to cancel its mercantile character. The Olivetti exhibition stores abroad were completely surreal. The first of these was created in New York, on fashionable Fifth Avenue, by the BPR studio in 1954. It was followed by a store in Düsseldorf by Gardella, one in Venice by Scarpa in 1957–58, and a Paris store designed by Albini and Held in 1958. Thus, the Italian architects who had contributed most to the renewal of museum design were entrusted with charging Olivetti's objects with an impalpable "aura."[8]

Adriano Olivetti's relationship to the urbanistic operations that he himself had initiated in Ivrea and the Canavese was less felicitous. In 1938, Adriano had asked Luigi Piccinato to draw up a master plan for the commune of Ivrea. The plan was never adopted by the communal council; nevertheless, it provided guidelines for the two quarters of Canton Vesco and Castellamonte. In 1952 Olivetti again solicited a study for a plan on a regional scale. This time the designers were Quaroni, Fiocchi, Ranieri, and Renacco, supported by a large team of sociologists, economists, and specialists in agricultural and industrial problems. The moment seemed to have arrived for Italian culture to try out techniques of analysis on the most diverse aspects of regional structure, taking advantage of the opportunity to update interdisciplinary techniques of real scientific value. In other words, it was a matter of substantiating the slogan "urban planning for cultural unity."

Intellectuals were less interested in the final result—the projected plan—than they were in the *process* by which it was developed. Furthermore, the complex organization set up for the analysis of the Canavese territory, which should have led to exemplary publications, demonstrated the way in which intellectuals less organically tied to Olivetti's ideology interpreted the concept of "community." Under the aegis of an enlightened impresario, culture reaffirmed itself, attempted to overcome the barriers of specialization, and revealed itself as a mass of communication techniques. The myth of the interdisciplinary approach was welded to the myth of community. This revealed, however, that the only real community that might be concretely organized—in a later and exceptional situation—was the community of *clercs*.[9]

The plan for Ivrea represented the sum of theories and models circulating in Italian culture at the time joined, for official duty, to Olivetti's idea of a "community" made to fit human beings. The plan, presented unsuccessfully in 1954 and revised in 1959, provided for a controlled expansion of nuclei together with minor centers of production, for the development of separate industrial zones, and for the creation of two office districts with urban and regional responsibility. One of these districts would lie beyond the Dora and would be connected by the bridge designed by Quaroni, Zevi, De Carlo, and Musmeci.

But the process that led to the plan and the difficult relations between intellectuals and corporate interests caused deep disappointment. For Quaroni this process proved once again to be unsatisfactory and incomplete: even the myth of an interdisciplinary approach proved illusory. This disappointment was reflected in singular fashion at the tenth Triennale of Milan in 1954. The exhibit on urban planning, organized by Quaroni, Giancarlo De Carlo, and Carlo Doglio, was provocative. The three short films presented there—especially Elio Vittorini's *A Lesson in Urban Planning*, which featured Giancarlo Cobelli as protagonist[10]—sent urban planners a severe and acerbic warning. As De Carlo wrote, "They specify up to what point they are willing to risk a confrontation with reality: to bring into urban planning the collaboration of all the active forces implicit in the culture and to devise the means that would make possible an effective participation of the collectivity." But the provocation had no effect. "The inscrutable high priests," De Carlo continued, "have disdainfully rejected the provocation and have not responded."[11]

The rethinking of planning techniques proposed by intellectuals like De Carlo and Quaroni only touched the surface of the web of plans, institutions, and structural reforms. Political analyses of the real situation were inadequate in responding to the substantial failure, in the south and in contact with Olivetti, of the generous effort of *Aufklärung* urban planning. In light of this failure, an attempt was made to translate the ideology of community into direct political action: in 1958 Adriano Olivetti himself participated in the political elections. The anachronism of the third force route thus became fully evident. Moreover, by the end of the fifties Olivetti's dream had already been shattered by the firm's attempt to enter the electronics market, by a financial crisis, and by the Olivetti family's loss of absolute control over the firm. Adriano, who died in 1960, would never witness the transformations that the firm was to undergo, changes that would not only include a revision of his social programs, but would also feed an international market image quite different from the one that prevailed in the fifties.

3
The Myth of Equilibrium: The Vanoni Plan and INA-Casa's Second Seven Years

The profound modification of the Italian economy during reconstruction was provoked by the pursuit of international capital. Moreover, the lagging role of public enterprise took priority over those sectors of the ruling class still entertaining despotic fantasies. Italy's entry into the CECA (the European Coal and Steel Community), with the subsequent expansion of iron metallurgy, especially affected the mechanical sector, underscoring the necessity for a long-range strategy to transform the entire society. At the end of 1954, the Vanoni plan appeared to meet that need. By maintaining the increase in national revenue at a rate of 5 percent and by providing additional jobs outside of agriculture, the plan was to develop the efficiency and competitive capacity of the productive system, setting as a goal the creation of 4 million new jobs. A program providing guidelines for the growth of national capital was thus established: the specifics of its realization would depend strictly on the political variables bracketed by the model. Only in this way can one explain the abandonment of some of the "propelling sectors" of the economy in favor of others that would soon turn around like a boomerang against the strategy of development. The large infrastructures necessary to reorganize the countryside—the highways and distribution lines for natural gas—actually supported the expansion of private consumption (the automobile industry, for example), encouraging the formation of metropolitan areas, and proving themselves incapable of reversing existing tendencies in the geography of development. The dream of *equilibrium*, which was at the base of the Vanoni plan and of the most advanced attempts of the Catholic movement in those years, was shattered when it encountered a strategy that, *without a plan*, focused on the building trades as a guaranteed means of consolidating the various strata of the landed bourgeoisie and cementing the alliance between the latter and Confindustria through collecting land revenues and realizing its contributions to the productive system.[1]

"The policy of the building sector," the Vanoni plan stated, "will have to be to promote or restrain investments in the construction industries insofar as the demand for consumer goods unrelated to housing is respectively insufficient or excessive in relation to the possible process of expansion." The urbanization process begun in Italy in the fifties had nothing to do with such a conception of the building industry as a "shuttlecock." It seemed that the misgovernment of local administrations was being institutionalized, while construction standards and the master plan were considered less binding. The availability of housing was expanding in an indiscriminate fashion, reducing the amount of low-cost housing and following the laws of land speculation. Meanwhile, an increase in construction costs, which corresponded to a tenfold increase in the price of lands suitable for construction, caused the price of new buildings to triple between 1953 and 1963, and the level of capital in the fragmented building industry remained low, allowing the industry to profit from its deliberate backwardness in an economic as well as political sense. It has been estimated, furthermore, that the number of housing units built annually went from 543,000 in 1951 to 1,970,000 in 1961, with an annual average of 1,400,000; the construction industry as a whole in the period considered was developing at the rate of approximately 12.1 percent, against 8.2 percent in the industry in general. As for the average annual salary in the sector, it registered a 4.5 percent increase for a group of workers that represented 28 percent of the total number of industrial workers.

The Vanoni plan, consequently, did not lead to an effective line of economic policy, but served instead to unleash a conflict within the Catholic movement that would only be resolved when the power of the most reactionary forces was consolidated. In this period the governing power block was happily promoting unbalanced development and was willing to pay, through the swelling of parasite sectors, for the risks provoked by the heavy obstacles impeding the entire mechanism. In contrast with these policies, all attempts to superimpose programs that might displace interests and historically impossible alliances upon such a fluid institutional picture appeared like enlightenment rationality.

Italy's building policy took shape through a collage of arrangements defined by sector, rather than by way of programmatic declarations. The initial law of INA-Casa was amplified by two other provisions, the Tupini law on cooperative housing of 1951 and the Aldisio law, which launched an incremental fund for construction. The aim was to offer housing on credit and financial arrangements that privileged various small businesses, thereby shifting interests—especially with the Tupini law—to a market accessible to average-income groups. The wild urban development that resulted from this indiscriminate increase of available housing inadvertently encouraged migration toward developed areas and urban centers, providing industry with untrained reserve labor that would, for the most part, be reabsorbed by the construction industry. This explains why the building industry remained at a low technological level, even after it had overcome the contingent conditions of reconstruction. The decay and congestion in urban centers, along with rent control, cleared the way for a clean-up of portions of historical centers by real estate interests. Meanwhile a luxury market was being created for historical centers not only by the appeal of the antique and the exhaustion of desirable areas outside the urban cores, but also by the tendency of many official functions to remain within them. (This was true as long as historical centers were not directly affected by aggressive speculation, as in Milan.)

Urban culture responded in two ways to this cycle triggered by centrist forces with the backing of big industry, which, until the phenomena it had induced proved an impediment, aspired to capital from financial speculation. On the one hand, there began an intense muckraking campaign under the banner of morality. In 1957 the association Italia Nostra was founded under the initiative of Umberto Zanotti-Bianco; the column written by Antonio Cederna for the *Mondo* periodically attacked the mistakes of the "housing vandals," and thereby contributed to halting demolition and to saving of parks and green spaces from subdivision. The defamation suit brought against the *Espresso* by Salvatore Rebecchini, auditor of Rome, shed light on the process and extent of land speculation, as well as on the connections between administrative corruption and economic power.

On the other hand, there was a movement toward an abstract refinement of the discipline's methods, a search for an "indefinite technique"—indefinite above all because devoid of situations and clients whose interests coincided with those of a "balanced region," and indefinite because constrained to continual statements of principle regarding the conditions justifying its existence, such as an end to the free market system for real estate, or at least greater public control of it. It was no coincidence that the INU proceeded, between 1952 and 1958, to examine all possible modes of intervention, while the few plans drawn up were ignored or rendered inoperative through the mechanism of "variants."

It was left to the architects to design the INA Casa housing. Experience in that field was not acquired in vain, and a self-critical revision was the first step in redefining limits to be applied to the new areas of research.

The ideas of community and the formal reticence that had characterized the ideology of the neighborhood during INA-Casa's first seven years were in fact exhausted at the beginning of the second seven years. And it was again Quaroni who picked up the threads of previous experience in a memorable essay published in the review *La Casa*, and who completed a process of self-criticism that led, in 1957, to the San Giusto quarter in Prato.[2] The architectural lesson of the 1956 projects for the Genovese churches of San Gottardo and the Sacra Famiglia certainly formed part of Quaroni's radical revision. If the first, which remained at the idea state, tended to become an urban hinge rooted in the physical nature of the site—a knot of traffic in ascending levels—the second skillfully took advantage of an area closed in by buildings and by a high supporting wall crossed by two roads at different levels (figure 37). The church, dominated by a compact tower penetrated at the corner, again provides continuity between overlapping urban channels; it is a monumental visual fulcrum, standing out at the center of an ascending series of small stairs. The balance achieved here between the search for a hitherto unformulated code, devoid of concessions to romanticism, and the search for a dialogue between a strongly structured object and its urban site is one of Quaroni's greatest accomplishments.[3]

Not only the Genovese churches but also the project for the bridge over the Dora in Ivrea is closely linked to the project for the San Giusto quarter. The complexity of the city could not be overcome by dividing it into discrete elements, yet this was the "condition" imposed by the policy of INA-Casa. The only option left was to assume these contradictions and give them full expression. The composition begins in plan with a tower module; this is then amplified in a second module "with courtyard" in which a "pinwheel" positioning of cells is repeated until it is finally set free from the preestablished geometric figure in a free and continuous grouping of courtyards.

In a brusque and significant move away from the "poetics of the neighborhood"—contradicted only by the still "peasant" treatment of the front elevations—Quaroni prepared, in Prato, the materials that would lead to the most problematic of his works of the late fifties, the CEP complex of San Giuliano in Mestre (figure 71). The closed courtyards no longer interpret sociological dictums: it is the fabric that counts here, its openings and adherence to multiple modules. The quarter no longer "resolves" itself; it is no longer put up for ransom. It is only what it can be, and does not try to ennoble its own alienation.

It is telling that one finds similar themes—the closed courtyard taken as a module, the defining of an extendable mesh, and a conscious self-discipline—in another key quarter built during INA-Casa's second seven years. This one, on Via Cavedone in Bologna, of 1957, was executed by a team headed by Federico Gorio and including Marcello Vittorini and Leonardo Benevolo.[4]

Any remaining populist tendencies were purely vestigial. The urban type was now crucial, as was a technological control that seemed to foreshadow new possibilities for design. Neorealism was, however, demoted uncritically to the pragmatic level. The recourse to a tested morphology such as the closed courtyard avoided obvious historicizing references; the attempt to impose a severe "realism" was resolved in reticent simplifications. The unattainability of the city, which Quaroni's project had denounced implictly, was accepted in the complex on Via Cavedone with serene resignation.

But a willingness to experiment characterized the phase that opened the second seven years. Also in Bologna, in the complex on Via della Barca of 1957–62 (figure 38), constructed by the group led by Giuseppe Vaccaro, a rigorist of the old guard, the neighborhood units were interpreted as a continuous fabric interrupted only by a long, curved, and arcaded building placed on the central axis. Once again, the residential quarter was trying to emerge from isolation, picking up motifs from the historical city, articulating its functions timidly. The obvious ideological *décalage* turned these quarters into experiences of "waiting," but it also made possible work that used typological aggregates only as images. This was the case with the housing complexes in Galatina (Lecce) (figure 39) and in Ascoli Piceno (1958), executed by the Cicconcelli group with Luigi Pellegrin's decisive contribution. Pellegrin strongly reflected the lesson he had learned from Wright. His interpretation of Wright, as opposed to Carlo Scarpa's, refused mannerist solutions and revealed itself as a meditation on the qualities of space and objects. The analytical bent of this solitary investigator is evident in his schools in Urbino and Sassari, designed in 1956 in collaboration with C. Cicconcelli, and in the residential units he designed for Rome. His approach demonstrated, in the quarters of Galatina and Ascola, that the linguistic deficiency affecting most of INA-Casa's designers was anachronistic. Especially in Galatina (figure 39), the reiteration of the housing units, placed at a forty-five degree angle to the street grid, and the treatment and number of connecting elements allowed the complex to formulate its identity: a convulsive one marked by restless interruptions.

The supremacy of Quaroni's inquiry was thus countered by Cicconcelli and Pellegrin's search for finite results. On the other hand, Ridolfi's INA-Casa interventions in Naples (the apartments on Via Campegna and Via Chiaina of 1956) in Conegliano (1958–60), in Mareno (1958), and in Treviso (1956–58), can only be appreciated as variations on familiar typological and formal experiments. In these buildings the lack of interest in the scale of projection and the concentration of interests on the built product revealed their limitations.

Another isolated achievement is the Forte di Quezzi quarter in Genoa (figure 40), begun in 1956 and constructed by the Daneri group,[5] perhaps the most spectacular residential complex constructed during INA-Casa's second seven years. It was above all a demonstration of the architect's consistency. As he had done in the houses by the water on the Lido of Albaro, begun in 1934, and in the Bernabò Brea quarter and in the Forte Quezzi complex, Daneri compensated for self-imposed formal limitations with a serious inquiry mindful of such recognizable models as the serpentine and "dancing" blocks of Le Corbusier's *Plan Obus* for the Algiers hills. But one can see in the sinuous blocks at Forte di Quezzi not only a response to the landscape—one that faithfully follows its topographical curves, breaking up into typologically complex units, and enriched by internal services, loggias, and pedestrian paths—but also an attempt to consolidate an urban fragment that "exposes itself" as a living contradiction. The public pedestrian level that interrupts the two central blocks is to be read in the context of the difficult dialogue with the site: the complex contracts and expands elastically, opening itself "to the theater," then pulling back into itself. Daneri's design speaks serenely of the intolerable conditions imposed by programs of public intervention. He responded to Quaroni's problematic research with an image and a structure that placed in tense opposition the limitations of the intervention and its frustrated aspiration to become part of the city.

In the end, the examples emerging from INA-Casa's second seven years—to which one must add many routine, disconcertingly provincial realizations, such as the residential village in Ricciano (Pescia) by the Gori group or the Acilia quarter of 1957–59 by the Perugini-Del Debbio group —make it clear that the de-creased emphasis on public construction and its methods pro-duced brilliant but forced attempts and experiments recalling past motives. In speaking "of other things," one dirties one's hands to save one's soul; accepting the limitations of the real, one designs suggestive "mistaken ciphers."

But what is even more significant is that in these quarters the ideology of "living" survived only as a simulation. The "search for a place" in Forte Quezzi was, in fact, simulated. So was the typological research in Galatina, and so was the methodology with which the San Giusto quarter attempted to make itself convincing. The quarter was not in the city, yet its dynamic was hidden by its realization: whoever played such a game could only produce "honest dissimulation." The immersion in realism thus produced the sleep of reason. And demons would soon appear to reverse the mood that had generated the mythologies of the postwar years: the ideology of realism would soon be replaced by a revived quest for utopia.

But first one had to exhaust the motives that gave rise to autobiographical narcissism, or to make them move forward.

4
Aufklärung II: The Museum, History, and Metaphor (1951–1967)

The frustrations experienced by Italian architects in planning public housing were offset by achievements in the field of design and especially by accomplishments in museology. In designing "houses of art," the best Italian architects undoubtedly unleashed otherwise repressed aspirations: here their relationship with history was obligatory and direct, and strictly intertwined with pedagogical duties.[1] Museum architecture seemed to sum up the principal themes of the fifties, now cleansed of unnecessary appurtenances. These themes ranged from the "civil" role of form to the encounter between memory and innovation, to the recovery of modes of representation associated with special occasions. In this context, the design of the Palazzo Bianco in Genoa by Franco Albini 1950–51 (figure 41) immediately became a necessary point of reference for a culture intent on safeguarding, in all situations, a reassuring equilibrium.[2] Albini's design is a masterpiece of its kind: the extreme and rigorously developed museological function is accompanied by a refined neutrality of the decor displaying works; at the same time, it allows other signs to shine through like filigree, reducing them to respectful interlinear glosses of patiently reconstructed textual fragments.

Albini's museum "style" was thus defined; it would later on be expressed in his restoration and design of the Palazzo Rosso in Genoa of 1952–61, and would reach its peak in the Treasury Museum of San Lorenzo of 1952–56 (figures 42–43).[3] In the subterranean space of San Lorenzo, three *tholoi* of different diameters intersect an inverted hexagonal container endowed with ancillary spaces. It was a precise allegorical program, not unrelated to Caterina Marcenaro's intervention: the shrine of the Holy Grail was coupled with the memory of the treasure of Atreus. Albini managed, however, to sublimate the esoteric nature of his referents. The dialectic between spaces, the variations of light, the dialogue between the glass cases and the ambiguous suggestiveness of the interconnected organisms articulated one of the most original ingredients of Albini's poetics: a surrealism all the more subtle in that it was resolved in technically faultless vocabulary. Albini's "buried architecture" possesses its own language. Isolated from the external world, it elicits a dialogue between technological elegance—a further tool for achieving supreme detachment—and forms. This dialogue exalts an unreal dimension: the dimension, to be precise, of abstraction as "suspended image." It was the same abstraction that characterized Albini's interiors: ephemeral containers for magically transported historical obects. Thus, in the didactic exhibit "The Evolution of the Bicycle" at the 1951 Triennale, in the "16th-Century Genovese Textiles" and "Miracle of Science" rooms at the Palazzo Grassi in Venice in 1952, in the Salone d'Onore at the tenth Triennale of Milan in 1954, and in the later Palladio exhibit at the Basilica of Vicenza, Albini created masterpieces of representational virtuosity and dreamlike suggestiveness. His lyricism resided in the erect, suspended, and reinforced frames that—as Fagiolo has noted—resembled "larvae or surrogates of architectural structure."[4] Albini's severity alludes to an *absence* without ever becoming tragic.

One finds a "magical abstraction" in Albini's interior design, as well as in his San Lorenzo Museum. It is less perceptible in works such as the terraced complex of communal offices behind the Palazzo Tursi in Genoa of 1952–62, where the lyricism of the *intérieur* is replaced by a formal play *en plein air*.[5] Yet it would be a mistake to think that museum architecture constituted an isolated experience for Albini. Whereas the design of the INA office building in Parma (figure 23) relates to that of the Palazzo Bianco (figure 41), it is undoubtedly true that the Treasury of San Lorenzo (figures 42–43) prepared the way, through its use of allegory, for the projects for the Rinascente department store in Rome (figure 70). But in the fifties it was the "scale" of Albini's interventions that set the standard. Compared with the quiet murmur of Albini's apodictic signs, Carlo Scarpa's museum projects appear too expressive. And the critics, even those who favored the maestro from Venice, expressed their perplexity with Scarpa's work at the Correr in 1953.[6]

On the one hand, then, there was Albini's "let it be" attitude; on the other, there was Scarpa's magisterial narration. The situation was potentially explosive. Scandal erupted in 1956, when the Museo del Castello of Milan (figure 44) was opened to the public. Designed by the BPR studio, it became the target of an animated controversy that continued, two years later, when the BPR completed a building destined to become symptomatic of the Milanese climate in the late 1950s: the Torre Velasca (figure 45).[7] In fact, the Museo del Castello and the Torre Velasca faced the same problem: the handling of artifacts. For the BPR, and especially for Rogers, who opened the debate on existing conditions in *Casabella*,[8] only manipulation—appropriation through physical intervention—could make an archaeological field historical. Whether the "field" was a museum or a city, history assumed its character though intervention in the form of projects; the many legacies combined in a project gave rise to contaminations, to works that were in some way "dirty." But it was impurity that made the "game of recognition" possible. Architecture, tainted by ancient artifacts, recognized the legitimacy of its own tradition. These artifacts could, in fact, use the "new" as a kind of litmus paper, as a questioning mirror that could provide a *principium individuationis*.

The redesign of the Museo del Castello was eloquent (figure 44). In contrast to Albini's cautious treatment, the BPR chose a completely and powerfully present scenography that introduced—in the medieval street pavement of the Sala degli Scarlioni and the "fence" of the Sala delle Asse, in the dreamlike placement of armaments in the Sala Verde and the protective display of the *Pietà Rondanini*—multivalent resonances between the pieces exhibited and the exhibition architecture. The installation manifested an anxiety about communication, about the relationship between private and collective memory. The problem was how to make the private memory of the intellectual speak—a memory considered, as if by consensus, the keeper and executor of all obligations to the collective memory.

The Torre Velasca (figure 45) attempted to fulfill, in its own way, these same "obligations." The BPR, working for the Rice company, built the tower on a site that had been devastated by bombing, 450 meters from the Piazza del Duomo.[9] The planning of this building, which was to provide stores, commercial space, offices, studios, and residences, began in 1950–51, when a real estate agency acquired this property in the center of Milan. The structure was to be made of steel; defined by geometry and modules, rising like a monolith, the proposed tower had a tripartite composition: a projection at the entrance on Via Velasca, a vertical body with slabs bound by pilasters, and a double cube jutting out over the street below. The use of steel was initially rejected because of its high cost. The final project was drawn up between 1952 and 1955 and built from 1956 to 1957. The tower now became a compact, solid body, with ribs restraining the internal tensions of an image meant to be unique against the Milanese skyline. The connection between the main vertical block and the projecting body above was accomplished by means of slanted struts. Haughtily rolled up in its materiality, the tower expanded toward the sky like an energized volcano, assuming the appearance of a medieval tower paradoxically magnified. It stands as a "homage to Milan," achieved through means that could not yet be accused of historicism. The Velasca took its place in the city, commenting lyrically on an urban corpus about to disappear. Once again, the expectation was that a catharsis would emerge from intentions hidden in the recesses of a single object.

In fact, the Velasca, like the Castello Sforzesco Museum, was intended to "teach people how to see." Underlying resonances generating this form stirred public "consciousness" to take part in a collective *epoché*, a radical reconsideration of the new in light of the *temps perdu* it encouraged people to seek. Enzo Paci was the "philosopher" of *Casabella* for good reason, and he and Rogers were united by the lesson they had both learned from Antonio Banfi. But the Torre Velasca, wrapped in its ambiguous aura of implied meanings rediscovered through analogies, is above all a symbol of Italian architecture in the fifties: in the *great museum* that is the historical city, it seems fitting to find a "house" that gives signs consolation for their alienation, that protects them from the future and reassures them of the validity of their "moral" stands.

The BPR achieved similar though formally less interesting results in a later work, the complex in Piazza Statuto-Corso Francia in Turin sketched out in 1955–56 and constructed in 1959. The notion of "existing historical factors" contributed decisively to the BPR's discontinuous experience, which encompassed the epos of the Velasca and the Turin tower's emphasis on structure, as well as the cautious alliterations of the restoration of the Casa Lurani Cernuschi on Via Cappuccio in Milan of 1959.[10] This was an architecture that reflected on everything—the past, the city, and the possible dialogue between intellectuals and the masses—less than on itself. Mediated by Rogers' theoretical teachings, they were destined to generate a new chapter in the autobiography of Italian architecture. The tomb that the BPR built, with the collaboration of Carlo Levi, for Rocco Scotellaro in the Tricarico cemetery in 1957, constitutes an allegory for the mood inspiring these works. It is an archaic reminiscence in masonry, providing a view of the Basento valley through a crack in its sloping border. The poet's verses are inscribed in stone, and their rich nostalgic content also speaks for the architects: "But one does not turn back on one's way / Other wings will flee the nests of straw / For the ages die slowly / The dawn is new, is new."[11] And yet, the "new dawn" seemed inaccessible to a culture that always chose, in order to recognize itself, the path of "pensive suspension." This path would be taken not only by the BPR, but also by Ignazio Gardella in his house on the Zattere in Venice, completed in 1958 (figure 47).

This house constituted a kind of coda to the Torre Velasca, one that was greeted at the time as indicative of a dangerously evasive historicist climate. With its calculated asymmetry, its notched details, and a facade presented as a "commentary" on the typology of the Venetian aristocratic palazzo, the house clearly sought a dialogue with its exceptional location. Gardella's revisionism expresses here an unstable equilibrium between the rarefaction of linguistic techniques, intimacy of scale, and formal prudence. Such a precarious balance had also characterized the Terme Regina Isabella at Ischia (figure 22), the church at Cesate of 1956–58, and the tourist hotel complex at the Colletta, Arenzano, constructed in 1956 with the collaboration of Marco Zanuso. Yet these works are rich in nuances that differentiate them from his Galleria d'Arte Moderna in Milan and the Olivetti refectory in Ivrea, the most "classical" of Gardella's works of the fifties (figure 46). It is almost as though Gardella had two antithetical personalities, linked only by a taste for "educated revision."[12]

Gardella was also working with already formulated languages; he could only play with them in a peripheral way, eroding them a little or testing their resistance. In the end, even though he would never again produce anything as fine as the Alessandria clinic, Gardella's "peripheral" work after the war was not very different from the work he had done in the thirties.

But the "scandal" caused by the house on the Zattere (figure 47), which Argan called the "Ca' d'Oro of modern architecture,"[13] went beyond Gardella the individual. It became part of an international debate over what Banham has called "Italy's infantile retreat from the modern movement." The cornerstone of the scandal, in reality, was neither the Torre Velasca nor the house on the Zattere, nor Michelucci's Borsa Merci in Pistoia, but a work by two young designers from Turin, Roberto Gabetti and Aimaro Isola: the Bottega d'Erasmo in Turin begun in 1953 (figure 48) and featured in a memorable issue of *Casabella continuità* in 1957. Planned and executed with great refinement, the Bottega d'Erasmo presented itself as a well-calibrated synthesis of compositional savvy and allusive language. A real flirtation with the golden age of Italian and European nineteenth-century high-bourgeois architecture emanated—without ever becoming direct quotation—from the dense and surprising treatment of surfaces, which, broken and folded, suggested hermeticism. Compared to the Velasca, the BPR tower in Turin, or the house on the Zattere, the Bottega d'Erasmo had the merit of eliminating all mediation, of defining the new referent that validated the autobiographical vocation of Italian architects. The controversy was not, however, the result of a direct analysis of the work. It began when Gregotti, editor of *Casabella* at the time, read the letter that Gabetti and Isola had enclosed with the photographs of the Bottega. Perplexed, Gregotti dictated to Rogers a commentary that set in motion the debate on the so-called "neoliberty."[14] The polemic grew out of the statement that the modern movement had failed, that its ethical ideals, by now formulaic, had become superfluous. As long as the "recovery of values left untouched" by the founding fathers did not injure the fortress of the modern movement, any incursion into heterodox linguistic areas seemed justified and healthy; once the protective nets of theory had been removed—verbally, furthermore—it seemed necessary to direct anathemas against those proclaiming a crisis.

Yet the Bottega d'Erasmo, as well as Gabetti and Isola's other significant works—the Borsa Valori in Turin, begun in 1952 with Giorgio and Giuseppe Raineri, the competition project for a convent in Chieti of 1956 (figure 49), or the Equestrian Society's offices in Turin at Nichelino of 1959—did not present revisions of recent discoveries. Seen from a distance in time, they do not seem to justify the fuss that, for the most part, was due to the hidden problems they brought out and to their capacity to bring to light—through extreme ambiguity—the oscillating content of repressed introspection, cathartic intimacy, and the theoretical moralism characteristic of the new Italian "maestros." For the attention paid to "existing factors" and to context was but an extreme attempt to anchor the profession in a stable port, to flee the tempest threatening this fragile vessel sailing without any lights to illuminate the menacing icebergs surrounding the institutions.[15]

There was in this a kind of phobia about formal codification: Rogers had said that only "method"—perhaps only the method of "the orthodoxy of heterodoxy"—could mediate between history, existing factors, and the modern movement.[16] This idea relates to another aspect of the debate in those years: the late work of Mies van der Rohe and Le Corbusier met with indifference or mindless prejudice. Argan accused the chapel of Ronchamp of irrationalism and mysticism, although Rogers defended it on an ideological level; the Seagram Building was seen as an unexpected revival of neoclassical monumentalism. Only Giuseppe Samonà and Aldo Rossi engaged in textual analyses of Ronchamp and the convent of La Tourette, respectively. But the significance of these works (and of the capitol of Chandigarh) for the themes of compositional virtuosity, the play of "differences," and memory remained a dead letter for Italian culture that, for the moment, was privileging other readings and turning toward more accessible texts and exemplars.

The echoes of *communitas* were like the prince's kiss that has the power to bring the sleeping beauty back to life: the semantically neutral imagery of the radical and elementarist avant-gardes made it possible not to define the limits of the languages used. Meanwhile the dogma of "continuity" became more and more compromised.

It is perhaps not so daring to say that the atmosphere enveloping the high points of Italian architecture in the fifties was Lukácsian, though none of the protagonists of that era seem to have meditated on Lukács's *Theory of the Novel* or on his *Soul and Form,* which had not yet been translated into Italian. Yet all of them participated in the nostalgia that this Hungarian philosopher experienced for a mythic time in which "being" and "form" coincided: the time of the great classical epic. And like Lukács they seemed aware that the division between the self and the world, between "inside" and "outside," between soul and action, provoked by the corrosive intervention of thought was, if not remediable, at least artistically representable. Nostalgia for totality and the effort to describe the situation by means of fragmentation can be seen in the allusive forms created by the BPR, Ridolfi, and the young Milanese designers, and constituted a heritage that would greatly influence the architecture of the 1960s and 1970s. Without such premises, we cannot understand the formation of the poetics of Canella, Gabetti and Isola, Aldo Rossi, and Gregotti.

In the meantime, on a formal level, it was discovered that the cautionary stance taken by the Italian masters in their revisions could now be abandoned. This was the path followed by Gabetti and Isola, and the term "neoliberty" certainly did not pay homage to this phenomenon. The two Turinese designers turned toward a history as impalpable as the one that, under their guidance, Vittorio Gregotti, Gae Aulenti, and Guido Canella would seek between Milan and Novara.[17] The common thread linking the efforts of this generation was a revolt against the "fathers," who were guilty of having transmitted illusions now harshly exposed and whose "continuity" was still obstinately celebrated. The bourgeoisie, which should have received the ascetic message of purism and avant-gardism, revealed that it did not know what to do with the proposed spiritual regimens. It was better to design an "armchair for crying" for that bourgeoisie and recognize that it had conquered all enlightened utopias. This was what Gregotti, Meneghetti, and Stopinno would do with their "Cavour armchair" of 1959, harking back to influences that were timidly mindful of Vandeveld's *coup de fouet*. Or they could place themselves under the wing of an ancient father like Alessandro Antonelli, as an alternative to Labrouste or Baltard, to create works that were carefully crafted, like the residential center for workers of the Bassi in Cameri of 1956. The same Novarese studio chose Perret as a temporary point of reference, finding in him a *décadence* suited to the foggy atmosphere of "sad Turin" as opposed to Rogers' canonical reading of Perret of 1955.[18] The result was an office building in the historical center of Novara built in 1959–60 (figure 50), an involuntary homage to the thematics of "existing conditions."

Meanwhile, Canella's essays on the "Amsterdam school" and on Dudok, like those of Gregotti and Aldo Rossi on Antonelli—the Milanese "Novecento" would eventually be revalued by Muzio and De Finetti, not to mention Aldo Andreani—transformed the work on the "prehistory of the new."[19] It was no longer a matter, as it had been in naming Zevi's review, *Eredità dell'800*, of annexing larger portions of the recent past onto the antechamber of a mythical "modern movement." History, which now provided examples for private exploration, was broken into discontinuous fragments, then reassembled as a discrete system.

Such a phenomenon was characteristic not only of architectonic culture. It is significant that between 1954 and 1959 the film directors Fellini and Antonioni endowed neorealist language with nuances of intimacy and used it to describe the relationship between depth psychology and the realm of dreams. Significantly enough, *La Strada* and *L'Avventura* suspended events in ahistorical spaces, and in *La Dolce Vita* and *La Notte* the alienation of the subject reflected that of the metropolis. Nor is the argument altered by the fact that such alienation was interpreted idealistically and presented with phenomenological overtones. Having stressed the autobiographical aspect of neorealist poetics, we can now see a continuity between the events that characterized it and those that tried to surpass it. The search for an identity was once again at stake, a search that questioned its own function, and which could only be answered by delving into subjectivity to find the umbilical cord tying the unhappy *savant* to collective society.

The methods chosen for such excavations were also revealing: they spoke of a solitude that had become acceptable, of an uncertainty about social existence that seemed to be the only discourse worth communicating. The irrational components of such methods, especially on the part of architects, were severely tested. Yet the conflict had repercussions on the international scene. As is known, in 1959 Banham thundered against "Italian historicism," which he accused of betrayal.[20] The condemnation was aimed not only at the youth who exposed their desires in the 1960 exhibit "New designs for Italian furniture," organized by Gae Aulenti and Guido Canella[21]; their immediate "fathers" were also condemned. Nor was that sufficient: at the Otterlo convention, Rogers, Gardella, and Giancarlo De Carlo were rudely attacked for the Torre Velasca (figure 45), the house on the Zattere (figure 47), and the houses in Matera. Only De Carlo succeeded in countering the accusations of "deviance" by reaffirming the freedom from prejudice that characterized his commitment to antiformalism— one of the motives that had led him to make a noisy exit from *Casabella's* group of directors—and by adhering to the work and initiatives of Team X.

In 1958 Paolo Portoghesi spoke out in defense of "neoliberty." His article, which appeared in *Comunità,* constituted the first recapitulation of Italian work associated with the autobiographical tendency and the recovery of a humanism aimed at combating alienation. Not coincidentally, the essay bore the title "From Neorealism to Neoliberty."[22] Portoghesi's intervention clearly contained an element of self-justification: it called for the construction of a *koiné* in places where its presence was not burdened by other interests. In fact, for Portoghesi the recovery of the historical dimension played a very different role from the allusive and docile one it had played in Piedmont and Lombardy. Initially interested in the philological and critical analysis of Borromini's works, which he saw as the paradigm of a human condition whose ambiguity originated in the Roman *genius loci,* and later interested in eclectic architecture of the nineteenth century, Portoghesi continually translated his plunge into the past into projects. His theoretical base was a criticism of the conditions of the "bad modern" and of reification initially linked to the philosophies of Catholic progressivism.[23] His resulting production found its *raison d'être* in the hybrid. In this sense, the neobaroque modulations of the Villa Baldi in Rome of 1960–62 went much further than the programmatic and rarefied monumentalism of the competition project that Portoghesi submitted, with Gianfranco Caniggia and Paolo Marconi, for the Biblioteca Nazionale in Rome. This project foreshadowed a "manner" proud of its own involutions. Following a score whose musical notations had been replaced by graphic games, Portoghesi intoned in falsetto a song of victory over the "inhibitions of modern architecture."[24]

It would, however, be wise to set aside all moralizing in evaluating the new interest in the academy—in the most genuine sense of the word—which was rising among the younger generations at the end of the fifties. The academy stood for the transmissibility and perfectibility of experience, as against a reigning, even didactic dilettantism; it meant loyalty to rigorous codes in the face of tiresome empiricism; it meant upholding Catholic culture—which was in large part responding to these stimuli—and a new opposition to the ruling ethical laxity. In the end, the young neoeclectics and the Pevsnerian defenders of a clean continuity, including Leonardo Benevolo, aspired to the same ethic. Certainly it was a matter of different interpretations, but the appeal to morality was once again the weapon needed to fight off the well-organized from the forces of vulgarity.

Saverio Muratori became the interpreter of the rigorist works and critique of the modernism that were proffered here and there as antidotes to the disorderly debate. He had been significantly influenced by Scandinavian neoclassicism, to which he, along with Fariello and Quaroni, had resorted before the war in projects for the imperial piazza of the E42. The structural severity of Muratori's projects for the Roman Auditorium and the Tuscolano I quarter was only a pretext for the search for objective laws to guide composition, beginning with miscellaneous data on various themes. Muratori's views included an acute perception of the "crisis in values." His criticism of modern "bewilderment," of relativism, and of the ephemeral, tended to *reconstruct what had been shattered* by invoking certain laws, rediscovered by subjectively rupturing the "oblivion of Being" and conquering the disease that had generated actual "dissociations." Muratori did not live out this crisis, he exorcised it.[25] He did not invoke history, but that which, in history, seemed to resist change. On the one hand, he was looking for forms to suit materials endowed with internal coherence: dome-shaped or arched masonry, for example. On the other hand, he was trying to derive certainties from an analysis of urban structures. Urban analysis, as it has developed in Italy from the 1960s to the present, is undoubtedly indebted to Muratori's studies on Venice and Rome.[26] These studies, moreover, downplayed the interest in the *structure* of ancient fabrics, making the debate on "existing conditions" anachronistic and lending a different dimension to the theme of historical centers. Muratori's contribution was weakened by his nondialectical movement from typological analysis to project: his arguments against subjectivism and the "poverty of the modern"—Bonatz and Fahrenkamp versus Mies—led him to design not only the

ENPAS offices in Bologna, an undoubtedly valuable creation of 1952–57 (figure 54), but also the mediocre central offices of the Democrazia Cristiana in EUR of 1955–58 (figure 53), a structure content to be a dignified anachronism. Not coincidentally, one of the first student revolts in the field of architecture was directed against Muratori's teachings in Rome, which were targeted as the weak point in an institution deaf to the most acute demands of the time.

Yet having recognized the intrinsic weaknesses of Muratori's architecture and the concision of a few of his historical and structural analyses, one must stress the fact that at the heart of his work there was a desire not only for rigor but also for unity and legibility within the architectural bodies, a desire set against the judgment and conceptual poverty of architecture in the 1950s and 1960s.

The renewed call for the city "as it was" and for building types that slowly and collectively evolve, assumed questionable aspects in Muratori's teachings, but reflection on these themes proved fertile for a few of his students, including Gianfranco Caniggia. Again, Muratori undoubtedly created a form that reflected the "crisis of the modern." But given his rigorism, which was inimical to all "libertine" attitudes, it would be ungenerous to consider him a forerunner of so-called postmodernism. The study of the building type as an "a priori synthesis"—existing before reflective consciousness—and of a logic capable of connecting urban fabric, streets, and topographic structure, enabled Muratori to plan a quarter in Magliana in 1956 and several interesting solutions for its expansion in 1957. The theme was "open" development, one capable of changing into an urban *continuum* while maintaining a coherent relationship with its site. It was polemical in comparison to the typical abstractions of the INA-Casa quarters. Muratori, who died in 1973, would try to apply the same method to the Venetian situation in his entry to the competition for the CEP at the Barrene of San Giuliano, especially the third solution (figure 72). But, especially after 1963, he dedicated himself almost exclusively to the study of urban realities, reducing his own involvement in design almost to zero.

In the fifties, however, the recourse to history—as a discontinuous field for the young designers of the north and as a structural root for Muratori—often resulted in experimental antidotes seeking to counteract the impact of divisive forces. The appeal to totality hiding behind such reflections barely dissimulated the nostalgia for an intellectual work being carried out in ritual forms and priestly vestments.

This was even true, in spite of appearances to the contrary, for the troubled history of urban planning in those years. While Quaroni, as we have seen, was seeking complex new modes of intervention for cities and territories that had not yet been fossilized in a priori schemas, Luigi Piccinato and Giovanni Astengo were consolidating a discipline that seemed more and more inoperative, though endowed with canonized models and refined techniques of analysis. When regional planning was officially launched in 1952 under the auspices of Salvatore Aldisio, the minister of public works, in conjunction with the INU congress dedicated to that theme, Astengo was engaged in the writing of the two methodologically rich volumes of *Criteri di indirizzo*. But the "good government" of the territory, evoked by the image of Lorenzetti's Sienese fresco, was only a dream for *philosophes*. In the absence of responsible institutions and real political direction, not to mention laws governing the use of land, the studies for the plans for Campania, the Piedmont, Lombardy, and the Veneto were destined to remain pure exercises.[27] The scientific urban planning heralded by Astengo could only withdraw to the scale of small communities with rich historical associations; it was in Assisi, however, that Astengo experienced one of his most burning defeats. Nor would the "model" fare any better when repeated by Piccinato in the master plans for Matera, Aquila, Padua, Siena, Benevento, and Carrara. These plans were deficient not only because they adhered excessively to the model in question. Piccinato's urban planning had its own, independent, coherence. The identification of major axes, the placement of alternative nuclei of office buildings in the historical center, and the technique of zoning constituted interpretations of the 1942 law, carrying to completion the work of the discipline's "fathers." (We are thinking here not only of Stübben and Eberstadt, but also of Piacentini and his 1916 proposal for Rome.) But the discipline became ornamental under the influence of the economic ideas supporting it; to grasp this, historical analyses would have to dispell certain illusions. This was unthinkable in the crusaders' climate of Italian urban planning in the fifties, a climate in which the very use of the term "planning" was greeted with suspicion, and whose character was reflected in the troubled experience of the master plan for Rome (figure 55).[28]

In 1954 it was decided that a new plan for the capital should be implemented, following a report delivered at the Campidoglio by the liberal councilor Storoni in December 1953. The plan adhered to the lines appropriately drawn by the Lazio section of the INU: the campaigns of the progressive press against building speculation and administrative corruption seemed about to produce concrete and far-reaching results, and Roman culture took advantage of the occasion to form a coalition for what would be a lengthy battle. While the Lazio section of the INU was functioning as a pressure group and the population, including those in higher education, was becoming increasingly aware of the problem, the Great Commision for the plan proceeded amid compromises and jurisdictional confusion. Meanwhile the CET—the Committee for Technical Execution, featuring the strong personalities of Quaroni and Piccinato[29]—elaborated a schema that immediately became the object of controversy and provoked further study. The CET's plan represented both a summary of current models and a decidedly innovative hypothesis. The idea of salvaging the historical center through unidirectional expansion and the shifting of tertiary structures into a belt zone was adapted to Roman reality with a decisive urbanistic "invention": the eastern zones of expansion were welded to the surrounding territory on one side and to the historical nucleus on the other by means of office buildings located on a heavily traveled corridor and on the three poles of Pietralata, Centocelle, and EUR. The scheme was flawed by conventional zoning and a lack of concern about the relationship between housing and the workplace. Nevertheless, this project— which had taken shape in the absence of an economic plan and of prospects for feasible industrial projects—remained the most advanced product of Italian urban planning in those years.

The simple prospect of a plan was, however, enough to motivate forces of large and small speculation to form a coalition capable of political and cultural expression. The argument used to shelve the CET's proposal—the absence of an intercommunal plan—was a mere pretext. In June of 1959, after laborious polemics, the communal administration adopted the "council's plan, " a document that primarily reflected the desires of the construction industry and landowners. Quaroni, who had been skeptical from the beginning and considered the climate for real planning immature, reflected the disappointment experienced by the Roman intelligentsia in a clever essay, "An Eternal City: Four Lessons from 27 Centuries."[30] But the Rome plan had indirect historical consequences. Above all, the fact remained that the plan's very method was a blunted weapon, and not only for want of popular support or a political will to sustain it. Its intervention, restricted to a single aspect of a single economic sector—the use of land—did not justify hopes for different social and productive orders, hopes raised by a culture that was too interested in its own traditional methods and was still faced with an ineffectual concern for capitalist development. In order to offer true technical contributions to the political parties, it was necessary to enter directly into the "game" and to transform the appropriate cultural equipment along with it. But the daily debate over the plan also familiarized public opinion with the theme of the future of the city. Accusations no longer appeared only in the columns of *Il Mondo, L'Espresso, Il Contemporaneo*, and the daily papers published by leftist parties: Rosi would soon describe Neapolitan urbanistic speculation for the filmgoing audience in *Mani sulla città*.

While the INU was preparing, with its *Codice dell'urbanistica*, to launch its great challenge as an independent body, Italian urban planning, in possession of an elegant international review, was forced to withdraw to a position of defense. In the meantime, architectural culture witnessed the sporadic emergence of theories offering new approaches to the definition of the urban form.

Parallel to the historicist and intimist *tendenze*, there developed a *tendenza* soon defined as "neorationalist," while formal inquiries coming from more experimental and less "orthodox" investigations were beginning to separate architectural design from its referents. A competition served to catalyze forces grouping under different banners. Neither the BPR, Albini, Gardella, Quaroni, nor the northern revisionists participated in the 1957 competition for the new Biblioteca Nazionale of Rome, which was to be located in the neighborhood of the Castro Pretorio. Younger energies entered the scene, along with that eternal child, Giuseppe Samonà, and used the competition as a stimulus for a revision of methods that had come into question or simply as a pretext for programmatic declaration.[31] The emerging groups greeted each other's proposals with scorn. The projects of the Benevolo-Giura Longo-Melograni groups and the Manieri-Nicoletti group (with Giuseppe Vaccara as consultant) were radical in their decisive and critical reinterpretation of the method and stylistic elements of the International Style. In 1958, such an affirmation of orthodox continuity could only seem polemical, aiming at the historicist *tendenze*—which were, incidentally, documented in a few of the plans submitted to the same competition—as well as at more cautious revisionism and the neorealist tradition. The operation bypassed the quality of individual projects: whereas the Vitellozzi-Castellazzi group dedicated itself to anonymity with its mute winning project, the tradition upheld by Benevolo, Giura Longo, and Melograna seemed adapted to a new Italy, a country that was entering into international economic competition and consequently not wishing to disperse its energies in marginal research. Benevolo in particular was interested in announcing a new, self-critical turn: he retracted the populism of his first projects, such as that submitted to the competition for the Torre Spagnola quarter in Matera. The approach that, in the next few years, would lead him to outline his *History of Modern Architecture*, was already clearly delineated.

That approach, however, could only seem reductive to someone like Samonà, who considered modern architecture a vast heap of unresolved problems that deserved reflection beyond any "prospective" vision. From 1953 to 1958, Samonà had wisely borrowed Perret's use of structure as a compositional device for his blocks at the Palazzata of Messina, and had demonstrated that there was no "objectivity" in the "material" he manipulated with somewhat emphatic severity. But, along with Egle Trincanato, he had already experimented with achieving unity through breaking down elements in the INAIL offices of 1950–56 near San Simeone Piccolo in Venice, a text of fragments and oblique messages (figure 56).[32] The composer's wisdom lies not only in his capacity to elaborate, explain and "comment" upon a style, but also in his ability to complete and comment upon an urban site. In Samonà's project for the Biblioteca Nazionale of Rome, the basic theme was the same, though the point of reference had been changed. The materials and monumental language of the late Le Corbusier were borrowed again; but it was a code assumed only conditionally, a pretext used to declare the necessity of "classic" mastery, to escape a petty debate beginning to enjoy its own provincialism. The assurance with which Le Corbusier's language was reworked by Samonà in an austere binary structure—a tall L, tied diagonally to a slab scored with hermetic signs—recalls one of the many opportunities lost on postwar Italian architecture, while explaining its isolation. Samonà responded to the method proposed by Benevolo with the fecundity of language, of the "full word": too full to be comprehended in those years, and yet prophetic of a climate needing contemporary, crosscultural infusions to affirm itself.

Carlo Aymonino did not present a product, but rather a dense and austere programmatic manifesto. He too was in search of a way out, not wishing to remain stranded upon the shoals of the impoverished realism that characterized his previous professional experience. He too turned to modern architecture for referents whose complexity did not exclude symbolic values; he too was ready to undertake, temporarily, an operation of rereading. Exploring the polysemy of the sign and the modularity of spaces, Aymonino hoped to find in Aalto the source of a writing of accretion and eventual outbursts; it is significant that at the end of his voyage he encountered the sugary aggregations of Willem Marinus Dudok.[33]

The dualism of Aymonino's Biblioteca Nazionale was clearly provisional, though it seemed, upon publication of the results of the competition, like a novelty of unexpected promise. It was, however, more difficult to grasp at the time that the complex poetic embraced by Aymonino actually had its roots in the neorealism he had implicitly retracted. Yet the experience of the Tiburtino proved to be the distant source of this search for structures that had in some way absorbed an urban polysemy, and that functioned in the city as variables tied to a morphological theme—a theme that would characterize Aymonino's work from then on. Aymonino perfected his lexicon of rhetorical flourishes in his projects for the industrial technical institutes of Lecce and Brindisi, in his condominium on Via Arbia of 1960–61, and in his dense complex on Via Anagni in Rome of 1962–63. But for Aymonino individual buildings were only in vitro experiments, brief moments in a development that would ultimately reach an urban scale.

The recovery of the representational value of the image was, moreover, a constant temptation for Italian architecture in the late fifties. That temptation was present in Milan in the work of Vico Magistretti, a skillful professional capable of modulating disturbing volumetric aggregations, like the building for the *L'Abeille* society, designed with G. Veneziani in 1959–60 (figure 57). It also dominated Vittoriano Viganò's Istituto Marchiondi Spagliardi in Milan Baggio of 1953–57 (figure 58), which was greeted as an example of almost Japanese "brutalism" deriving from Le Corbusier.[34] This same nostalgia for representation informed the work of Caccia-Dominioni, though more superficially (figure 62),[35] and rendered ponderous the work of Figgini and Pollini, both the Chiesa della Madonna dei Poveri in Milan of 1952–54 (figure 61) and the house on Via Circo of 1954–57. Gino Valle skillfully joined it with a poetics that overcame Mangiarotti's objectivism and Marco Zanuso's abstract elegance (figures 63–64).[36]

Valle was also committed to formal revisions that resulted in constructivist vocabulary.[37] His location, geographically peripheral but in touch with a specific clientele, removed him from both the ruling ideologies and the autobiographical wave. The high degree of professionalism he demonstrated in the condominium on Via Marinoni in Udine of 1958–60, in the monument to the Resistance in the same city, designed for a competition in 1958 and executed in 1967–69, and in the condominium on Via San Francesco in Trieste of 1955–57, led to a work—the Zanussi offices in Porcia, Pordenone of 1959–61—that attracted international attention. The building offered a multivalent image of industry: the handling of structure spoke of the potential of industrial work, translating its reality into serene formal discourse. Valle responded to the tormented appeal of high Italian architectural culture with an anti-intellectualism satisfied with its safe insertion into the world of production. The line of work heralded by the Zanussi offices has continued without interruption up to the present; it seeks to realistically assess the capacity of planning to influence immediate industrial reality.

In the 1950s, in the struggle to define areas in which the power of speech might dissipate the clouds of alienation, Valle's work seemed courageous. The tension that informed the whole and the resolution of details in the Zanussi offices were built on a tradition dissipated by Melchiorre Bega's flat exercise, the Galfa skyscraper in Milan of 1958, and also by the more pretentious but equally empty exercise of the Pirelli skyscraper by Ponti, Fornaroli, and Rosselli of 1955–58 (figure 65).

Yet Valle's building was destined to become an object for architectural pilgrimages in the Veneto, and the works of Gio Ponti, Melchiorre Bega, and Luigi Mattioni—the designer of Milan's first skyscraper in 1950–55, of the Diaz center in 1953–57, of the San Babila center in 1954–57—gave shape to the new third force of Milan. International vestments were in tune with the need for security that leaders of the Italy of the economic "miracle" opposed to the haut bourgeois conscience as expressed in the Torre Velasca (figure 45). This need for security, moreover, was felt in vast sectors of architectural culture. In this sense, the "recourse to Bakema" apparent in the Pharmacology Institute of the Roman Città Universitaria of 1957–60, by Claudio Dall'Olio and Alfredo Lambertucci, was equivalent to the crisp Esperanto of the third volume of offices on Via Torino in Rome designed by Libera,

Calini, and Montuori in 1956–58.[38] The "international" vocabulary, manipulated with assurance by architects of the caliber of Libera and Moretti, working here with Vittorio Cafiero, Amedeo Luccichenti, and Vincenzo Monaco, also gave life to the Villaggio Olimpico in Rome of 1957–60, in a zone enriched by the Stadio Flaminio and the Palazzetto dello Sport by Vitellozzi and Pier Luigi Nervi.[39] The Olympic complex was one of the few Roman interventions of the late fifties endowed with dignity: the long arched blocks define an urban landscape alternately capable of recovering the value of the street and of confirming a poetics of indeterminacy exempt here from the rhetorical excesses of a few of Moretti's contemporary and later works, like the apartment building in Monte Mario of 1961–62 and the Watergate apartment complex in Washington of 1959–61. The fact remains, however, that the quarter in the Flaminio is a fragment of the "Rome of the Olympiades": a fragment of a colossal speculative operation grafted onto an athletic event and offered as an unconvincing polemic of urban development.[40]

Roman professionalism was, therefore, once again able to participate in the problematics of a high culture expressing disorientation; participation extended even to the relationship between the discipline and politics that high culture claimed as its own. In the pages of *Casabella* the debate shifted to history, while European works were considered in a new light. But even that debate now seemed limited, compromised by an unproductive elitism. Intolerance would soon manifest itself in short-lived efforts as a few exponents of the newest generation gathered around new reviews such as *Superfici* and *Argomenti di Architettura*, and young architects formed the Società di Architettura e Urbanistica (SAU). From 1957 to 1963 the SAU presented itself as more than a group expressing a *tendenza;* it saw itself as an eclectic association of moralists in search of an ideology. Only a generic morality, in fact, could have reunited architects like Benevolo, Aymonino, Valori, Giuseppe Campos-Venuti, Melograni, Vittoria, Bruschi, Manieri, Moroni, and Insolera. The insistence on methodological problems and on a "commitment" to resolving the larger problems presented by the reality of Italian society was in curious contrast to the works of these architects who, with a few exceptions, could only agree on minor abstractions and who were ready to disband upon collision with contemporary politics.[41]

In 1959 the endeavors of the SAU "group" received a reply in the "broad" initiative instigated by Zevi, who demanded an end to cliques of *tendenza* and promoted INARCH, the National Institute of Architecture. Manufacturers, architects, building engineers, and entrepreneurs were called upon to collaborate in a national body, or, at the very least, to resolved their conflicting interests. Accusations of corporatism were scornfully deflected by Zevi, who stressed the dialectical function of an organized encounter of forces destined to collide anyway.

INARCH was riddled by the tensions that characterized the INU, but most of the grand objectives stated by Zevi in his promotion speech were never met. Yet even the formation of INARCH was a symptom of aspirations alive in the late fifties. To appreciate this historically, one must realize that soon afterward the debate on the political formula of the center-left would splinter the big Italian parties and provoke adjustments and reformulations of the entire culture.

Leonardo Benevolo's *History of Modern Architecture*, which appeared in 1960, was influenced by this climate. This historical project was based on a desire to clarify, even at the cost of oversimplification, and on a need to draw a coherent and progressive line comprising the "tradition of the new." In Benevolo's work the Modern Movement theorized by Pevsner in 1936 became a solid edifice, in whose shadow anxieties and worries might find rest and satisfaction. The works chosen as examples in the final pages were also reassuring: an inexorably reductive reading crushed the dazzling testimony of the late Mies, while the "furors" of Le Corbusier and Wright in the 1950s and 1960s were considered with skeptical compunction. In addition, Bakema and Van den Broek and Arne Jacobsen were seen as timely perpetuators of Gropius's monumental orthodoxy. But Benevolo was not interested in setting one language against another. Instead, his power lay in his demonstration that the modern movement began and developed as a complex project intended to relocate human activities within the context of a reformed collective life.

Benevolo's *Storia* stood, in 1960, as a kind of dam against all deviance, but also as a *rappel à l'ordre* and a calming *summa*. The sociological and political perspectives that inform Benevolo's work were equally vague. What counted for him, as he stood on the threshold of a new historical phase in the country's development, was that architects should free themselves from the debt to Zevi, Rogers, and the revivalists. Benevolo's method was even more endebted to post-neorealist reductionism than it appeared to be at the time. Nonetheless, Benevolo's historiographical revision, which also sought a political base for intellectual work, was definitely overdue. His optimism, appearing nine years after Argan's tormented reading of Gropius's Weimar period, reflected a defensive stance.

Not even a work of unquestionably high quality, like the new Rinascente department store in Rome, executed by Albini and Franca Helg on Piazza Fiume in 1960–61, seemed conscious of the new problems.[43] In passing from the initial project of 1957–59 to its eventual execution, Albini's "machine" experienced a noticeable reduction in tension (figure 70): the steel structure knowingly juxtaposed with a blind volume was replaced by a rippled screen of an inert pink color, incised by a structural grid and interrupted on the side of the piazza by an all-too-welcome large window. The Rinascente exhibited its own reification, for it entered too readily into a dialogue with the urban environment; as an experiment on the theme of "existing conditions," it went too far afield. The equilibrium achieved in the INA building in Parma (figure 23) was not to be found here. Albini and Helg's Rinascente made it obvious that the theme had been exhausted along with its motives. The problem of a dialogue with existing structures took on another dimension: within the INU, analyses of the physical form of city and country were leading to an alternative line without resorting, at least not verbally, to the habitual identification and denunciation of bureaucratic channels of intervention.

One should be aware, however, that such an alternative line was often upheld by the very protagonists of an architecture of self-reflection, who maintained as their basic objective "full expression" in the methodology of urban and rural intervention, not realizing that their research paralleled the search for full expression in the object itself. The effects of this singular coincidence would soon become evident, when the two scales of operation were united in a continuum that functioned as a magnet for divergent forces.

It was no coincidence that at the INU Convention round table in Lecce[44] in 1959, Giancarlo De Carlo, Piero Moroni, Quaroni, and Eduardo Vittoria all agreed that the term *"urbanistica"* had been exhausted, and then proceeded to subsume it under the term "architecture." Having effected this artificial synthesis, they imbued it with meaning, ignoring all limitations of scale and all methods of communication. Protected by a word, the will to power was free to roam in the magical terrain of the "city-region." As terms were coined, the dreamed-of control extended to the new dimensions evinced by the implosion generated by the mass media, by the technological progress and the absence of limits that changes in the scale of life and the urban scene seemed to have introduced. Once again, the intellectual attempted to recognize himself as he entered a room of distorting mirrors, and could only express shock on seeing his reflected image. He did not find himself in a space suffering from the reality of the rural south, but on a metaphysical trip in a technologically over-equipped, hypothetical missile. The "land of the baroque" was abandoned in favor of a voyage to the realm of "invisible cities."

In the same year, 1959, Giuseppe Samonà's *Urban Planning and the Future of European Cities* also broached, though with greater deliberation, the theme of the extra-urban scale. The examples of Greater London and the French *grands ensembles* were assumed as the pretext for an interpretation of the environment's physical form that suggested a profound restructuring of the discipline. Two elements emerged from this ferment. On the one hand, the visible was stressed; on the other, urban planning as a "model" entered a critical phase, while "regionalist" thematics were unconsciously revived. This crisis of the model, however, had no institutional referents: the critique of the "city as form" and of neighborhood poetics liberated the political valence that had in some way been contained (or compressed) in those operative instruments. A twofold operation, then, took place in the late fifties. The worn relationship of plan and institutions was cast aside, at least theoretically, as the focus shifted onto the *problem* of new subjects and new techniques for new institutions; the theme that had emerged into the reassuring current of the "will for form" was immediately redirected, and the problem was thus prevented from erupting.

The examples put forward at the round table in Lecce were picked up at a later competition destined, like many others marking the stages of our history, to become the focus of a cultural debate that nonetheless produced few concrete results. In this same year of 1959, Italian urbanists were preparing to participate in the competition for a CEP quarter in the Barene of San Giuliano, in Mestre, in a strip facing the Venetian lagoon.[45]

The project proposed by the Quaroni group sparked a debate that would have broad repercussions (figure 71); in effect, it signaled a decisive stage in the development of international architectural culture. In this project, Quaroni concentrated the positive results of his incessant criticism, the intuition of untried planning methods suited to large-scale design, a disinterested reading of the historical morphology of the Venetian lagoon, and an attention to visual communication aimed at a densely stratified mass public. The shapeless, aleatory quality of the zoning and the formal rigidity of architectural articulation were rejected in favor of a "town design" that set its principal components within a weft of relations, but did not define the forms of individual parts. This aesthetic of the undefined was, however, deliberate. The big semicircular edifices facing the lagoon linked to form an enormous belt opening out to the urban fabric and then radiating inland. The project alluded to the urban lesson of Venice's historical fabric: an allusion perceptible on a structural, rather than visual level. The intense stratification of the city, the intersections of its multivalent images and the eclecticism informing it were organized by Quaroni into a large-scale network of signs animated by a vitality that also influenced the design method. The discovery of the immense communicative richness of the aleatory approach was translated into a "plan-in-process," an "open work" of urban scale. Quaroni sketched out many typological inventions for the configuration of fabrics, but they were not binding. The urban design freed the architectural configurations, giving them full autonomy within a system of pure relations.

Quaroni's project for the CEP of San Giuliano not only buried, for once and for all, the ideology of the quarter and its attendant microsociology; it also served as a solution and turning point for the entire experimental phase comprised of the complexes built during INA-Casa's second seven years. A new discipline was in the works. Its origin was certainly Quaroni's reflection on the American metropolis as well as his critique—much more profound than that of Alexander—of all theories of urban development based on "conforming additions." The *manifesto* legible in the CEP project has, not coincidentally, been crucial to all research in progress now.

Yet Quaroni could not immediately follow up on the turning point he had helped bring about. In his studies and final solution for the partition plan for the Lido di Classe in Ravenna, designed with D'Olivo, Antonino Manzone, and Antonio Quistelli, work initiated in 1959 produced new results. But in 1962, the Quaroni group's project for the office district of Turin resorted to an ambiguous identification of urban projection with expanded architecture.

Quaroni's project for the CEP in San Giuliano, however, set in many ways the groundwork for the new climate of the sixties. It appeared, in fact, at a moment in which Italian intellectuals were becoming aware of a new reality: convulsive urbanization and the diffusion of mass communication had effected profound transformations in society and individual behavior. These changes, along with rapid economic growth, encouraged the formation of interpretive models that quickly replaced those of the preceding decade. Neorealist myths were replaced by technological ones, though consideration was given to the legacy of the avant-guarde. It was not, then, a question of implementing the technique that Pier Luigi Nervi had triumphantly celebrated in his Palazzo and Palazzetto dello Sport in Rome and his Palazzo del Lavoro in Turin (figure 66), nor was it a matter of simply assuming the new rites of an "affluent society." The new work was warranted instead, on the one hand, by a reality that seemed to be overturning all established models in its unbridled course and, on the other hand, by a methodological crisis of instruments reflected in the anxieties that produced Libertini and Panzieri, Franco Fortini, and Elio Vittorini's "heterodox Marxism."

The ferment resulting from these reflections created a widespread antiideological climate. In the meantime, a context favoring the institutionalization of planning policy arose because of the following factors: Colombo's thesis on the necessity— including and indeed focused on the industrialized areas of the North—of investments in production for underdeveloped areas; Pasquale Saraceno's call for the use of public capital in the development of a self-propelling economic system geared toward full employment; the tendency of the most advanced minds in business to focus on the increasing global demand; and the notion of national control of the market, to be facilitated, according to Ugo LaMalfa's note of 1962, through the planning of investments.

When the INU presented its own plan for the *Urban Planning Code*, it carried out a conclusive and double initiative: the time for abstractions had passed, now was the moment to engage in a more articulate dialogue with political parties. The ideal image of the *Code* did constitute, in fragments, an occasion for some significant political encounters. But the entire concept of urban planning would be overhauled in the early sixties.

More methods had to be applied in the country: it was no longer a question of the old myth of the interdisciplinary approach, itself a reflection of Olivetti's "republic of the intellect." The founding of research organisms like the ILSES (the Lombard Institute for Economic and Social Sciences), in which the urbanist De Carlo and the economist Sylos-Labini participated, displaced the terms of the dialogue between methods, greatly clarifying the relationship between analysis and intervention. In 1962, a convention in Stresa organized by the ILSES took stock of international experiments and indicated that the theme of the city-region was of critical importance.[46] The convention in Stresa proclaimed the end of the "model," of the global form imposed upon an urban dynamic. De Carlo, in concluding the proceedings, spoke of the city-region as a set of dynamic relations, instituted within a territorial galaxy of specialized installations homogenized by those interrelationships. It is clear that the intervention into a constantly changing entity could not pretend to attain a "form" without making a conceptual leap. The attack that De Carlo and Quaroni had launched in 1954 against the Italian urbanistic tradition was turned into a working methodology. The same Rome plan now appeared, in light of the new views, almost too concerned with imposing an impossible control on the complex form of an oversized city. The studies for the intercommunal plan of Milan (figure 73), which witnessed the participation of, among others, De Carlo himself, made another appeal for a formal skeleton—a "turbine" design, whose extremities would function as territorial unifiers of an organism with many centers—but only as a support for successive interventions, not all of which could be "designed."[47]

The idea of "grand scale" immediately became part of the mythological baggage of Italian architectural culture. Those who thought they should adhere to Elio Vittorini's invitation to take hold of the new reality created by the industrial universe were drawn to automation and cybernetics or to models of spatial economy. They were mesmerized by the uncontrollable and projected their own dissimulated emotions onto images of the future. As for the populism and sociology of the 1950s, the referents and methods had changed, but not the intellectual attitudes. It thus came about that the new gaps created by the analyses of the ILSES and the conclusions of the convention at Stresa were filled by the implications of Kenzo Tange's 1960 projects for the Boston Bay and for Tokyo, which were published in detail. *Casabella* entered a new era with a sequence of monographs dedicated to the American scene, to office districts, to the "city-region," to the Milanese intercommunal plan, and to large national and international competitions. Kevin Lynch's studies of the structure of urban sites and of their identifiable traits were fused with images of a culture that was turning technique into a fetish. It was important to make sacrifices to the new totem, without acknowledging that reality had been sublimated into it. The feverish enthusiasm for the "large dimension" still sought places to realize forms. Despairing of affecting general levels, these places were identified among the ganglia of the territorial organism, which was seen as a structure undergoing constant change. It was hoped that the supporting skeleton, the bony structure and brains of this magnetic field, would eventually become apparent. The office districts were disruptive nuclei at the same time capable of gathering the forces interacting within the region. The projects elaborated by the research of the architecture school in Rome in 1961–62 tried to define the office district of the capital,[48] and the 1962 competition projects of architects like Aymonino, Canella, Quaroni, Samonà, and Aldo Rossi for the office district of Turin sang apologies to the service sector, confronting, like "machines" filled with promises, regional concerns. The synthesis between architecture and urban planning, recommended in 1959 at the round table in Lecce, now identified its field of application. Symptomatic, however, were the megastructures that filled the architecture magazines: projects Paolo Ceccarelli immediately criticized as expressions of "opulent urban planning."[49] Many, such as Aymonino's and P. L. Giordani's project for the office district of Bologna, remained the unrealized fantasies of Italian communal administrations.[50] There was an attempt to control what were emerging as feasible possibilities and to use design to enter the citadel where power supposedly reigned. There was a desire to subject that sacred stronghold to form, to seek compensation in unconscious exorcism. If realism had tried to join the language of the "people" to the language of the cultivated class, that very class of cultivated people now sought to give voice to the anonymous think tanks in which they—for simplicity's sake—were concentrating power.

This phenomenon occurred in a particular form in Italy, but it also appeared on the international level,[51] reflecting a profound malaise over the limitations of architecture and trauma over the establishment of "planning" as an autonomous discipline. While the new "international utopia" was taking root, that malaise also manifested itself in more traditional spheres, with intolerant gestures interpreted as architecture's response to the provocation of Action Painting. The most famous was that of Michelucci's church at the entrance to the freeway between Florence and Bologna, designed in 1960–62 and opened in 1964.[52]

With his Chiesa dell'Autostrada (figure 74), Michelucci made a singular attempt to force architectural logic, exposing a battle between matter, endowed with explosive force, and structure, which he paradoxically deformed. The result, a hurried grouping of spaces and random objects, did not derive from the patient, autobiographical labyrinths lying in the folds of the Ronchamp chapel. Rather, it was the outcome of a kind of ongoing protest Michelucci waged against the formal imperative. Here was yet another place that called for participation and lived experience, and that looked on geometry as constraint. In spite of its proximity to the speeding highway—or perhaps because of it—the architecture of the church seeks to ignore the possibility of "composing." Decomposed, the Chiesa dell'Autostrada seems to warn the inattentive driver. He is not obliged to stop and contemplate the church, but is instead presented with a mass of materials violated in order to demonstrate the unnaturalness of the "false modern." Michelucci's neoexpressionism progressed through an entire range of variations on the "uncomposed"; his language became an increasingly coherent system of torn membranes, magical ruins, twisted and interwoven paths, material and structural clots, from his Chiesa di Borgomaggiore in San Marino of 1961–66, to the Chiesa di Longarone of 1966–78 (figure 76), perhaps the masterpiece of his last phase, to the Chiesa di San Giovanni Battista in Arzignano near Vicenza, of 1965–67. On the other hand, the dynamic of the sign and the envelopment of forms reached a *horor vacui* of Piranesian dimensions in a series of projects: his churches and parochial centers of Montalbano Jonico and Sesto Fiorentino, his memorial to Michelangelo in the Apuanian Alps, his thermal complex near Massa Carrara (figure 75), and his lemon-house at the Villa Strozzi in Florence.[53]

It was in the early sixties, however, that Michelucci's new research had the greatest influence on the "manner" of the Florentine school.[54] Working independently of each other, Leonardo Ricci and Leonardo Savioli translated Michelucci's "furor" into structural brutalism in the Sorgane quarter near Florence of 1963–66. Ricci's long residential block impatiently untied syntactic knots, in search of typological renewal (figure 77), while Savioli's apartment house on Via Piagentina in Florence of 1964 (figure 78), played with material excrescences, exaggerated objects, and formal paradoxes. Everything ran to excess in Ricci's project for the Village of Olives in Riesi, Sicily in 1963: here inhospitable caverns open up like fossils of prehistoric animals, mimicking an "absolute natural" reminiscent not only of Finsterlin's organic amoebas, but also of André Bloc's *habitacles* and Fredrick Kiesler's gestural landing.

Direct cultural stimuli stood behind this anxiety over semantic richness. Above all, it reflected the expressionist era, but it also expressed a desire to communicate uncertainty and the problems it generates. Finally, it conveyed anguish over a "loss" compensated for by increasingly insistent attempts to apply semiological research to architectural analysis. It was no coincidence that in 1964 this climate gave rise to the exhibit "Michelangelo the Architect" at the Palazzo delle Esposizioni in Rome, in which Zevi and Portoghesi portrayed Buonarroti as a raging iconoclast extending his hand across the centuries to Pollock and Frank Lloyd Wright.[55] With this exhibit, "normative criticism" may have reached its low point: the reinvention of Michelangelo—whether the Michelangelo of the Florentine fortifications or the improbable "urbanist Michelangelo"—functioned in fact as a retrograde force, the one that Zevi would perpetuate when he proposed a reassessment of Erich Mendelsohn a few years later. A poetics of heroic sublimation was offered to disillusioned and frustrated intellectuals. Moreover, this poetics encouraged them to don prefabricated garments of sorrowful fury. Italian neoexpressionism—interpreted in cleverly fashioned forms by Marcello D'Olivo in the Villa Spezzotti in Lignano Pineta of 1958 (figure 79) and in the resort in Manacore del Gargano of 1964, as well as by Guido Canella, who requires a different sort of analysis—resembled a thin veneer that had been applied to an exhausted discipline. Like any cosmetic, it served to conceal the reasons for that decadence, creating an illusion of eternal youth, instead of seeking roles best suited to the new, emerging conditions. The critics who were enthusiastic about Michelucci's Chiesa dell'Autostrada thus joined the chorus celebrating the realization of that "ambiguous traitor's" aesthetic.

The ethic that emerged from the models proposed by this kind of historiography was, significantly, a loser's; it was the creed of someone who needs to be vanquished in order to sing his own heroism. There was ample reason to be perplexed when that criticism then claimed the duty to choose, as contemporary examples of "anticlassical" language and nonconformity, the flat technological exercises of Moshe Safdie's Habitat in Montreal and the elegant but rarefied disjunctions of the Passarelli studio's building on Via Campania in Rome of 1963–65 (figure 80).[56]

The critics' disorientation reflected, however, an uncertain reformulation of roles occurring in the light of a more precisely defined political demand and a persistent confusion of needs. The hostility toward the social sciences once experienced by the communists had vanished; but the dream of generic employment and the myth of abstract humanism had both been miserably exhausted. In this void the labor parties called for technical support, which, in the absence of comprehensive reorganization of intellectual work, was offered in accordance with inactive methodologies. Typical, in this regard, was the compromise that in December 1962 enabled the Roman council to adopt a master plan drawn up by a commission that had composed it with an eye on the politics of the center-left (figure 55).[57] The oversized scale of the plan, the vagueness concerning expansion, and the zoning— generic for the existing or completing sectors, and based on inadequate nuclear models for those recently created ones—added up to an office zone inherited from the CET's scheme: an uncertain technique came to the aid of a basically static urban policy. The sole innovation lay not in the design, but in the accompanying norms, foreseeing the creation of an "urbanistic observatory" indebted to the Geddesian Outlook Tower and capable of following the dynamics of urban and territorial development. Not coincidentally, this proposal remained a dead letter.

Confirming that the 1962 plan was an inoperative design, a dissemination of equipment, services, and installations progressively lessened the significance of the notion of an eastern office zone. This idea was compromised, furthermore, by the increasing saturation of available land. Above all, EUR signified to the south an efficient business district and a residential area for the upper middle class: the showy internationalism of the ENI skyscrapers and of the Ministry of Finance—the latter designed by C. Ligini, G. Marinucci, and R. Venturi from 1958 to 1962—in the zone looking over the lake, along with Nervi and Piacentini's Palazzo dello Sport, constituted the urban "gate" to the south, while the office buildings by Luigi Moretti and Vittorio Ballio Morpurgo of 1963 functioned, with their sophisticated abstraction, as propylaea on the opposite side of the central axis. Italy's confidence and optimism as it "modernized" itself in the midst of a real economic miracle were evident in the new EUR, the only real administrative pole of the capital. That pole featured—and later not just meta-phorically—elements linking the official expressions of the Fascist era to those of the Christian-Democratic regime.[58] And in 1962 it was Moretti who confirmed, with his INCIS district near EUR (figures 68–69), the administration of the multifunctional installa-tion that the management of the extraordinary commissary Virgilio Testa had grafted onto the remains of the buildings executed for the E42.[59] It echoed, in a minor key, the formal linguistic and typological models used in the Olympic quarter. But the construc-tion of the INCIS, as well as of the long, hyperrationalist blocks by Pietro Barucci for the nucleus of office buildings on Piazzale del Caravaggio of 1968, encouraged building speculation that no public program had taken the responsibility to coordinate, between the Cristoforo Colombo axis and the golden suburb of Casal Palocco.

EUR and the axis it marked were not the only elements at variance with the guidelines of the master plan. The new magis-trates' courts, designed by the Perugini-Monteduro group, were constructed between 1959 and 1969 on Piazzale Clodio. The project's remarkable formal chastity, largely due to Vittorio De Feo's design, did not compensate for its unfortunate location. In the meantime, the execution of the Vitellozzi project for the Biblioteca Nazionale at Castro Pretorio of 1959–67, the RAI-TV office building on Viale Mazzini by Berarducci and Fioroni of 1963–65, and the sporadic interventions in the area of Piazza Fiume/Via Veneto—which included Albini's Rinascente and the purist, prismatic office building by Montuori and Calini on Via Po—focuses on a zone adjacent to the historical center, making a reconversion of *tendenza* problematic, to say the least.[60]

The eastern complex, which had been the focus of the debate leading to the 1962 compromise, thus remained the object of academic experimentation. It was followed by a singular initiative, in which architects of the caliber of Quaroni, Zevi, Fiorentino, the Passarellis, and Morandi, with the advice of Gabriele Scimemi, became associated from 1967 to 1970 in the Asse studio, formed in order to plan the entire office zone (figure 81).[61] It was obviously an enterprise that intended to exploit all of Roman architectural culture for promotional purposes. The architects responded to the immobility of the institutions with their own techniques, offering a project to the city for free, in the hope of removing, with an appropriate publicity campaign, the obstacles blocking the renewal of urban organization. Theirs was an appeal to the freedom that had been granted to the separate, experimental laboratory; the result of this appeal was a "useless machine" that sought to liberate itself from its own reified condition through the application of mute geometric codes. The chasm opened up by this condition of abstinence rendered excessive the perverse game imposed in university classrooms anxious for new purity. The monstrous animal testified to a collective neurosis, to an impotence devoid of pathos, and to the anachronism of operations still influenced by third force attitudes.

Without becoming "technicians," the architects involved found themselves competing with technique and forcing it into a sterile marriage with flimsy metaphors. Yet they achieved much on their own. The Passarellis showed that they knew how to manipulate a variety of languages correctly and professionally (figure 80), while Riccardo Morandi remained the most true and inventive of Italian structuralists (figure 67). As for Quaroni, he pursued his tormented research, indulging in Kahnian modulations in the governmental center in the Kasbah of Tunis of 1966–67, elaborating systems of control for an urban scheme full of imagination, as in his master plan for Bari of 1965–73 and his studies for that city's seaside promenade, and finally engaging in a weighty reflection upon the modes of configuration in his project for a church in Gibellina of 1970 (figure 82), in which the encounter between purity and impurity pursued a dialectic resembling personal confession. The experience of the Asse studio would prove to be profitable only for Fiorentino, who would later on draw from it a complex for Corviale (figure 117).

The time of forced *koinés* had passed, and it was too late to reaffirm the improbable preeminence of an intellectual work too unsure of its own aims to convey progressive messages. Besides, the hopes that had been raised by the first center-left hinged on the renewal of the legislative methods that were attracting attention. This period saw the development and maturation of roles directly implicated in the administration of various sectors of the construction industry and of urban development, with precise references to the strategies of political parties, and of the socialist party in particular. It was not just a matter of technocratic myths. The most pressing need was to create renewed technological and institutional structures adapted to an efficient strategy of reform; only later, motivated by new disappointments, would architectural culture address the problem of theoretical reflection. But from the early sixties on, technicians like Michele Achilli, Baldo De Rossi, Giuseppe Campos-Venuti, Marcello Vittorini, Edoardo Salzano, and Federico Gorio sought positions within organizations run more or less directly by parties of the left, here bypassing the roles traditionally assigned to architects and urbanists. The work they did for bodies like GESCAL, ISES, and the communal administrations—not to mention the Parliament—was anything but transparent. Their commitment did not, however, lead them to expect catharsis from the manipulation of forms and the excited elaboration of models. They too were subject to an illusion originating in an ideologically distorted reading of the real. Nonetheless, it was difficult to ignore—all consequences and moral considerations aside—the concrete contribution made by that reading, if only its dissection of exhausted disciplines and its suggestions of their potential usefulness.

This was the climate in which architectural culture confronted the theme proposed by the new "167" law of 1962, concerning the public acquisition of lands for economical public building. In comparison to the general expropriation favored by the socialist left and the communist party, the new law was undoubtedly a compromise. Nor did it replace the plans for laws that the Christian Democrats would manage to set aside, disowning its minister, Fiorentino Sullo, who had made himself the interpreter of the INU's votes and of the instances of reform. By freezing portions of urban areas, the "167" would not act as a controlled price list in the real estate market, but rather would have the opposite effect. But in a city like Rome it seemed like a good stance from which to wage the battle for small-scale reforms.

Priority was given to coordinating organizations in the sector of economical public building; equally important was the integration of their intervention with the actions of private companies, effected through the creation of master plans. The programs of the "167" were in fact understood as minutely detailed plans. In the meantime, the GESCAL, founded in 1963, replaced INA-Casa, inserting itself into the above programs on the basis of a ten-year plan. The ISES replaced UNRRA-Casas and turned toward social construction with unclear objectives.[62] The functioning of these new institutes turned out to be anything but easy. The interventions did not meet the demand, and the GESCAL study center, which had raised many hopes of typological and productive renewal, revealed itself to be a mere reservoir of techniques. It barely lasted two years. The control of urban development was eluding the projects of the public sector. There was, however, in the design of the "167" quarters, a concentrated and renewed will for form on an urban scale previously seen on a theoretical and experimental level at the end of the 1950s. In the project for the Tor de' Cenci quarter, Aymonino and Maria Luisa Anversa addressed a deferential homage to Quaroni's CEP of San Giuliano, enclosing the space within two semicircles. In the projects for the quarter in Casilino of 1964–65, the group headed by Quaroni experimented first with a morphology of elastic signs, then with forms seemingly inspired by the visual experiments of "op art," and finally settled on the solution of a "fan" as the metaphorical explosion of a hidden nucleus. The Spinaceto quarter, executed between 1964 and 1970 by the Piero Moroni-Nico di Cagno group, is dominated by a typological contamination that has been mistaken for richness; it stands like a program disguised as form, as an unnecessary variation. The "167" would be interpreted with noteworthy results only in the Corviale complex (figure 117), and the complexes of Vigne Nuove[63] in Rome and Gallaratese in Milan (figures 113–115). But by then illusions about the efficiency of the new legislative technique had been dispelled.

The debate, which had been sparked by the discovery of the "new dimension" and by the identification of *town design* as an autonomous ordering tool, was destined to subside and then enter a critical phase following its confrontation with reality. Moreover, as illusions about the first center-left gradually crumbled, the new technical/political roles were also affected by the demiurgic syndrome. It has been said that in those years, "the architect who wished to escape the cliché of the artist fell into a new and definitely clownish role ... his *livre de chevet* became the last issue of the *Journal of the A. I. P.*, he deserted art exhibits, and the bulletin of the ISTAT excited him more than Gadda or Montale."[64] This blunt assessment of an intellectual group that, in some way, was trying to move the debate on design onto relatively new ground might seem ungenerous. The members of this group attempted to transform themselves from "organic intellectuals" into "organic technicians"; but theory was still an undefined abstraction, and the battlefield contested by political forces was strewn with mines. There was ample opportunity to analyze the terms of the debate, and this was reflected in the work of the most committed designers, especially the "masters." These "disturbing muses," who had burdened entire generations with their doubts and ceaseless reflections, gradually lost their position as central points of reference.[65] Both Gardella and Albini seemed to be using makeshift language to protect themselves from the assault of problems they considered skeptically: the rarefied elegance of the Milan subway of 1962–63, of the Villa Corini in Parma of 1967–70, of the Luigi Zoja baths in Salsomaggiore (designed in 1963 and constructed from 1969 to 1970) (figure 83), and of the SNAM office building in San Donato Milanese of 1970–72, added little to Albini's poetics. In the same vein, the results achieved by Gardella in the resort center of Punta Ala of 1962–65, and later in the Chiesa di Sant'Enrico in Metanopoli of 1963–66 (figure 84), express a disorientation that has only been resolved in very recent works.[66] As for the BPR, they did not go beyond aphonic professionalism in the IACP complex of Gratosoglio in Milan, begun in 1963, and they showed sure signs of fatigue in their works "for exportation," like the Olivetti center in Barcelona of 1965. The thematics that had led them to the center of the international debate had obviously been exhausted: the building they executed in Piazza Meda in Milan (figure 87), in its attempt to enter into an allusive dialogue with the cylindrical drum of the Pellegrinian cupola of San Fedele and the adjacent works of Figini Pollini and Caccia-Dominioni, stands as a distorting mirror of the Milanese real estate system.[67]

Nor did the quest for a coherent approach, like that underlying the works Ridolfi executed in Terni in the sixties—the houses of Staderini (1960), Briganti (1962), Pallotta (1961–63), and Franconi (1960), or the multipurpose complex of the Fontana Brothers of 1960–64—cross known boundaries. Ridolfi's philosophy of "doing well" lost its baroque nuances, especially when applied to reweaving the urban fabric of Terni, which had been chosen as the site of a mediation between differing worlds meeting in the poetics of the increasingly isolated craftsmanship of form. That philosophy did, however, recharge itself with unexpected expressive "furor" in a singular project, which became Ridolfi's definitive farewell to the cultural battle. The project was for an AGIP motel in the Settebagni district of Rome, near the Autostrada del Sole, designed in 1968 (figures 88–89).[68] As though retracing its origins, the disjointed and violently twisted tower of the AGIP motel explicitly referred to—while ignoring its twentieth-century values—the "restaurant tower" that Ridolfi had designed in 1928. Reacting to the results of a fictitious "economic miracle," the architect violated his own forms. He represented them as shaken by an impetuous wind, and showed himself mastering a difficult geometry, responding with stupefaction to an overwhelming universe that simultaneously attracted and repulsed him. It is perhaps not coincidental that Ridolfi's AGIP tower, with its plan based on a ten-point star, recalls one of the skyscrapers of Fritz Lang's *Metropolis*.

Ridolfi too came full circle here. "Realism" came to express the "passion for the night" nesting in its folds; that same passion also led Ridolfi to focus with suspicious frenzy on his projects for the Casa Lina in the Marmore of 1966 (figure 90), for the Casa De Bonis of 1971–75 in Terni, and for the enlargement of a house in Norcia of 1976–77: three extreme works that testify to his voluntary exile.[69] In fact, the carefully crafted excitement of these projects, with their plans in the shapes of stars, polygons, and ovals, gathered quotations and allusions that had nothing to do with "professional integrity": so much so, in fact, that one is led to believe that Ridolfi had decided here to *consume compositional materials and to abrade technologies*, thereby remaining consistent with one aspect of the poetics he had expressed early on in the towers on Viale Etiopia and later clarified in the Scuola Media in Terni. The image of imminent collapse, crystallized in the AGIP tower, thus revealed itself to be allegorical.

The corrosion of a geometric solid is also the main theme of one of the projects executed shortly before Ridolfi's dramatic death in 1984: the last version of the office building for the Terni Council, designed in 1981. Ridolfi, Frankl, and Domenico Malagricci created an oval structure marked by a peripheral crown of pilasters. The work stands as the paradoxical outgrowth of the Palazzo Spada, but the regularity of the scheme contrasts with the corrugated and varied surface and with the broken rhythm of the openings and panels. As always in Ridolfi's later work, a cult of complexity and a tormented relationship with numerous traditions led to an excessive result, the mastery of which contrasts with his preceding, more peaceful 1978 version on the same theme, as well as with the stellar structure of the 1967 version. Ridolfi's later changes literally consumed the initial matrices—the geometric stability and an artisan's skill—emphasizing the dialectic between structure and instability that had characterized the AGIP tower. Further evidence of this material and volumetric expressionism can be found in studies for the Casa Francucci in Arrone and especially in the transformation of the Casa Luccioni in Terni of 1977–79, where Ridolfi and Frankl were working on a building that Ridolfi had built in 1951. One can clearly see the motifs of continuity and discontinuity that mark the evolution of Ridolfi's poetics.

This was the Ridolfi whom, beginning in the mid-1960s, a few young architects chose as a point of reference for their disinterested analyses and reinterpretations of projects. Nothing expressed more explicitly the cultural distance separating the two generations than Leonardo Benevolo's article in *Casabella*, seemingly intended as an obituary for Ridolfi, given its severe judgment of Ridolfi's most expressive postwar works.

Nonetheless, neither Ridolfi's coherence nor Carlo Scarpa's— another architect in exile, but for different reasons—would constitute "lessons" for the new generation of the sixties. When Ernesto Rogers died after a long illness in 1969, Samonà and Quaroni became, in their fashion, the current "masters,"more because of what they did not say than for what they said, and because of their Socratic didacticism. But their hermetic and suggestive teachings became progressively more confined to university classrooms, where they fed uncontrolled currents and were soon revealed to be contingent by transformations within the discipline and its institutions. It was, however, significant that in the sixties their most productive contribution was not from their projects, but their intentions, which those projects only rarely succeeded in translating. In the end, the large-scale design that characterized the work of Quaroni's students constituted an experiment that lent itself to the most disparate formal programs, causing boomerang effects that could then be more closely examined. Similarly, the "grand manner" Samonà used in the SGES-ENEL offices in Palermo in 1961–63 and in the details of the competition project for the offices of the National Insurance and Credit Institute for Communications in the same city (1963), followed a compositional style unrelated to the experiments he submitted to the competitions for the office district of Turin, the Tronchetto of Venice, and the "narrow metropolis."[70]

The fact remains that the desire to be at the forefront of structural changes affecting society and the national countryside was separated from the critical use of reliable languages. This separation was perhaps intended to break those languages into fragments and to exhaust their possibilities. This happened in the cooperative on Via Palmanova in Milan, designed by Gregotti, Meneghetti, and Stoppino in 1962–67, as well as in the excited articulations of the house on Via Conservatorio in Milan by Magistretti (1966), in geometries decomposed into clever games by Nino Dardi,[71] in the skillful reinterpretation of the brutalist lexicon of Giancarlo De Carlo's University Colleges of 1963–66 (figure 110), in the softened expressionism of Carlo Aymonino (the multipurpose building in Savona of 1963–66 and the competition project for the Teatro Paganini in Parma of 1964), and in the much more hostile expressionism of Canella, Achilli, Brigidini, and Lazzari, as represented in the civic center of Segrate of 1965 (figure 125). But these works did not satisfy their creators, whose intentions constantly exceeded their capacity to articulate them in form.

In order to evaluate correctly the architectural experimentation of the mid-1960s it is necessary to return to the convulsive debate initiated by the literary, musical, and pictorial neo-avant-gardes—supported by editors like Feltrinelli and reviews like *Il Verri*, *Quindici*, and *Marcatré*—which responded in their own way to Vittorini's exhortations in *Menabò*. The usefulness of language was at stake, as well as its capacity to convey information by means of difference, transgression, and "semantic distortion." The renewed interest in semiology and linguistics was in fact based upon an interpretation of form as a potential complex of relations. Information theory, popularized by Umberto Eco, supported the poetics of the aleatory, of the "open work," of the initial form perennially awaiting completion by its inhabitants. For an art that had lost meaning or that was not able to suggest a way to untangle meaning, the neo-avant-gard*e vague* seemed reassuring. Moreover, the polemics surrounding the *work* again raised the issue of the fossilized relationship between ideology and writing; the dominant theme to emerge was that of a language cleansed of superstructural dross. A difficult choice had to be made: between "apocalyptic" and "integrated" architecture.

The effect was profound. In the fields of music, literature, and the figurative arts, one of the main characteristics of the modern *project* became apparent, namely that it had appointed itself overseer of the individual *case* and functioned as a malleable technique, as a group of strategies open to the unexpected. There was no nostalgia for the irrational in the reflection on the avant-garde, but rather a recognition of the new forms taken by the *project* (which was political *and therefore* technical, above all). There seems, however, to have been no awareness of this in the architectural debate of those years. The review *Edilizia moderna*, edited by Gregotti, explored the notion of polysemy in its various forms, while a project like Maurizio Sacripanti's for the new theater of Cagliari (1965) drew as much on the poetics of the aleatory as on that of the programmed event.[72] Furthermore, had not the work of Aymonino and Canella already been influenced by a multivalent, ambiguous, and contradictory atmosphere? Italian architects did not need to be coaxed by Robert Venturi to absorb the message of *Seven Types of Ambiguity*. That message was a form of realism: reality, no longer synthesizable, was multivalent, and could be read as a continuous flux of superimposed texts. To encompass the contradictory in objects that challenge their finished character meant to examine what had escaped rationality's reductive interpretation. At the 1964 Triennale, dedicated to "free time," this expressed itself by overcoming the boundaries of the theme. Communication techniques overlapped onto each other, especially in the introductory "kaleidoscope" organized by Gregotti, Meneghetti, Stoppino, Peppo Brivio, and Umberto Eco, and in a series of explorations dominated by Luciano Berio's *Omaggio a Joyce*, Tinto Brass's films reflected in six mirrors, a soundtrack composed by Balestrini, and images by Achille Perilli. But the Italian sector, managed by a group led by Gae Aulenti and Aymonino, also used a variety of techniques including collage, shock with multiple effects, and happenings.[73]

The contrived disorientation characterizing the magical caverns of the thirteenth Triennale projected some of "miracle" Italy's major problems onto imaginary spheres, perhaps by enlarging and echoing Picasso's *Race to the Sea* (figure 91). But inquiry into the informative capacity of nonverbal communication eventually diverged from analytic knowledge, even though *Casabella* focused on the Italian coasts, tertiary infrastructures, and the adaptation of green spaces to the urban scale. This same Triennale, however, was entered by way of an enigmatic iron bridge with a triangular section. The bridge was cut into two pieces, one of which was shifted forward: Aldo Rossi thus linked Muzio's building to the park hieratically. Opposing the formal wasteland inside the exhibit, Rossi's bridge spoke only of the limits of vision. The challenge was significant, and prophetic regarding developments being consolidated in research. Gian Ugo Polesello grasped this; commenting on Rossi's bridge, he made reference to Wittgenstein's "mystique."[74]

The possibility of replacing the poetics with an architecture based solely on *relations* had a further result: first in 1965–66, at the tenth INU Convention in Trieste, and then in a monographic issue of *Edilizia moderna* dedicated to the geography of the countryside, questions were raised about intervening in a landscape by speaking in its own terms.[75]

The transformation of nature into culture, foreshadowed here, had nothing to do with the utopianism that had prospered between 1962 and 1964, nor did it convey ideological messages. This too was a sign of changes that intellectuals were experiencing: Emilio Sereni's analyses of the history of the Italian agrarian countryside and Lévi-Strauss's work on the consequent form of particular anthropological structures encouraged research on the legibility of the countryside and of installations. These experiments, which were intended to go beyond Kevin Lynch's naive psychology, eventually led to Luciano Semerani and Gigetta Tamaro's projects for Trieste begun in 1969 (figure 97) and to Gregotti and Purini's large-scale projects (figures 120–121).[76]

The effect of this overlapping of themes and suggestions, benefiting from increasingly frequent exchanges with experiments occurring outside of architecture, was to multiply possibilities infinitely. If, on the one hand, the "bla-bla-bla" denounced by De Carlo at the INU Convention of 1965 was a reality not overcome until today, on the other hand, the improvement in the overall quality of "current architecture" also elevated its highest achievements, while historiographical inquiry addressed in a new way the problem of its relationship to planning.

A competition once again provided the opportunity for a comprehensive picture of the new cultural climate and a test of the fluidity of institutions. In 1967, the competition for the new offices of the Chamber of Deputies in Rome, which would have no positive results, offered Italian architecture another occasion for confrontation, which the best used in order "to speak of other things."[77]

The location of the new offices in the middle of the historical center and next to the building by Ernesto Basile was in fact a sign of the public sector's substantial incapacity to program in a simple, "convenient" way the basic services required by the community. Only Italo Insolera rejected the given theme and presented a proposal of conventional interventions, aimed at a large sector of the wedge between the Via del Babbuina and the Via Ripetta; it was another effort in vain, however. The inadequacies of the competition program did not "scandalize" Quaroni, Samonà, Aymonino, Portoghesi, or Sacripanti (figures 92–93). To benefit from the occasion, they decided to approach it with an attitude "beyond good and evil": they sought to test the limits of their renewed faith in the specific instrument of form. All this, of course, came *avant le déluge*. Furthermore, these projects seemed too shaken by uncontrollable forces to present a catharsis for architectural design. The disenchantment with which the Italian intelligentsia faced this competition was the sign of an ideological indifference that had become widespread, as a consequence of the new climate, and whose roots were barely covered by disciplined commitment.

This did not prevent architects like Quaroni and Samonà from proposing projects that would not only stand among the best of their production but actually helped them to do so. Placing his project with perfect ease in the heart of the Rome he loved and hated, Quaroni did not hesitate to include a laborious and varied accumulation of episodes and fragments, as he searched for a monumental language capable of commenting on the contradictory relationship with the *genius loci*. A geometric frame formed by four axes meshing with the urban context cuts into the closed mass of the building, like a solemn and polyvalent hinge, a neobaroque synthesis of rationalizing instances and unorganized elaborations (figure 92). Compared to Quaroni's tangle of geometric forms, Giuseppe and Alberto Samonà's project seems more reflective and more carefully mediated (figure 93). If Quaroni's antecedents lie in Poelzig and Mies's skyscrapers of 1919 and 1921, Samonà's lie in Le Corbusier, whom he explicitly cites in the *main ouverte* at the top of the project. The Musée de la Ville et de l'Etat of 1935 was a special object of meditation for these designers. But the aerial weft of steel supporting the volumes floating at various heights, the paradoxical inversion of functions between weight and support, and the play of transparencies charged Samonà's proposal with barely concealed irony, one that recalls Klee as well as the rarefied artificiality of "third style" Pompeian painting. Samonà's project had a precedent in the project for regional offices for ANAS in Palermo; but the new nonchalance of his architectural language foreshadowed the most committed of his experiments in the 1960s, especially his projects for the Banca d'Italia in Padua and the Sciacca Theatre (figures 107, 109).

The experiments of Aymonino, Nino Dardi, and Luigi Pellegrin were less surprising. Their projects resembled "geometric games" declined with various inflections. These projects—like Portoghesi's, for that matter—only constituted stages in an approach to "manners" already consolidated. Furthermore, in the whirl of formal ideas emerging from the many projects submitted to the competition, it became evident that the lessons of Louis Kahn, Giurgola, and Paul Rudolph had been assimilated: if nothing else, Italian architectural culture was now more astute and more enlightened on the formal level. This was marked by two extremes: the projects of Maurizio Sacripanti and of the Roman group GRAU. Sacripanti had already experimented, as we have seen, with an architectural language greatly influenced by the poetics of the aleatory in his project for the theater in Cagliari and in his winning project for the competition for the Peugeot skyscraper.[78] He presented his work for the competition for the offices of the Chamber of Deputies with the motto "homage to Mafai"; a more appropriate motto would have been "homage to Rauschenberg," subtitled "a flower for Sant'Elia." In fact, Sacripanti's project was an orgy of exploded spaces, objects amassed and violated, and hallucinatory volumes: architecture was represented as a diseased ruin, as a nausea provoked by obscene objects that had become too familiar. The exaltation of the machinist myth was grafted onto this decay, uniting Sant'Elia with Rauschenberg. Sacripanti pursued his depiction of contemporary anxiety in his project for the Osaka pavilion (figure 94), while adapting the machinist pole of his poetics to a usable structure in his project for the new Museo Civico of Padua. His "junk sculptures" followed a path that has barely softened in his more recent projects.[79] The Apollonian abstraction of the GRAU group immediately responded to Sacripanti's "rage." Adhering to a poetics that had already been tested—in the competition project for the new Palazzo dello Sport of Florence—the GRAU hyperbolized its search for a formal logic that would be contained in its search for self-verification. Symptomatic of a generation that contemptuously rejected the ideologies superimposed on the specificity of architecture, the GRAU's work provocatively demonstrated an attitude whose roots lay in the "verification of powers" that Fortini had recommended in the early sixties. But in this particular case, neohumanistic abstractions took DellaVolpi's aesthetics as a theoretical base. Form withdrew into its own world and did not converse with the "other." The GRAU did not maintain this position for long: its competition project for the new State Archives of Florence of 1972, for example, was contaminated by a yearning for symbolism (figures 98–99).[80] But in 1967, the hermetic realms in which the GRAU manipulated its geometries marked a *tendenza* seeking to recover the absolute autonomy of the object in the Italian climate. This is seen in the projects by the Manieri-De Feo group and by Gian Ugo Polesello, which were submitted to the same competition. The debate over the coherence of Italian architectural culture on the threshold of 1968, spurred by the analyses of the projects submitted to the Roman competition, indicates a widespread anxiety, surely not obscured by more self-confident work. Thus began a phase of "waiting" for an architecture seeking new roles, aware that ancient and recent myths were worn out. Nor was anyone deluded by the nonchalant satisfaction with which self-reflection was being exhibited.[81]

5
New Crises and New Strategies (1968–1975)

On the threshold of 1968 the uncertainties that plagued intellectual work came face to face with weighty data about the very structure of the profession. An inquiry regarding the architecture school at the Politecnico of Milan and covering the years 1963–69 revealed that only 36 percent of the school's graduates were actually practicing the profession: 57.5 percent held salaried jobs, and 6.5 percent were either unemployed or employed outside the field. In addition, one ought to consider that in the early sixties nearly 60 percent of graduates in architecture were supporting themselves by teaching in primary and secondary schools, while the general figure for juvenile unemployment in 1968 amounted to approximately 600,000, which was equivalent to 10 percent of the total work force. The situation was far beyond "frictional": on the contrary, it seemed pathological.

Low employment rates were not the only problem. A rough estimate of the cubic meters constructed in Italy by architects amounted, in 1974, to a figure somewhere between 2 and 3 percent of the total. And one should remember that this history is founded on a selection made within a small percentage of relevant works. Furthermore, the vague title of architect, especially after the events of the sixties, seemed an anachronism dear only to those afflicted by incurable nostalgia. Nor did the opening of graduate courses in urban planning—in Venice in 1970, due to Astengo's initiative, and in Reggio Calabria in 1975—respond to an analysis of the concrete situation of the discipline. But while the latter was being dismembered and new sectors of intervention were being opened, the notion of *town planning* celebrated by those graduate courses fossilized a section of the discipline that should have been the object of ruthless critical discussion. Meanwhile professional outlets remained compromised by the fact that the title of *studio* received little professional recognition. If one also considers that in the meantime the percentage of public building, relative to private, passed from 25 percent in 1951 to 6 percent in 1968—finally reaching a low point of 2 percent in 1973 and later—one can better understand the structure of the sector compared with the formal contortions of architects "who designed in order not to think" and with the rebellious explosion of 1968. That explosion, insofar as the architecture schools and cultural institutions connected to architecture were concerned, only resulted in superficial modifications, hasty reflections, and demagogic attitudes resolved in collective débâcles. The protests directed against the INU and the Milan Triennale, not to mention the block of teaching activity, only revealed the fragility of those institutions and their functions. The attempt to force the "militant-student" to participate in struggles on construction sites and in villages, on the one hand led to the formation of neighborhood committees, but on the other hand rendered the analysis of "urban malaise" increasingly academic, in a wretched manifestation of political intervention and a distorted attempt to escape subjectively the grip of the "profiteers."

The most disinterested analyses of the "Marxism of the sixties," of new waves of struggle in the workers' movement, and of the new forms assumed by those same struggles followed paths having little to do with the ruling demagogic programs in the architecture schools. Yet in the wake of 1968 and its most palatable slogans, movements delineated in the preceding years took root and soon occupied the spaces left vacant by a culture that had become the object of more immediate protest. Once again, there was an appeal to the avant-garde, this time for its desecrating power. In a course held by Savioli and Santi on the "Space of Involvement," an attempt was made—due also to the intervention of

Ugo La Pietra and Ettore Sottsass—to use the strategies of pop art. The Florentine group Archizoom, which emerged from this course, sought an art that would function as a liberating psychophysical therapy devoid of codes, and called upon its audience to participate in a destructive and cathartic orgy.

The theses of "radical architecture" were thus defined.[1] On the one hand, the program inherited the destructive desires alive in Florence since the early 1960s; on the other hand, they flaunted anti-institutional goals, appealing to the "negative" block of recent avant-gardes.

The intention was to haul a mythical proletariat onto the stage of psychedelic action, rather than into the experimentalism of the Gruppo 1963. The Archizoom group's *No Stop City* and Superstudio's *Monumento continuo* of 1969 turned the project into dream material transcribed with an irony "that made nobody laugh." In the vignettes that illustrated *No Stop City*—a continuous urban structure devoid of architecture—neoprimitives living in an absolutely barren environment use small airconditioners, expressing a monstrous marriage between populist anarchism and liberating events influenced by those of France in May 1968.

Following this path, it was not difficult to achieve an intellectual playfulness, irresponsible in that it was deduced from a hasty reading of "new left" reviews such as *Quaderni rossi, Classe operaia*, and *Contropiano*. But, even though Strum and 9999 completely rejected the project, Ettore Sottsass and the groups Archizoom and Superstudio once again poured their ironic vein into design. Their designs conquered a market that had remained closed to the products of neoliberty; their desecrations, justified by appeals to Duchamp, finally gained international recognition at an exhibition organized by Emilio Ambasz at the Museum of Modern Art in New York in 1972: "Italy. The New Domestic Landscape." For a few years, the banner of antidesign, behind which an astute marketing operation was unfolding, also controlled the editing of *Casabella*. In 1964 the editor took power away from Rogers, and thus unwittingly signaled the conclusion of a cultural cycle, while critics like Menna and Restany prophesied "esthetic civilizations" and "total arts." At the other extreme were *tendenze* sharing with these arts and civilizations an attitude of defiance toward consumer society. Beginning in the early 1960s, Louis Kahn's work was watched in Italy with an interest strengthened by a tendentious reading of Galvano Della Volpe's esthetics. If the contingent was the extreme form of a universe sacrificed to the laws of the marketplace, the recovery of the concept of the "work," of its "semantic unity," and of the totality of experience it presupposes, was the only specific contribution made to design. Kahn, moreover, offered a recovery of a historical time free of romanticism: his allusions to late antiquity and to Piranesi appear to be the choices of "logical antecedents," results of "determined abstractions." In reality, what makes one consider Kahn immediately after closing the *Critica del gusto* is the "order" that transpires not only from his work as an architect, but also from his work as a theoretician. The mystical afflatus accompanying that order seems negligible; the richness of the sign and of formal organization in Kahn's works turns them into theorems that can be extrapolated from the context of their existence. Seeing himself as chief defender of "anticlassical" codes, Zevi greeted Kahn's work first with diffidence, then with a more decidedly critical attitude. Kahn's work, however, immediately became known in the architecture schools. Between 1963 and 1965 the phenomenon that in the fifties had focused attention onto the "youth of the rank and file" in Milan repeated itself: Marxist students elaborated projects that were stigmatized as "academic" by repentant academicians, who thus expressed their insatiable need for clarity.

Rigorous composition as the "recovery of nuance" had already been adopted by Muratori, followed by Aldo Rossi's and Giorgio Grassi's first influential works; it appeared, altered by various intonations, in the works and projects of the GRAU group, the Stass studio, and Vittorio De Feo. And though the geometric exasperation of the GRAU remained confined to pure programming, works like the residential unit in the Serpentara in Rome, the project for the office district of Grosseto by the Stass, and the Technical Institute for Geometricians in Terni of 1968, by De Feo and Erico Ascione, turned self-verification into a cause for pride. De Feo, in particular, demonstrated in his Institute in Terni that it was possible to adopt simultaneously the lessons of Ridolfi, Kahn, and Venturi, and that one could assume *Complexity and Contradiction in Architecture* without falling into the pitfalls still ensnaring the recent advocates of the "Post-Modern." The result was the compact composition of the project for the tourist complex in Abbadia San Salvatore of 1970, the pop image of the typical Esso station of 1971, and the laconic homage to De Chirico and Malevich in the competition project for the Palazzo Municipale of Legnago of 1974 (figure 96).[2]

In such works—and in Franco Purini's and Laura Thermes's first projects, which were stimulated by Sacripanti's experimentalism and Quaroni's systematic doubt—architecture attempted self-recognition. Having destroyed all the ideologies to which it had previously appealed, the only remaining possibility was architecture as self-reflective exercise. Architecture had gone from embracing populism to withdrawing into autobiography, it had traveled through the utopian explosion to the "sign as such." It had progressed in fits and starts through the stages of an exploration resembling the frustrated efforts of Kafka's land-surveyor trying to reach the ineffable Castle.

It was, however, impossible at the end of the sixties, to appeal to these intellectuals to give technical substance to the socialist strategy of reform worn down by daily compromise, by the adversary's skill, and by the increasing divergence between uncertain progress within the institutions and the movements of the "new" working class. One deduces that the invitation to make oneself as "candid as serpents" was actually welcomed by the GRAU, the Stass, and De Feo—not to mention Quaroni and Samonà—in spite of their serene, formal contemplation. But these architects gave way to Giorgio Ruffolo, Marcello Vittorini, Giovanni Astengo, and Baldo De Rossi, technicians capable of formulating a program of national scope, the urgency of which was dramatized by the paradoxical destruction of hydrogeological and historical resources. In July 1966, an entire section of the city of Agrigento crumbled under the weight of massive residential units illegally constructed across from the Valle dei Templi; in November of the same year the Arno overflowed and flooded

Florence, destroying an incalculable artistic and historical legacy. Meanwhile the Bastions of Venice proved incapable of protecting the Serenissima's lagoon, and the public was shocked by the disaster of the Vajont. Technical and political response came from the socialists in *"Progetto 80."*

But whoever thought in 1970 that the *Progetto 80*, drawn up by a team in the finance ministry, was a complete elaboration of a "plan for the capital," was confusing an abstract exploit with a real strategy. The analyses and proposals of the *Progetto 80* were essentially the result of an exercise that, beneath ambitions and desires for programs, hid a stalemated situation and a naïve technological optimism intrinsic to the political neutrality of the project. The *Progetto* did not foresee any basic modifications of the system of national production, nor did it modify the institutional framework or the management of economic power in order to permit working structural modifications. Instead, it sought refuge behind smokescreens: the *myth of equilibrium* was updated with the catch-phrase "territorial vocations." Once again, impracticable "corrections" were proposed for a system based on imbalances. This did not mean that the "impoverished planning" of that document (Asor Rosa) was completely useless. It served, at least, to polarize debate and to keep intellectuals occupied at a politically uncertain time. However, the methods that the *Projetto 80* specified for control of the countryside and rearrangement of production extended to a national level: "rebalancing" was pursued through the reorganization of metropolitan systems, of a national infrastructural system, and of a national program for leisure time.[3]

The fundamental urban "invention" that was to enable a realization of these objectives was the "metropolitan system." The *Progetto 80* took upon itself the entire mythology of the city-region, isolating systems seeking a new equilibrium, systems based on existing agglomerations, and alternative systems. The "ashes of Geddes" could thus be offered as a final remedy to a patient with an incurable disease.

Nor could the effort that socialist culture made in elaborating the *Progetto 80* be accused of technocracy. More ideological than technical, this document remained, among the frustrated aspirations of

Italian programming, evidence of the subjective limits of intellectuals believing it was their new duty to direct their talents toward concrete political intervention. It was, perhaps, proof of the absence of an effective technique, of an appropriate rapport between revitalized techniques and mass strategies.

In the big trade-union controversies of 1968–69, the organized workers' movement developed new modes of struggle that reformulated the problem of housing and regional organization. On November 19, 1969, the Italian workers accepted the invitation of the unions to declare a general, twenty-four hour strike. The aim of the strike was to insist on the organization of the city and countryside: the factory projected itself onto the social realm, the wage issue spread to unforeseen areas of concern. Class movement had reached a turning point: the parties were forced to consider the politics of building in a new light. Fundamental institutions were attacked; neither old techniques nor abstract rationalizations could be counted on to offer suitable responses. Instead, outmoded aspects of the discipline were displaced by a social subject armed with tools previously used to attain sectorial objectives. While Parliament was engaged in a wearisome discussion leading to the housing law of 1971, the struggles continued, creating in the process mobile organizations, such as tenant unions and neighborhood committees. The immediate effect of the latter was a diffusion of the tension surrounding general objectives, and a fragmentation of those objectives. But by this time it had been demonstrated that the connection between culture and mass movements could no longer be established by making "big syntheses" or by simulated models. A new chapter opened for the intellectuals in search of social identity. This search would be enlarged after the results of the 1975 and 1976 elections, which formulated for the working-class parties the problem of the management of cities and regions burdened by disastrous precedents and an impracticable legislative order.

In the meantime, the response to the workers' struggles of 1968–69 passed through the regional institution at the beginning of 1970, and resulted in the approval of the new construction law of October 22, 1971. The law was meant to curb real estate speculation, to assign to public power a broad range of duties of urban and territorial order—public housing, factories, tourist complexes, etc.—to democratize and decentralize management, and to coordinate initiatives. Naturally, such an administrative reform had to account for the traditional, centralized structure of the State: in the design resulting from this complex of measures, the region emerged not only as an interlocutor relative to the source and a mediator in centers of power holding a monopoly on public services, but also as a possible site of arbitration for social conflicts, when not serving as a buffer.[4] On the other hand, the end of the boom in speculation was sanctioned by the 1971 law: from then on, archaic forms of collecting revenue, such as that garnered from urban property, as well as the waste brought about by the free market in real estate, were recognized by more attentive capitalist groups as factors inhibiting development and further retarding the lagging sectors. But big industry needed administrative structures capable of channeling conflict outside of the workplace: regions were established, respecting the constitutional datum only when the need for such channeling was dramatically evident. Industry also needed to restructure the building sector in a way that would transcend its use in an exclusively "conjunctural" key. Such a structure would have to assure the continuity in the productive process, thereby affecting both the price of and demand for materials. It is significant that Law no. 865—finally approved by the Parliament in a compromise that reduced its range and made its application difficult—was not concerned with the modification of the financial or credit mechanisms controlling the sector.[5] The new law was thus contradictory. On the one hand, it supported the conception of social security and health insurance pursued in Italy by INA-Casa and the GESCAL. On the other hand, it responded to the need for a new notion of the social uses of revenue, for a planned politics of social investment.

This did not oppose the line of the major entrepreneurial forces. The latter, organized in the ambit of the ANCE and of Confindustria—the "integrated construction firms"—functioned in the parliamentary debate by playing the trump card of crisis and occupational blackmail, but only because their design sought to force the law to leap forward. The new yardstick for production was of regional dimensions and the problem was how to use the new regional powers. The controls held by financial capital, which had remained untouched, guaranteed this end.

A new institutional armature and a new capitalist strategy were thus delineated in the early 1960s, serving a politics of rationalization no longer motivated by the ethical and enlightened considerations of the preceding decade, to embrace a large-scale system of production. Once again, ideology was supplanted by reality in a climate dictated by the conflicting requirements of politics and of the dynamics of development.

It was no coincidence that, already by the beginning of the seventies, a few of the large private industries, like FIAT and Montedison, and also some partially state-controlled industries—IRI and ENI—became involved in the building sector. It was the end of an era that had considered construction the handmaiden of depressed sectors. The problem now facing nationalized industries was the monopolization of the production of social facilities—residences, schools, hospitals, etc.—affecting the real estate market, the supply of materials, and the coordination of supply and demand. An entire cycle became the object of planning. A formula that seemed able to translate this into regional dimensions had been introduced by Colombo, the president of the Council. He accepted a few of the recommendations made in the *Progetto 80*: the program "new urban systems," to be realized through public intervention and by firms controlled by the state, was broadly expanded. The documents of FIAT and of ISVET agreed upon "systems" in which the residential question would be inextricably linked to the reorganization of commercial structures and urban services: graduated economies, indispensable technological leaps, the management of new centers of development within economic regions, and the management of social infrastructures all formed a whole. In this context, even the dialogue between capitalistic initiative and democratic institutions was programmed. The regions were entrusted with promotional roles,

which were subtly turning those regions into consenting managerial bodies. The triumphal entry of big capital into the social arena
required a conciliatory cooperation on the part of democratic
institutions.

The most sensational project to emerge from this strategy was
the so-called "Nolana city" of 1969. This intervention, promoted
by SICIR, a firm financed by FIAT and IRI, envisioned a new
integrated structure near Naples modeled after the one large
industrial complex already in existence, Alfa-Sud.[6] The residential
zone, designed for 50,000 inhabitants but capable of expanding to
accommodate 200,000, was set along a highway axis linking the
complex to Naples, to the region, and to a new structure of services
of regional scope including a 5,000-bed hospital and a university
for 10,000 students. A pragmatic assumption of urbanistic megastructures was projected: in a chronically underdeveloped and
overcrowded region, a hypertechnological axis, superior to the
most recent English New Towns in the quantity and quality of its
services, was to be created. A similar conception was guiding the
project for intervention in the region of Ottana, in Sardinia, which
was entrusted to the ENI and the SIR. Once again, public and
private capital were combined in a proposal for a regional restructuring supporting a chain of new chemical factories.

The policy of intervening in the South with "cathedrals in the
desert" was, however, only completed in theory. The Ottana
project still adhered to the logic of a strong concentration of capital
for factories served by a limited work force, while the scandal of
the new steelworks of Gioia Tauro was a response to the unrealized "Nolana city" project. A further political response to the
jacquerie exploded in the subproletarian unrest in Reggio Calabria,
skillfully maneuvered by the parties of the right, which the state
was forcing to spend hundreds of millions for a doomed enterprise.

The fact remains, however, that at the beginning of the seventies
the emergence of the regional and urban problem as a domain for
capitalist intervention led to the creation of new financial and
organizational structures by the large companies: FIAT created
FIAT Engineering and SITECO for the planning and execution of

industrial, commercial, residential, and tourist complexes; the ENI worked through TECNECO and ISVET; Montedison created Montedil; the SIR launched a program for the manufacture of plastic building materials; the IRI created Italstat, a financial agency that in 1971 absorbed the Società Condotte d'Acqua, the major building firm in Italy that had executed the Mont Blanc tunnel, the viaduct of Polcevera in Genoa (designed by Riccardo Morandi), the underground parking lot at Villa Borghese in Rome, and the Palazzo dello Sport in Milan. In the meantime, research bodies based on mixed capital were created, like Tecnocasa, whose funding came from Italstat, ENI, Montedison, and FIAT, while in 1973 the Tuscan region drew up a contract with SVEI—a firm that relied on the equal participation of Italstat, ENI, and Montedison— for the construction of 20,000 units of low-income housing.[7] In contrast with this revival of capitalist initiative, which turned the proposals of the 1960s intelligentsia into anachronisms by stretching their limits, was the effort of the cooperative movement—and especially of the National League, in which the "red" cooperatives merged—to tie their production of residences and their demands to union politics. This dialogue between productive and political bodies was a difficult one. There were also the internal difficulties of the same cooperatives, whose principal objective—to give priority to common property—was impeded by credit policies aimed at the traditional political objective of individual property.[8] Furthermore, only in regions like Emilia, Lombardy, and Liguria did strong firms support cooperatives of production and labor; in other regions it was necessary to resort to private enterprise. But the "red" regions were not without contradictions. Subject to a competitive market, the cooperative enterprises of production and labor were forced to accept prices often beyond the reach of the residential cooperatives, so that products politically intended for the working classes were in the end used by the middle class. However, from the late 1960s on, cooperative building managed to construct complexes remarkable in their typological articulation and their search for significant urban images, like the Federcop complexes of Verbena in Ancona of 1972–75 (figure 100) and Astra in Terni, both by the Coper studio, the Barca and Steccone complexes in Bologna (a city in which 40 percent of the residential buildings are cooperative), and the complex of the "167" intervention by Casal dei Pazzi in Rome, also by the Coper studio, which was completed in 1977.

But the projects described so far remained theoretical. The strategies of the ruling class as well as of the cooperative movement, especially from 1973 on, were forced into a stalemate by the pressing economic crisis. Large projects of regional scale remained on paper, technological reconversion in the building sector remained hypothetical, and Italstat seemed to be spinning its wheels. Construction once again became a marginal economic consideration. Whoever had hoped, or feared, a sensational resurgence of capitalist initiative was forced to recognize once again that such enlightened dreams were an illusion. After ten years, the general strikes for housing still drew no response.

There remained, of course, a new residential quality in the articulations of a complex like Verbena: a reflection on international experiences and a commitment to simultaneously resolve technical, productive, and political problems had a positive effect in this case. But it also betrayed the violent impact that resulted when craftsmen of quality were forced to face the new demand. The Nizzoli associates, founded in 1965, ventured to design complex urban structures in the area of the new industrial center of Taranto; their results were disappointing both in the residential strip of 1972 as well as in their project for the offices of the Italsider company. Industry no longer inspired the totalizing solutions that Edoardo Persico's former collaborator reversed in his projects for Olivetti. But even an architect carefully focused on an inquiry into specific formal problems, like Luigi Pellegrin, seemed disoriented in the early seventies: there was no echo of Wright in his competition projects for the Zen complex in Palermo of 1970 or for the University of Barcelona of 1970, designed with Ciro Cicconcelli, both of which were wedded, as was the Liceo Scientifico ed Istituto per Geometri of 1972–76, to a process of technological transformation that was as professionally controlled as it was detached. The result of such a hybrid encounter between formal skill and systems of construction can be found in the prefabricated cells designed by Pellegrin for the SIR in 1974 (figure 101), as part of the intervention plan mentioned above. Its tubular elements—combined, multiplied, and superimposed—are not without irony. But they were evaluated in light of contemporary designs for the utopian cities hurriedly sketched by Pellegrin: once again, the motif of technique became a nightmare, an updated invocation of the decadent megalomania of *Alpine Architektur*.

If Pellegrin's involvement in the programs of the SIR placed in question the role of the design in the production process, the BPR's involvement in organizing the highway branches of Milano Nord and the highway encircling of Naples (1970–71) reduced design to a decorative backdrop, almost a landscape painting: in those places where the objectives of large public or private capital took shape, intellectual work was used either for technical support or seen as mere ornament. Those, such as the designers of the Castello Sforzesco Museum or the Velasca Tower, who had assumed the role of custodians of collective consciousness and memory now calmly accepted the task of attaching quality to programs of regional intervention that could not be controlled by knowledge on a par with that "quality."

Meanwhile, a new project developed within the democratic communal administrations that would influence the destiny of so-called "historical centers." Real questions were being asked about the economic and cultural productivity of overturning a *tendenza* in favor of the existing patrimony. It was a matter of protesting both the eviction of less prosperous tenants from those centers, and the processes by which the centers were being transformed into tertiary bodies or into residential districts for the upper class; it was also a matter of using the powers of the public sector to reclaim and conserve these areas.

The quality of responses to the problem suddenly improved with the initiatives taken by the commune of Bologna, which actively confronted the restoration of exemplary sectors on the basis of careful typological analyses and the experimental use of legal decisions to control the effects of such restoration. The problem was now seen to be political and technical, and not merely an abstract cultural phenomenon, as it had presented itself at the convention in Gubbio in 1960. The successes and failures of the Bolognese enterprise—which was followed by attempts in Pesaro, Rimini, and Brescia—powerfully formulated the problem of the reuse of existing structures as an alternative to the creation of new fabrics, and led to an awareness of the limits and obstacles involved in projects undertaken on a local level to succeed. These projects, moreover, often ran the risk of lapsing into ideological vice. The basic theme, which contained an ambiguous antiurban streak, was still that the recovery of the ancient fabric would restore an environment permitting balanced communities. The question of recycling buildings was left open, though this was a crucial issue not only for a city like Venice, which, in spite of the special law (or because of it) continued to experience a grave identity crisis, but also for eighteenth-century neighborhoods, and for the suburban fabric of Turin, Milan, and Rome. It was, however, independent projects that set the pace after the Bolognese experiment, in spite of the changed political orientation of many communal administrations. Relations between decentralized decision-making and institutional apparatuses shifted dramatically with the political equilibrium. The election of Giulio Carlo Argan, an art historian, to the Rome union from 1976 to 1979 seemed a delayed realization of Vittorini's dream of power in the hands of intellectuals. But good will and personal dedication proved unable to significantly influence a metropolitan body thus composed and compromised. Once again, the search for an effective rapport between techniques and power structures took priority, and on this rapport much of the future of Italian society would depend.

1. Nello Aprile, Cino Calcaprina, Aldo Cardelli, Mario Fiorentino, and Giuseppe Perugini. Monument to the Fosse Ardeatine, 1944–47 (Rome). The sculptures are by Mirko Basaldella and Francesco Coccia.

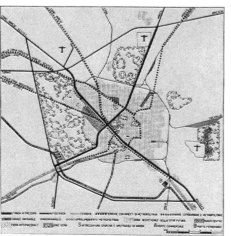

2. Ludovico Belgiojoso, Enrico Peressutti, and Ernesto Nathan Rogers. Monument to the Dead in the Concentration Camps in Germany, 1946. Milan, Cimitero Monumentale (Foto Monti).

3. The Italian CIAM Group in collaboration with Franco Albini, Piero Bottoni, Ezio Cerutti, Ignazio Gardella, Gabriele Mucchi, Giancarlo Palanti, Mario Pucci, and Aldo Putelli. Master plan for Milan, called the "AR" plan, drafted in 1944 and presented to the competition for such proposals organized by the Milan Commune in November 1945.

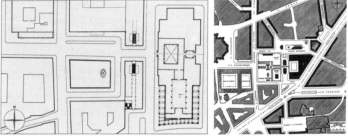

4. Giuseppe De Finetti. "Strada Lombarda" in Milan, 1944–46. Perspective of the new artery between Via San Paolo and the Cordusio.

5. Giuseppe De Finetti. Piazza Fontana in Milan, 1944–46. Above: perspective; below left: site plan, 1944–46; below right: site plan for the organization of the *"tre piazze"* in Milan, 1949.

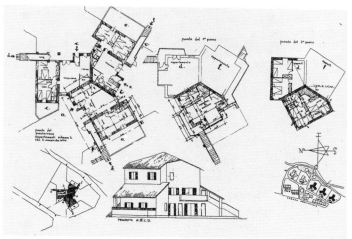

6. Aldo Cardelli, Arrigo Carè, Giulio
Ceradini, Mario Fiorentino, Ludovico
Quaroni, and Mario Ridolfi. Competition project for the passenger terminal of
the new train station in Rome (perspective), 1947 (Foto Cartoni).

7. Mario Ridolfi and Wolfgang Frankl.
UNRRA-Casas development in Popoli,
1950. Plans and elevation of an
apartment building arranged on three
levels.

8–9. Ludovico Quaroni and Mario Ridolfi (project managers), Carlo Aymonino, Carlo Chiarini, Mario Fiorentino, Federico Gorio, Maurizio Lanza, Sergio Lenci, Piero Maria Lugli, Carlo Melograni, Giancarlo Menichetti, Giulio Rinaldi, and Michele Valori. INA-Casa quarter on Via Tiburtina in Rome (view and site plan), 1949–54 (Foto Savio).

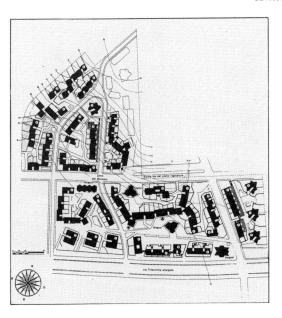

10. Franco Marescotti. The social cooperative center called "Grandi e Bertacchi" in Rome (view of the residential building), 1951–53.

11. Franco Albini and Luigi Colombini.
Rifugio Pirovano in Cervinia, 1949–51.

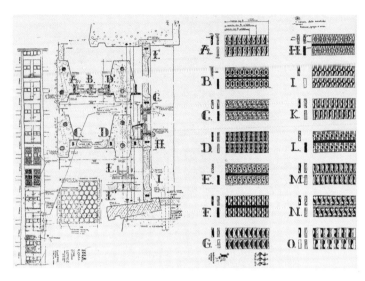

12–13. Mario Ridolfi and Wolfgang Frankl. INA-Assicurazioni residential towers on Viale Etiopia in Rome (design charts and view), 1950–54 (Foto Sforza).

14. Mario Ridolfi and Wolfgang Frankl.
Palazzina Zaccardi on Via De Rossi in
Rome, 1950–51 (Foto Sforza).

15. Arnaldo Foschini. Winning project
in the competition for the new branch of
the Banca d'Italia in Naples, begun in
1949.

16. Carlo Mollino. Sled-lift Station with hotel on Lake Nero in the Val di Susa, begun in 1946 (Foto Archivio Mollino).

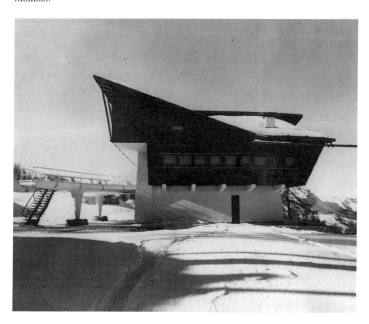

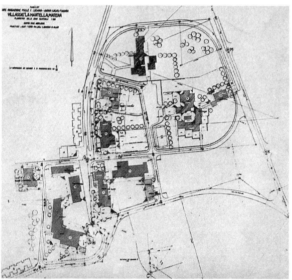

17–18. Ludovico Quaroni, Federico Gorio, Michele Valori, Piero Maria Lugli, and Luigi Agati. "La Martella" Village in Matera (view and site plan of the center), begun in 1951.

19. Luigi Moretti. Residential and office complex on Corso Italia in Milan, 1952–56 (Foto Monti).

20. Luigi Moretti. "Il Girasole"
(Sunflower) Palazzina on Viale Buozzi in
Rome, 1950 (Foto Sforza).

21. Luigi Moretti. Villa Pignatelli,
called "La Saracena" in Santa Marinella
(Rome), 1952–54 (Foto Monti).

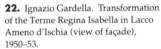

22. Ignazio Gardella. Transformation of the Terme Regina Isabella in Lacco Ameno d'Ischia (view of façade), 1950–53.

23. Franco Albini. INA office building in Parma, 1950 (Foto Monti).

24. Giovanni Michelucci. Studies for the reconstruction of the Ponte Vecchio area in Florence, 1945 (below: a view of Via Por Santa Maria looking toward Santa Maria del Fiore).

25. Giovanni Michelucci. Osteria del Gambero Rosso in Collodi, 1961–63 (Foto Serafini).

26. Giovanni Michelucci. Cassa di Risparmio in Pistoia, 1964–66. The building was constructed by transforming and enlarging that of the Borsa Merci, also designed by Michelucci, in 1949–50.

27. Franco Albini, Gianni Albricci,
Ludovico Belgiojoso, Ignazio Gardella,
Enrico Peressutti, and Ernesto Nathan
Rogers. INA-Casa quarter in Cesate
(Milan), begun in 1950.

28. Franco Albini and Ignazio Gardella.
IACP "Mangiagalli" quarter in Milan,
1950–51.

29. Giovanni Astengo, Sandro Molli Boffa, Nello Renacco, and Aldo Rizzotti. Study for the community center of the Falchera residential unit in Turin, 1950–51.

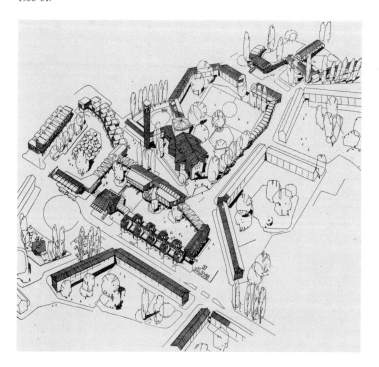

30. Adalberto Libera. Horizontal residential unit in the Tuscolano quarter in Rome, after the completion of construction, 1950–51 (Foto Savio).

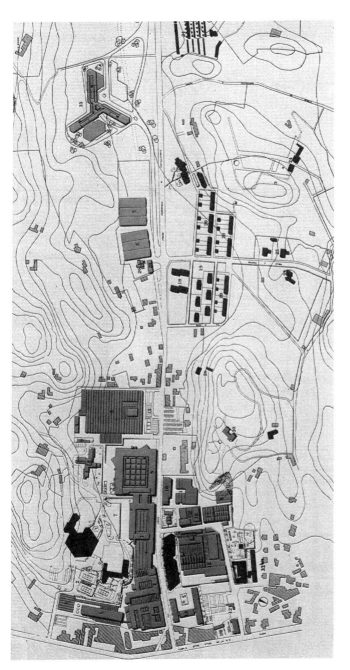

31. Site plan for the Olivetti industrial complex in Ivrea.

32–33. Luigi Figini and Gino Pollini.
Olivetti complex of social buildings in
Ivrea, 1954–57. Exterior and portico.

34. Luigi Cosenza. Olivetti establishment in Pozzuoli (detail), begun in 1951 (Foto Mulas).

35–36. Luciano Baldessari and Marcello Grisotti. Breda Pavilion at the Milan Fair, 1953–54.

37. Ludovico Quaroni, Adolfo De
Carlo, Andrea Mor, and Angelo Sibilla.
Chiesa della Sacra Famiglia in Genoa,
begun in 1956 (Foto Monti).

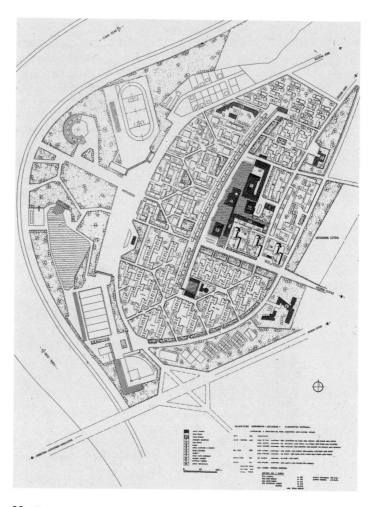

38. Giuseppe Vaccaro, Luciano De
Filla, Mario Paniconi, Annibale
Vitellozzi, Francesco Santini, Alfredo Le-
orati, and Umberto Chiarini (project
manager). Site plan of the coordinated
quarter (IACP-Bologna, INA-Casa,
INCIS, and UNRRA-Casas) on Via della
Barca in Bologna, 1957–62.

39. Luigi Pellegrin, Ciro Cicconcelli,
Franco Antonelli, Angelo Cecchini, and
Mario Roggero. INA-Casa residential
complex in Galatina (Lecce), 1958.

40. Luigi Carlo Daneri (coordinator),
Eugenio Fuselli (vice-coordinator),
Claudio Andreani, Robaldo Morozzo
della Rocca, Mario Pateri, Gustavo
Pulitzer, and Angelo Sibilla (project
manager). Residential quarter at Forte di
Quezzi (Genoa), begun in 1956.

41. Franco Albini. Layout of the Communal Galleries of the Palazzo Bianco in Genoa, 1950–51 (Foto Monti).

42–43. Franco Albini and Franca Helg. Treasury Museum of San Lorenzo in Genoa (view of a tholos and site plan), 1952–56 (Foto Monti).

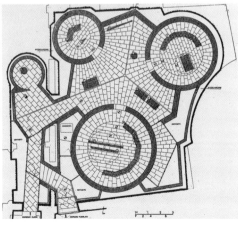

44. Ludovico Belgiojoso, Enrico
Peressutti, and Ernesto Nathan Rogers.
Restoration and layout of the museums
of the Sforzesco Castle in Milan, 1954–56
(Foto Monti).

45. Ludovico Belgiojoso, Enrico
Peressutti, and Ernesto Nathan Rogers.
"Torre Velasca" skyscraper in Milan,
1950–51. Construction completed in
1958 (Foto Monti).

46. Ignazio Gardella. Olivetti refectory
building in Ivrea, 1955–59.

47. Ignazio Gardella. Apartment house
in Zattere (Venice), 1954–58.

48. Roberto Gabetti and Aimaro Isola.
Bottega d'Erasmo in Turin (detail),
begun in 1953.

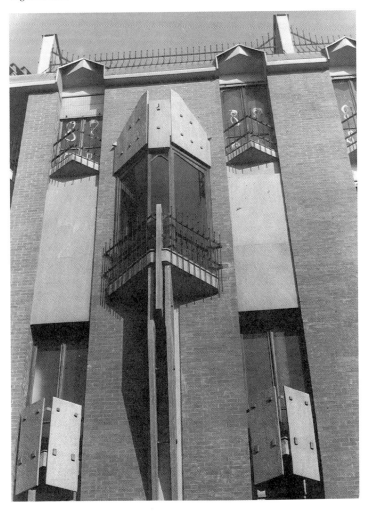

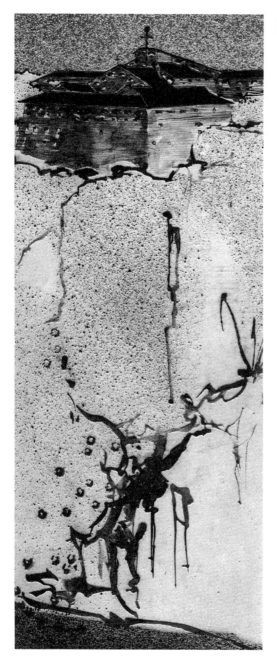

49. Roberto Gabetti and Aimaro Isloa Project for a convent in Chieti, 1956.

50. Vittorio Gregotti, Ludovico Meneghetti, and Giotto Stoppino. Office building in Novara, 1959–60 (Foto Monti).

51. Gianfranco Caniggia, Paolo Marconi, and Paolo Portoghesi. Competition project for the new Biblioteca Nazionale of Rome, 1957.

52. Paolo Portoghesi and Vittorio Gigliotti, in collaboration with Giuseppe Palma, Mario Alamanni, and Fabrizio Ago. Chiesa della Sacra Famiglia in Salerno (interior), 1969–73.

53. Saverio Muratori. Building of the Democrazia Cristiana in EUR (Rome), 1955–58 (Foto Sforza).

54. Saverio Muratori. ENPAS office building in Bologna, 1952–57 (Foto Monti).

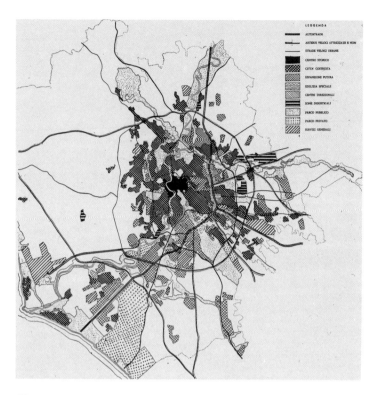

55. Special Office for the Master Plan.
The master plan for Rome, 1962.

56. Giuseppe Samonà and Egle Renata
Trincanato. INAIL center in San
Simeone (Venice), 1950–56 (Foto Monti).

57. Ludovico Magistretti and Guido
Veneziani. Office and residential
building of the firm "L'Abeille" society
on Via Leopardi in Milan, 1959–60 (Foto
Monti).

58. Vittoriano Viganò. Marchiondi Spagliardi Institute in Milan-Baggio (exterior), 1953–57 (Foto Monti).

59. Angelo Mangiarotti. Project for a square-based megastructure, in reinforced prestressed concrete, 1975 (Foto Casali).

60. Luigi Caccia-Dominioni. Villa on
Via XX Settembre in Milan,1954–55 (Foto
Monti).

61. Luigi Figini and Gino Pollini.
Chiesa della Madonna dei Poveri in
Milan (interior), 1952–54 (Foto Monti).

62. Luigi Caccia-Dominioni.
Residential and office building on Corso
Monforte in Milan, 1965 (Foto Monti).

63. Gino Valle. Offices for the Zanussi
industries in Porcia (Pordenone),
1959–61 (Foto Zannier).

64. Gino Valle. Offices and company
cafeteria of the Fantoni industry in
Osoppo (Udine), 1973–78 (Foto
Marpillero).

65. Gio Ponti, Antonio Fornaroli,
Alberto Rosselli, and collaborators.
Pirelli skyscraper in Milan, 1955–58. The
structures in reinforced concrete are the
result of the collaboration of Pier Luigi
Nervi and Arturo Danusso (Foto
Monti).

66. Pier Luigi and Antonio Nervi.
Palazzo del Lavoro in Turin (detail),
1960.

67. Riccardo Morandi. Automobile
Exhibit Pavilion in Turin, 1960 (Foto
Torino Esposizioni s.p.a.).

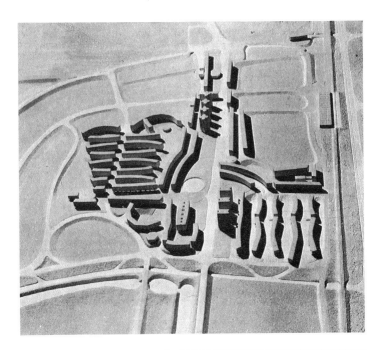

68–69. Luigi Moretti (urban plan),
Vittorio Cafiero, Ignazio Guidi,
Adalberto Libera, and collaborators.
INCIS quarter near EUR in Rome (model
and perspective drawing of a courtyard),
begun in 1958.

70. Franco Albini and Franca Helg.
"Rinascente" department store in Rome
(model of the first scheme), 1957–61.

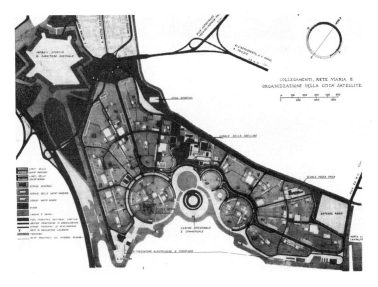

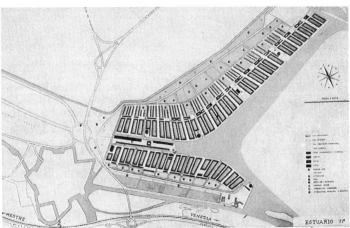

71. Ludovico Quaroni (project manager), Massimo Boschetti, Adolfo De Carlo, Gabriella Esposito, Luciano Giovannini, Aldo Livadiotti, Luciana Menozzi, and Alberto Polizzi, with the collaboration of Ted Musho. Competition project for the CEP quarter on the Barene of San Giuliano in Mestre (site plan), 1959.

72. Saverio Muratori (project manager), Renato Bollati, Sergio Bollati, Guido Figus, Paolo Maretto, Guido Marinucci, and Giovanni Mazzocca. Competition project for the CEP quarter on the Barene of San Giuliano in Mestre (site plan), 1959.

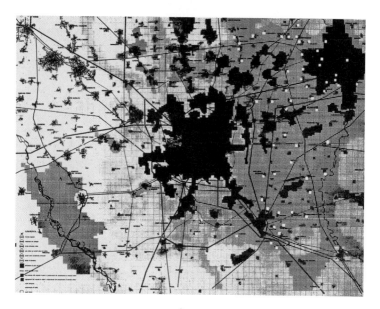

73. Study center for the Milanese intercommunal plan. Plan, 1963.

74. Giovanni Michelucci. Chiesa di San Giovanni Battista on the Autostrada del Sole in Campi Bisenzio (Florence), 1960–64 (Foto Monti).

75. Giovanni Michelucci. Study for the
San Carlo thermal complex in Massa
Carrara, 1978.

76. Giovanni Michelucci. Study for the
roof of the church in Longarone, 1968.

77. Leonardo Ricci. Residential
building in the Sorgane quarter in
Florence, 1963–66 (Foto Serafini).

78. Leonardo Savioli and Danilo Santi.
Apartment house on Via della
Piagentina in Florence, 1964 (Foto
Serafini).

79. Marcello D'Olivo. Villa Spezzotti in
Lignano Pineta, 1958.

80. Vincenzo, Fausto, and Lucio
Passarelli, in collaboration with Paolo
Cercato, Edgardo Tonca, Maurizio
Costantini, and Enrico Falorni. Residen-
tial building on Via Campania in Rome,
1963–65 (Foto Sforza).

81. The Asse Studio (Vicio Delleani,
Mario Fiorentino, Riccardo Morandi,
Fausto, Vincenzo, and Lucio Passarelli,
Ludovico Quaroni, Bruno Zevi, with
Gabriele Scimemi as consultant).
Proposal for the office district in Rome
(model), 1967–70.

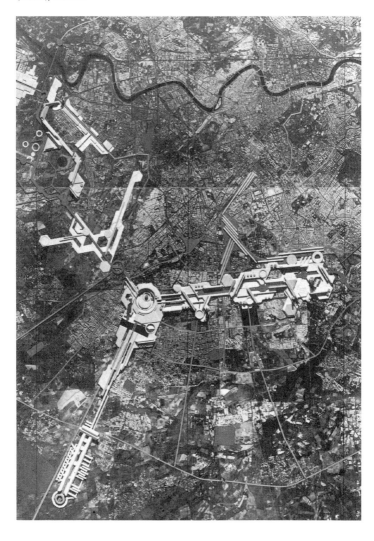

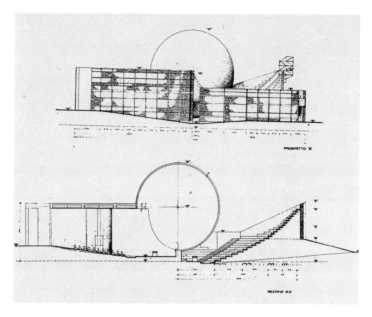

82. Ludovico Quaroni, Luisa Anversa,
and Giangiacomo D'Ardia. Project for
the new church in Gibellina (elevation
and section), 1970. The structures are the
result of Sergio Musmeci's collaboration.

83. Franco and Marco Albini and
Franca Helg, in collaboration with
Giuseppe Rizzo. New baths "Luigi
Zoja" in Salsomaggiore, 1967–70.

84. Ignazio Gardella. Chiesa di
Sant'Enrico in Metanopoli (Milan),
1963–66.

85. Ignazio Gardella, Anna Castelli, and Jacopo Gardella. Building for the technical offices of Alfa Romeo in Arese (Milan) (foreshortened view of the ramp), 1968–72.

86. Ignazio Gardella. Competition project for the new Theater of Vicenza (uncovered model), 1968 (Foto Mulas).

87. Ludovico Belgiojoso, Enrico Peressutti, and Ernesto Nathan Rogers. Office building of Immobiliare Cagisa in Piazza Meda in Milan, 1958–69 (Foto Nicolini).

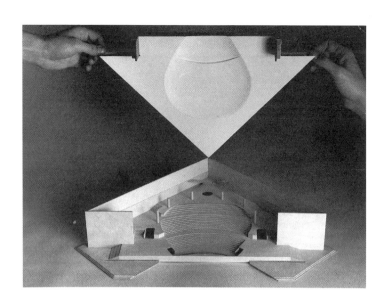

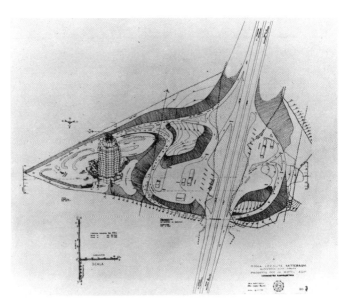

88–89. Mario Ridolfi, Wolfgang Frankl,
and Domenico Malagricci. Project for an
AGIP motel in Settebagni (Rome)
(axonometric and perspective study),
1968.

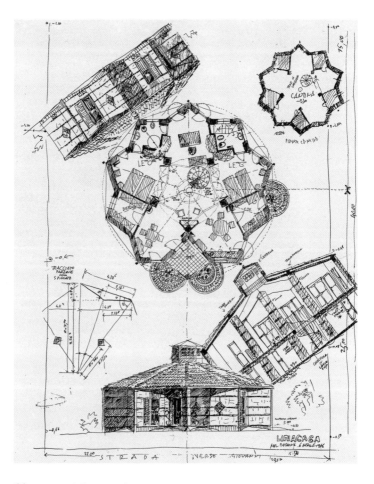

90. Mario Ridolfi. "Lina" house in
Marmore (Terni) (studies), 1966.

91. Gae Aulenti, Carlo Aymonino,
Steno Paciello, Ezio Bonfanti, Jacopo
Gardella, and Cesare Macchi Cassia,
with Antoni Ghirelli as design collaborator. "L'arrivo al mare": presentation for
the Italian sector, dedicated to the theme
"Leisure Time and Water," at the
thirteenth Triennale of Milan, 1964.

92. Ludovico Quaroni, Gabriella
Esposito, Marta Lonzi, and Antonio
Quistelli. Competition project for the
new office center for the Chamber of
Deputies in Rome, 1967.

93. Giuseppe and Alberto Samonà.
Competition project for the office center
for the Chamber of Deputies in Rome
(perspective), 1967.

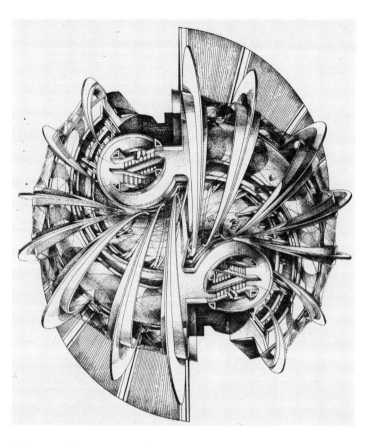

94. Maurizio Sacripanti. Project for the
Italian pavilion at the Osaka Expo, 1970.

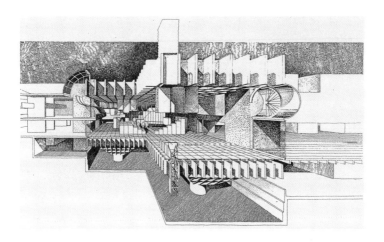

95. Maurizio Sacripanti. Winning competition project for the new Teatro Comunale of Forlí, 1978.

96. Vittorio De Feo, Errico Ascione, Fabrizio Aggarbati, and Carla Saggioro. Competition project for the Palazzo Municipale of Legnago (perspective), 1974.

97. Luciano Semerani and Gigetta
Tamaro, in collaboration with Adalberto
and Romano Burelli, Luciano and
Mariella Rossi, Emilio Savonitto, and
Vico Tramontin. Competition project for
the historical center of Trieste (aerial
view of the model), 1969.

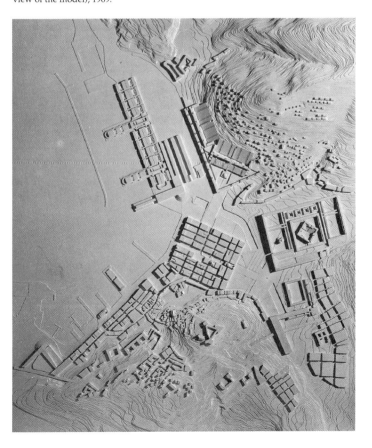

98–99. Alessandro Anselmi, Pierluigi
Eroli, and Franco Pierluisi (of the
GRAU). Competition project for the new
State Archives of Florence (perspective
facing the historical center; site plan),
1972.

100. Coper Studio. "Le Grazie" cooperative quarter in Ancona, 1972–75.

101. Luigi Pellegrin. Project for a modular cell in polyester resin for serial production (model), 1974.

102. Carlo Scarpa. Villa Veritti in
Udine, 1956–61 (Foto Monti).

103. Carlo Scarpa. Restoration and remodeling of the Biblioteca Querini-
Stampalia in Venice (detail of the
entrance), 1961–63 (Foto Monti).

104–105. Carlo Scarpa. Brion Tomb in the San Vito cemetery of Altivole near Asolo (interior and view of the funeral arch with tombs), 1970–72 (Foto Sforza).

106. Carlo Scarpa. Studies for the placement of the statue of Cangrande near the Castelvecchio Museum in Verona, 1964.

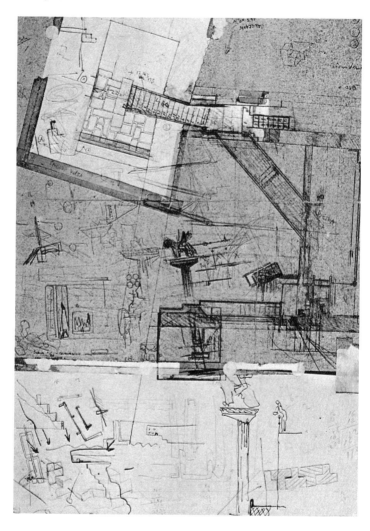

107. Giuseppe and Alberto Samonà.
New branch of the Banca d'Italia in
Padua (detail of the facade on Via
Roma), 1968–74 (Foto Sforza).

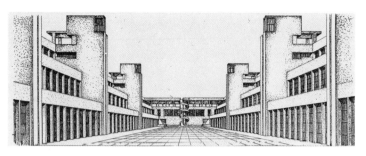

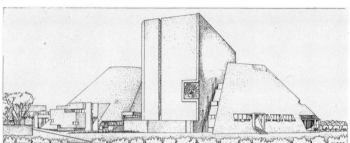

108. Giuseppe Samonà (project
manager), Alberto Samonà, Cesare
Ajroldi, Cristiana Bedoni, Mario Alberto
Chiorino, Mariella Di Falco, Carlo
Doglio, Giovanna Fartaglio, Francesco
Frattini, Rejana Lucci, Livia Toccafondi,
and Egle Renata Trincanato. Competi-
tion project for the new University of
Cagliari, 1972.

109. Giuseppe and Alberto Samonà.
Project for the Teatro Popolare of Sciacca
(perspective), 1974.

110. Giancarlo De Carlo. University
Colleges in Urbino, 1963–66.

111. Giancarlo De Carlo. "Matteotti"
quarter in Terni (view of a connecting
overpass), 1969–75.

112. Giancarlo De Carlo. Nuova
Facolà di Magistero in Urbino (view of
the skylight over the big lecture halls,
and of the restored and restructured
fifteenth-century convent), 1968–76.

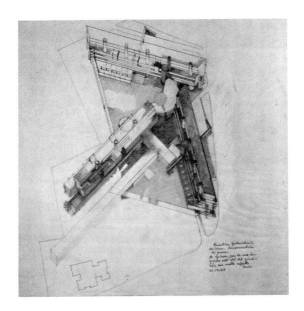

113-14. Carlo Aymonino, in collaboration with Maurizio Aymonino, Alessandro De Rossi, and Sachim Messarè. Monte Amiata residential complex in Gallaratese 2 (Milan) (axonometric study, 1968, and view of the entrance beneath the A1 building). The project was drafted between 1967 and 1970, and the execution was completed in 1973.

115. Aldo Rossi. Residential building in the Monte Amiata complex in Gallaratese 2 (Milan), 1969–70.

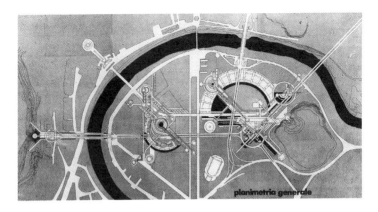

planimetria generale

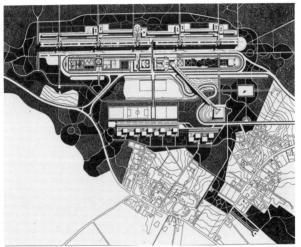

116. Mario Fiorentino (project manager), Giuseppe Cappelli, Gabriele De Giorgi, and Fabrizio Sferra Carini. Project for the office district of the urban sector Olimpico-Tor di Quinto in Rome (site plan), 1971–72.

117. Mario Fiorentino (general coordinator and project manager), Piero Maria Lugli, Federico Gorio, Giulio Sterbini, and Michele Valori (project manager), structures by Riccardo Morandi. Residential complex in Corviale (Rome) (site plan), 1973–82.

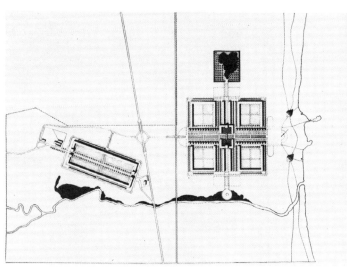

118–119. Mario Fiorentino. Project
for a residential complex in upper Lazio
(site plan and courtyard elevation),
1979–81.

120. Vittorio Gregotti, Francesco Amoroso, Salvatore Bisogni, Hiromichi Matsui, and Franco Purini. Project for the Zen quarter in Palermo (site plan), 1969.

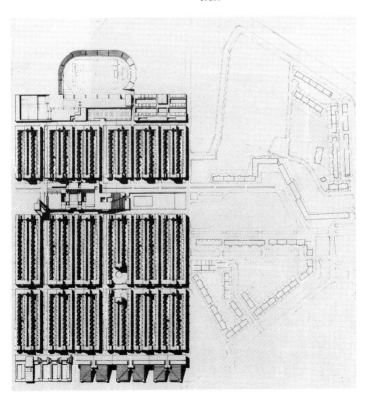

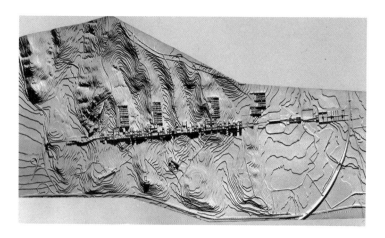

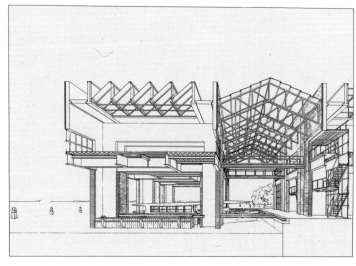

121. Emilio Battisti, Vittorio Gregotti, Hiromichi Matsui, P. Nicolin, Franco Purini, C. Rusconi Clerici, and B. Viganò (structures: G. Grandori; urban planning: Laris). Competition project for the new branch of the University of Calabria in Cosenza, 1975.

122. Vittorio Gregotti, Augusto Cagnardi, Pierluigi Cerri, and Hiromichi Matsui, in collaboration with Spartaco Azzola, Elvio Casagrande, Raffaello Cecchi, and Carlo Magnani. Project for the ACTV boatyards in Giudecca (Venice), 1980.

123. Roberto Gabetti and Aimaro Isola, in collaboration with Luciano Re. Olivetti residential center, 1969–70, Ivrea.

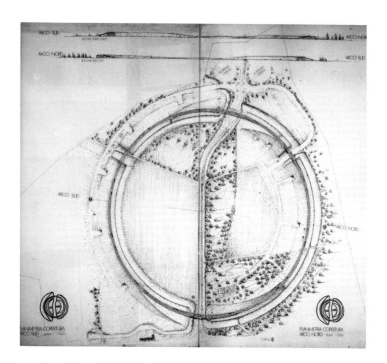

124. Roberto Gabetti, Aimaro Isola, Luciano Re, and Guido Drocco. Competition project for the Fiat office district in Candiolo, 1973.

125. Guido Canella, Michele Achilli, Daniele Brigidini, and Laura Lazzari. Civic center in Segrate, 1963–66.

126. Guido Canella, in collaboration with Michele Achilli, Daniele Brigidini, and Giorgio Fiorese. Civic center (the town hall-secondary school complex) in Pieve Emanuele (Milan) (detail of the town hall), 1968–81.

127. Guido Canella. IACP quarter in Bollate (Milan) (detail of the two-level structure over portico), 1974–81.

128. Gae Aulenti. Decor and remodeling of the Casa Agnelli (Lamb House) in Milan, 1968–69.

129. Aldo Rossi and Gianni Braghieri.
Competition project for the new
cemetery of Modena, 1971.

130. Aldo Rossi, Gianni Braghieri, and
Arduino Cantafora. Elementary school
in Fagnano Olona, 1972.

131. Aldo Rossi. Competition project
for the Student House in Chieti, 1977.

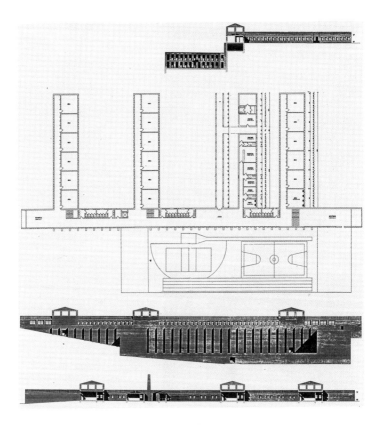

132. Giorgio Grassi and Antonio
Monestiroli. Project for a secondary
school in Tollo, 1975.

133–34. Franco Purini. Theoretical designs: *I paesaggi dell'architettura*, 1980; *La casa Romana*, 1979.

135–136. Franco Purini. Theoretical designs: *Due case*, 1980; *Studio per una colonna*, 1980.

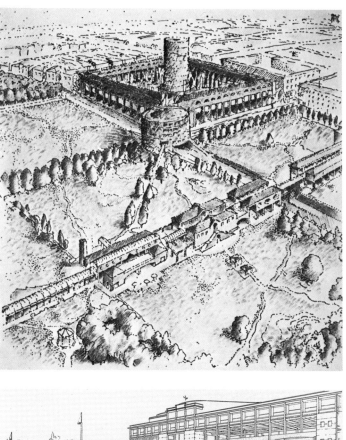

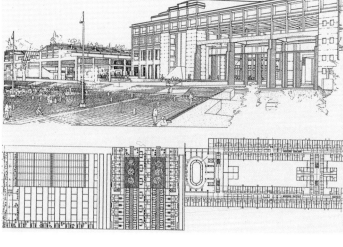

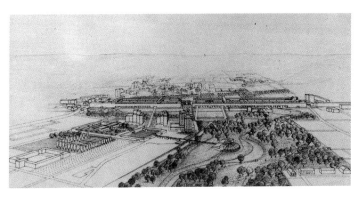

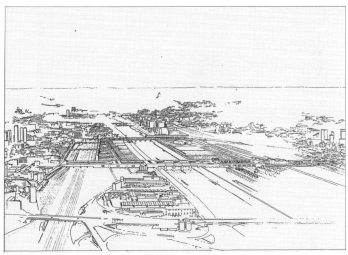

137. Roberto Scannavini. Design for the interstitial zone of the Mercato Ortofrutticolo in Bologna, 1984.

138. Gae Aulenti, Italo Rota, Luigi Mazza, and collaborators. Competition project for the restructuring of Fiat Lingotto in Turin (perspective and plan), 1983.

139. Gregotti Associates. Detailed plan for the area of Via Corassori in Modena (bird's-eye perspective), 1983–84.

140. Gregotti Associates. Project for a residential bridge for the Exposition Universelle of 1989 in Paris (bird's-eye perspective), 1982.

141. Gino Valle and collaborators.
Sketch in the course of execution for the
IBM buildings at La Défense in Paris
(detail).

142. Gianni Fabbri and Roberto Sordina. IACP residential nucleus in Mestre-Altobello (section-perspective of the V-shaped block), 1978–83.

143. Carlo Chiarini, Luigi Cremona, and Italo Melanesi. Residential complex in Tor Sapienza in Rome. The project dates from 1982–83 and was built in 1984–85.

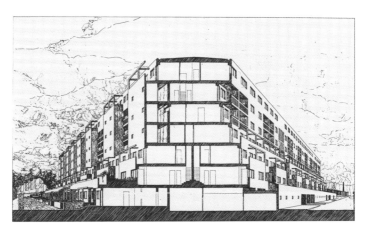

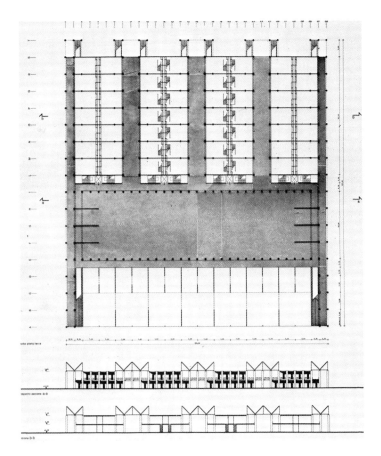

144. Gianugo Polesello (with
Francesco Panzarin). Project for a
market in Bibione near San Michele al
Tagliamento (plan of the ground floor,
elevation and section), 1980.

145. Luciano Semerani and Gigetta Tamaro (with Carlo and Luciano Celli and Dario Tognon). Nuovo Ospedale of Trieste in Cattinara (detail of the slab), 1965–83.

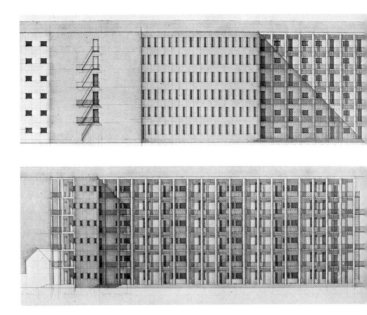

146. Giorgio Grassi (with Adalberto
Del Bo, Edoardo Guazzoni, and
Agostina Renna), project for the Lützowplatz in Berlin (detail of the elevations),
1980.

147. Guido Canella and Michele Achilli (with E. Mezzetti). Secondary school in Monaca di Cesano Boscone near Milan (view of exterior), 1975–83.

148. Roberto Gabetti, Aimaro Isola, and Guido Drocco. Residential building on Via Sant'Agostino in Turin (lateral view), 1980–83.

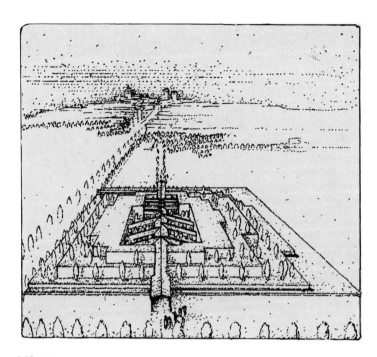

149. Roberto Gabetti, Aimaro Isola,
and Giuseppe Varaldo (in collaboration
with Guido Drocco and Enrico
Moncalvo). Project for the Judiciary
Offices in Alba (bird's-eye perspective),
1982.

150. Guido Drocco and Enrico Moncalvo. Competition project for the new Opéra in Paris on the Place de la Bastille (perspective), 1983.

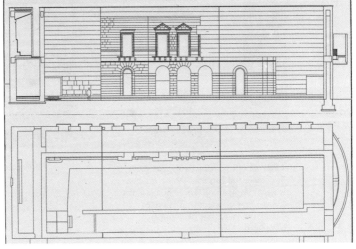

151. Francesco Venezia. Museum of Gibellina (view of the ruin of the Palazzo Di Lorenzo in its new setting). The project dates from 1981–82; the first phase was executed in 1984 (Foto Roberto Collovia).

152. Francesco Venezia. Museum of Gibellina (section on the courtyard and plan of the first floor).

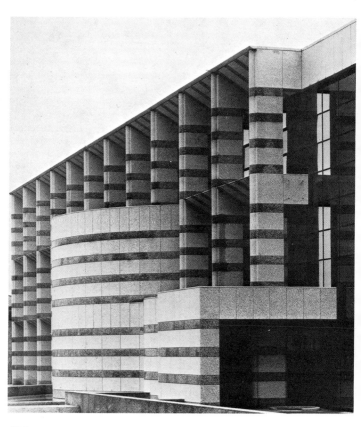

153. Adolfo Natalini (with Giampiero
Frassinelli and Fabrizio Natalini). Cassa
Rurale e Artigiana of Alzate Brianza near
Como (view of exterior). The project
dates from 1978; construction was
completed in 1983.

154–155. Alessandro Anselmi (with Paola D'Incecco, Andrea Salvioni, Hitoschi Tsubouchi, Margherita Tzifachi, and Roberto Ugolini). Project for temporary residences in Testaccio in Rome (model), 1983.

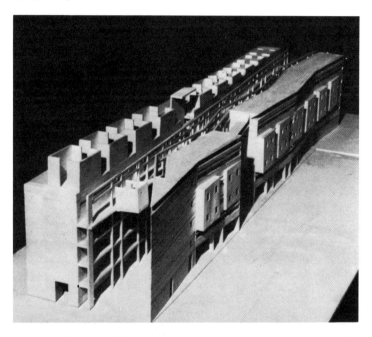

156. Franco Purini and Laura Thermes (with D. Modigliani). Project for the civic center of Castelforte near Latina (axonometric), 1984.

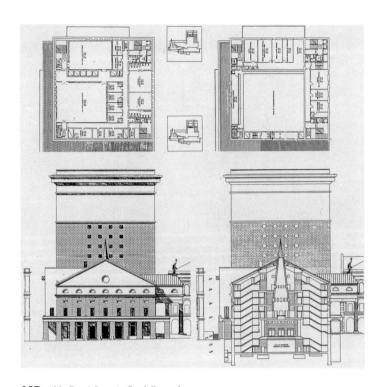

157. Aldo Rossi, Ignazio Gardella, and Fabio Reinhart. Project for the reconstruction of the Teatro Carlo Felice in Genoa (plans of the tower, elevation and section), 1981–82.

158. Aldo Rossi, Gianni Braghieri, and
collaborators. Project for an office
building in Buenos Aires (perspective),
1984.

159. Carlo Aymonino, Luigi Calcagni, Giampaolo Mar, and Gigetta Tamaro. Initial scheme for the new hospital in Mestre (perspective of the bed unit), 1984.

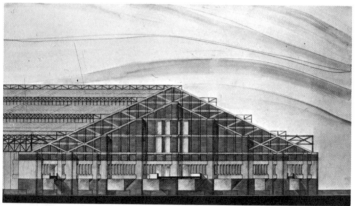

160. Gianfranco Caniggia, Romano
Greco, Gaetano Imperato, and
collaborators. Initial scheme for the
Palazzo di Giustizia of Teramo (model),
1968. The building was constructed
between 1975 and 1981.

161. Gianfranco Caniggia, Gian Luigi
Maffei, and collaborators. Competition
project for the new station of Bologna
(elevation of the bridge-station), 1983.

162–163. Pier Luigi Nicolin (with Giuseppe Marinoni). Project for the Accademia bridge in Venice (model), 1984–85.

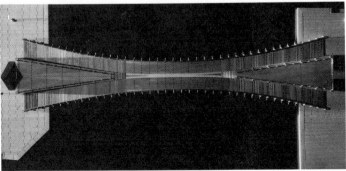

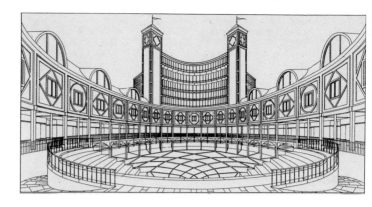

164. Paolo Portoghesi. Project for a
piazza in Latina (perspective of solution
A), 1984.

165. Paolo Portoghesi. Project design
for the Fortezza da Basso in Florence
(bird's-eye perspective), 1983.

166. Francesco Cellini and Nicoletta Cosentino (with Andrea Salvioni and Roberto Ugolini). Project for the Piazza della Repubblica in Turin (perspective), 1982.

167. Oswald Zoeggeler. Cooperative for nine residences in Chiusa near Bolzano (view of exterior), 1982–84

6
Two "Masters": Carlo Scarpa and Giuseppe Samonà

While prepared to face the new problems erupting in the early 1970s, architects were armed only with a renewed capacity for self-verification. Their corporate organizations did not offer methods for acting or learning, their cultural organs were too dispersed, and the specialized publishing business was inflated. Meanwhile, the "ideology of rejection" demonstrated its inadequacy, and technocratic arrogance proved its inefficiency. The best architects "wrote texts." Many found this path painfully limiting; others found that it concurred with the separatist attitude they had maintained all along. The youngest watched anxiously as this supposedly brief moment grew longer.

Not coincidentally, the highest level of formal coherence was found in the works of those who, seeking refuge from the surrounding commotion, isolated themselves. The detachment of the "outmoded" threw light on subjective and collective situations that allowed (or stimulated?) "the courage to speak of roses." Historiographical treatment must be suspended in the case of such golden, isolated individuals, and give way to "classical" monographs.

There is no other way to deal with a body of work such as Carlo Scarpa's (1906–78), which proudly defends the magic circle enclosing the architect and his own private *codes*. Scarpa's work should be treated in its entirety, but here we will focus on its isolation and uniqueness.[1]

There was no "decadence" in the Venice sung and experienced by Scarpa. Instead, Scarpa drew from Venice a somewhat perverse lesson, one that emerges from the dialectic between the celebration of form and labyrinthian dissemination, between the will for representation and the evanescence of what is represented, between a search for truths and the consciousness of their relativity. In the thirties, Scarpa's work began with a series of windows for the Venini of Murana and with the internal remodeling of the Ca' Foscari, done in 1936–37, where he referred to Arturo Martini's sculpture as well as to Braque and Léger. Already in those first efforts, an ironic smile could be detected in the work of this "wise artisan." His postwar work, which suffered no ideological traumas, adhered to a poetics of the object, rich in formal pleasures and attentive to Wright's heritage, but careful not to lapse into mannerism as it persisted in the elaboration of preciousness, evocation, and contrast. Scarpa cleansed Wright's syntax of all utopianism, turning it into a flexible means of meditation engendering convulsive and interrupted narrations. Phrases alluding to other phrases in an infinite chain of references characterize his projects for an apartment building in Feltre of 1949, a movie theater in San Donà di Piave, the Villa Zoppas in Conegliano of 1953, the Casa Taddei in Venice of 1957, and the Villa Veritti in Udine of 1956–61 (figure 102). Obstinately concentrated within the secrets of his discipline, Scarpa decomposed the elements of his language, pulling his spectator into a tangled universe of signs, the deciphering of which was somewhat facilitated by a deceptive hedonism. His articulation of distinct phrases was in fact hedonistic. Such phrases were crucial in the Venezuela pavilion at the Giardini of the Biennale of 1954–56, and even more so in the fragmented and precious spaces of the Olivetti store at the Procuratie Vecchie of 1957–58, in the Gavina store in Bologna of 1960,[2] and at the Querini-Stampalia library in Venice of 1961–63 (figure 103).[3] Interrupted and "figured" angles, dislocated planes, and water further diluting unstable forms: a true art of manipulation informs the fragments of words that seem "too rich." Language was in some way a pre-text for Scarpa, just as those monuments where he intervened with indisputable competence as a restorer or designer were also pre-texts. In the interior design of the Palazzo Abatellis in Palermo of 1953–54, in the Gipsoteca of Possagno of 1956–57 and in the restoration of the Castelvecchio Museum in Verona of 1964,[4] Scarpa enjoyed a private and metaphorically rich dialogue with history: the surreal placement of the equestrian statue of Cangrande della Scala in the Castelvecchio (figure 106) is typical of his simultaneously humorous and pensive rapport with the past. This is the main difference between Scarpa's attitude and the ambiguously tolerant or "reluctant historicism" of Rogers, Gardella, Quarini, and their immediate students. Scarpa also applied his irony to history, which he considered design material. Irony also colored his encounter with Klee, on the occasion of the 1948 exhibit. An impertinent and disenchanted comic vein sprang from the confluence of Klee's dreamy echoes of "cruel childhood," Mondrian's asceticism—which Scarpa also commented upon in the design of the Roman exhibit of 1956[5]—and Wright's "geometrical games."

The art of smiling whenever risks became too serious: this was another lesson that emerged from Scarpa's work, though his aristocratic reserve was tinged with immodesty. Scarpa's last major work was certainly "immodest": the construction of the San Vito cemetery at Asolo for the tomb of G. Brion, begun in 1970 (figures 104–105). "Necropoli ludens" are the words that have been used to describe this tormented sequence of formal episodes, frozen and overwrought—design was never a mere means for Scarpa—tunnel-like and metaphysical, laid out according to a plan based on secret rules. A homage to the "art of concrete and invention," the San Vito cemetery resembles a battlefield where forms—the little temple evoking the Oriental, the small pavilion and the covered passageway leading to the entryway, and the hermetic funereal arches covering the family sarcophagi—all play a partita with death. The secret nucleus of Scarpa's poetics does not really lie in his projects for the Vicenza theater of 1968, for the Banca Popolare in Verona, or for the remodeling of the Teatro Carlo Felice in Genova, but rather in the San Vito cemetery and the Casa Ottolenghi in Bardolino of 1975. These closed works beseech their "commissioners" to acknowledge the stubborn will to communicate of a Byzantine master who happened to live in the twentieth century, and who was consequently forced to use modern language to speak ancient truths.

But it is necessary, in analyzing the great cycle of Scarpa's architecture, to avoid the slippery and threatening terrain of mythology. Discontinuous form, the praise of the fragment, and the intense fashioning of materials and geometry are very different from the corrosions of Mario Ridolfi. The free associations of the Brion tomb, the dissonance of the project for the Casa Cassina at Ronco di Carmiate in Como, the studied complexity of the buildings for the Banca Antoniana in Monselice (1976–77) and for the transformation of the convent of Santa Caterina in Treviso into a museum (1974–75), and the hieratic tomb of Galli in the Genoa Nervi cemetery of 1978, give rise to a variety of recurring, de-formed "figures" that speak to each other in a kind of uninter-rupted dialogue. Scarpa's language, which is marked by gaps and interruptions, can be read as a musical score, the phrases of which are interwoven in a complicated pattern punctuated by pauses.

The experience of discontinuous historical space, the theme of Scarpa's masterful configurations for museums, was therefore a logical extension of the spatial dissemination that paradoxically supported the architectural "figures" on which he focused. This is so much so that it seems fitting to establish a relationship between the figurative worlds of Scarpa and Paul Klee. Echoes of Klee's *icons of the possible*—as Massimo Cacciari has called them—can be found in Scarpa's allusive spaces: a universe of coexisting possi-bilities has been left open and is expressed in multivalent forms, inviting one, especially in his last work, to embark upon interpre-tive voyages that question the "one-way streets" of the "bad modern." Ernst Bloch might have read, in Scarpa's details, positive responses to his attempt to recover the time of *experience.*

The later works of another isolated "master," Giuseppe Samonà (who died in 1984), were also imbued with ancient truths. Too often, in analyzing Samonà's work, observers take credit for a theme that he himself theorized: the indissoluble unity of different scales of intervention, ranging from the region to the individual building.[6] But this dated assumption, which was tied to the conditions of a debate begun in the fifties, has been verified in his recent projects, the fruits of an exceptionally creative period. The phase that began with his projects for the Biblioteca Nazionale of Rome and with the new Parliament offices (figure 93) continued with competition projects of a larger scale, like the "Metropolis of the Stretto di Messina" of 1969, and especially for the universities of Cagliari of 1971 (figure 108) and Cosenza of 1972.[7] A complex linear "machine" inserted itself—in the project for Cagliari—into existing urban centers, becoming entrenched in the ground; conversely, an "epic" game of forms took place in the internal courtyards. Samonà worked through paradox: his "composing," now more than ever, proceeded by subjugating fragments and affirming, with the dignity of past times, that his task was to rework the memory of an *ars antiqua* in modern terms. Operating in this way between historicism and antihistoricism, materiality and immateriality, the will for form and syntactic disintegration, he structured one of his most remarkable works, the new office building for the Banca d'Italia in Padova of 1968–74 (figure 107). The facade of this building on the Via Roma presents deformed allusions—the swollen or contracted arches at the base, the Ghibelline merlons united at the summit—the Via Tito Livio facade features neutral fields tormented by surrealistically isolated objects. "Composing" demonstrated its own limits here, encountering the art of "decomposition." A different discourse characterizes the civic, cultural, and commercial center of Gibellina of 1970–71, which exemplified the delays and corrupt lethargy of Italian bureaucracy, as well as what could happen when interests accumulate—with "exemplary" intentions—around a project for the reconstruction of a community affected by an earthquake. It is interesting to note that Samonà, Quaroni, Gregotti, and G. Pirrone felt they had to abandon all inhibitions in order to imagine an installation made of *objets trouvés*: their Gibellina appears to be the fruit of an impossible dialogue between interlocutors whose reciprocal mistrust led to hermeticism. This too was symptomatic: the natural disaster was not interpreted with the vision of Verga or Pasolini, but rather seen as an occasion to confront different approaches to the autonomy of language. In Samonà's case, Gibellina prefigured, on a smaller scale, his project for the public theater of Sciacca (completed between 1975 and 1979) (figure 109). An assembly of three peremptory signs shapes the body of the theater: a section of a cone and another of a pyramid face each other on opposite sides of an enormous parallelepiped, which holds the movable sets and the services of two opposite rooms. Recalling the Padua bank, but more markedly expressionist, the imperiousness of the project is masked by a whirl of references to Poelzig, Van de Velde, and Le Corbusier, while the entryway evoking an ancient post and lintel, the long external stairways inspired by Mayan temples, and the bucrane that crowns the summit of the small theater are caustic disruptions of the narrative.

With aristocratic detachment, Samonà exhibited the fragments of his own cultural autobiography in a ciphered code. The passion for autobiography was no longer concealed, nor did it assume tragic tones, as did Quaroni's. At most, it recalled a universe of lost "totalities," evoked in a climate devoid of nostalgia.

7
The Fragment and the City: Research and *Exempla* of the Seventies

The closed cycle completed by the works of Scarpa and Samonà clearly expressed the waste of energy that took place within the discipline as it struggled between incompatible duties. The capacity to draw poetry out of personally experienced contradictions was the flip side of a situation that had no support, either from universities surviving a chronic crisis, or from the institutions, or from cultural organizations. The INU had become increasingly specialized in its functions, and the INARCH had become ornamental, while the rapport between universities and local groups was problematic: research pursued in solitude, or in small groups conscious of their own contingent status, found no outlet. This provoked pompous and ineffectual gestures—like Zevi's request for retirement in 1979 to protest the governmental indifference contributing to the gangrene of university structures—and encouraged architects to withdraw into a limbo of invented spaces realized only on paper, as extraneous testimonies. In both cases, inquiry into the basic causes of the crisis was carefully avoided: such inquiry might have revealed that "small no's," although pronounced with vehemence, are actually "big yes's" offered without compensation to an enemy acknowledged only because unknown.

This explains the failure of the Zevis, Quaronis, and Samonàs from the mid-1960s on, as they faced the subjective duty of teaching. Quaroni, of course, was still influencing certain among the chosen, and Samonà could take credit for having catalyzed in Venice processes of transformation that were still in their "early stages." But it remained an issue of beginnings that these, like Socrates, would never go beyond. Nor could Quaroni, the most tormented and problematic of the protagonists of Italian postwar architecture and a master of doubt and self-criticism, vaunt, like Samonà, achievements that sublimated sudden or self-imposed failures. Doubt, moreover, led to a path marked by unexpected concessions and abrupt, inexplicable changes in direction. The magisterial hypothesis delineated in 1959 in the project for the CEP of San Giuliano (figure 71) was tenuously linked to the excessive machine of 1967 for the Parliament offices in Rome (figure 92); but in the large-scale design that Quaroni experimented with in the seventies, in collaboration with Salvatore Dierna and other young students, indifference toward materials led to an approach that had nothing to do with the formal macerations of the church in Gibellina (figure 82) or those of the Roman branch of the Banco di Roma, begun in 1970. An unusual grandiosity dominates Quaroni's projects for the universities of Cosenza, Mogadiscio (1973), and Lecce (1974): these projects seemed to have definitely exorcized the "tower of Babel."[1] In reality, Quaroni, who had laid the foundation for an entire range of ideas and subsequent disillusionment, was in these works stepping back without ado and adopting the stance of skeptical observer.

Other bearers of new professional tools appeared between the end of the sixties and the early seventies; almost all believed that utopia was a dull weapon, and that they had to obtain eloquent results. If the old masters had elaborated strategies, the new were privileging exemplary experimentation; if the former had been imbued with morality and myth, the latter would treat ideology lightly and would instead problematize analytic systems claiming to remain free of dross.

Italian architectural culture was thus able to produce four instances of residential intervention of international breadth in spite of the sudden slowdown caused by the 1973 crisis, the uncertain prospects of the public sector, and the state of suspended activity in the construction industry. These instances were: the

Matteotti quarters in Terni by Giancarlo De Carlo of 1969–75 (figure 111), Monte Amiata in Gallaratese in Milan by Carlo Aymonino and collaborators of 1967–73 (figures 113–114), Corviale in Rome by the Fiorentino group, begun in 1973 (figure 117), and Zen in Palermo by the Gregotti group of 1970 (figure 120). A comparison of these four is useful, for their methodological as well as exemplary value. Of all the baggage accumulated in the course of various programs for public construction, almost none is present here. The architects were well aware of the disruptive effect their project had on the debate over placing manufacturing industries in the heart of the development of the contemporary city. The ideas that they (fortunately) rendered concrete and verifiable closed an era and signaled a change in direction that would lead to numerous developments.

First let us consider the Matteotti village. It is impossible to evaluate this work without referring to De Carlo's complex research and its ramifications. De Carlo, who was committed to redefining concrete tools for the political development of architecture and planning, was also open to the methodological solicitations of American techniques of analysis. But he was prepared to make these react with Italian reality, and was conscious of the way in which different scales of design call for a modification of techniques. He accompanied the architectural work on groups of buildings like ILSES or the intercommunal plan of Milan with explorations of urban design, like his competition project for the University of Dublin of 1964. He directed an exemplary work of ongoing planning in Urbino, deepened and purified the language he had tested in the University of Urbino dormitories located in the residential complex La Pineta of 1968 (figure 110) and in the new Ospedale Civile of Mirano, begun in 1967, and in the project for the new University in Pavia of 1970–75. De Carlo's approach to form was flexible: an absence of prejudice enabled him to sift through a number of ideas clearly adhering to those of Team X, but leaning more toward the Smithsons' experimentalism than toward Bakema's peaceful certainties. Neither the brutalism of the Urbino dormitories, nor the elegant geometry of the Nuova Facoltà di Magistero in the same city (figure 112), could, for him, be reduced to a formula. What counted was the search for a method and, above all, a rigor, both of which might restore credibility to the discipline.[2]

It is therefore necessary to evaluate the utopian residue in the plan De Carlo drew up for Rimini, and the formal deviations present in his work, in light of the predominant theme informing them: the search for a security in design that contains the many demands of the client, the search for a technique that is "open" and capable of conversing with languages other than its own. It is undoubtedly true that all this was influenced by De Carlo's "anarchic" origins and his contact with the Advocacy Planning experiment that took place in the United States. But De Carlo was also capable of turning the mythology of participation into a flexible instrument of experimentation. The Matteotti village becomes incomprehensible if one merely challenges its ideological bases.[3]

In fact, the project's value lies not so much in its execution, as in the *process* that made it possible. In 1969, when De Carlo was called to the steelworks at Terni to design a complex on the site of the old village built in 1939 for dependents of the firm, he found himself at the center of a conflict featuring the communal administration, the city of Terni, and the workers' organizations.[4] Choosing the most courageous and innovative of the five different plans De Carlo had proposed, Terni intended to prove that its social politics, previously almost nonexistent, had changed course. De Carlo imposed, however, a process of design based on a continuous exchange with the workers at the Terni steelworks, an exchange not to be controlled by the firm and occurring outside of working hours. Beginning with an exhibit documenting exemplary cases of residential building, De Carlo opened the way for an operation that would have unforeseen effects. Participation in the project by its future inhabitants was definitely orchestrated by the architect: typological variability and the frequency of single units were determined by the workers. They selected a sunken base, with parallel elements on three levels, spaces for the entry of vehicles and private areas outside, and primary services on two levels of the transversal passages. The three-dimensional grid defined by De Carlo thus functioned as a mesh (rather than a point) of reference focusing the desires of clients whose former habits were undoubtedly modified by the didactic skill of the architect, joined by an engineer from Terni and a sociologist.

The image that emerged from this dialogue between intellectuals and consumers reflected the richness of acquired choices (figure 111). The clarity of the grid at the base is constituted by typological variation, diminishing concrete volumes, roof gardens, and various passageways. The severity of the language is softened by modulations and details approaching somewhat undisciplined urban "picturesque." But execution was interrupted by conflicts that compromised the operation: Terni chose as contractor an IRI partner, Italedil, and the management of construction was entrusted to Italstat, despite lower offers from local enterprises; construction turned out to be difficult; the builders conflicted with the designers, and De Carlo was not welcomed on the construction site.

In 1975, the 250 families chosen for the complex entered their new residences, but Terni, which had in the meantime passed from a socialist government into the hands of the Fanfani party, was no longer interested in an "enlightened" operation. As a result, the construction of services and the second lottery drawing for residences was put off indefinitely. As for the results of the participatory process that De Carlo had set in motion, they branched out into a number of directions: the neighborhood committee, along with the cooperative movement, proposed a self-run rehabilitation of old lodgings as an alternative solution to the new complex, a proposal that received the support of 98 percent of the residents but met with the opposition of the unions and the factory council; the communal administration, in its 1975 triennial plan for economical public construction, was inspired by De Carlo's methods; in 1974, the factory committee and the unions demanded a say in decisions regarding remodeling of the installations.

De Carlo had sought to redefine the relationship between intellectuals and production, and acted upon a single sector of a single "case"; the repercussions of his action related the theme to modes of production and their global management.

While the Matteotti village forces one to examine procedure, the Monte Amiata complex in Gallaratese presents itself as a completed object. The results that Aymonino achieved in the Monte Amiata quarter (figures 113–114) were arrived at through the thematic of the "new dimension," through the elaboration of working hypotheses regarding the formation of the city "in finite parts,"[5] and through a deepening of the formal themes previously formulated in the Biblioteca Nazionale in Rome. This is especially true of the residential building on Via Anagni in Rome of 1962–63, and the competition projects for the Teatro Paganini in Parma and the Ospedale Psichiatrico in Mirano, designed in 1967, in collaboration with Nino Dardi.[6] Moreover, the lengthy production of the complex—designed between 1967 and 1970, and built between 1970 and 1973[7]—served to clarify its structural characteristics. And in coinciding with the years of "grand illusion" and uncertainty, it also assumed value as a summarizing essay. Dominated by the office towers of Vico Magistretti, the complex is too open to its surroundings to be a self-sufficient entity; it is also too "designed" to be of methodological value. The complex, while painfully enunciating its own small scar, seems unable to "make order" in the suburban ocean of the Lombard metropolis, but is nonetheless intent on prefiguring more complex ways of life. But the intense life recommended here is lived mainly in forms: the four blocks spread like a fan, and based on the prototype of the open-air theater are rich in typological and formal motifs, from which the principal theme of the "essay" emerges: memory. The solemn cadences of the Karl Marx-Hof are evoked, along with the "non-form" and dreamy stupefaction of Stirling's St. Andrew Melville Hall: made of deformed materials alluding to different, unreachable orders, the complex, all-inclusive like a Fellini film, is heir to the deepest ideology of the "Roman school." Not coincidentally, its self-assurance is tempered by angular, empty, distorted, and convulsive solutions (figure 114). Laceration is the subject of this singular conglomeration of ideas, phrases, and multivalent images.

Nor was a "linear" discourse allowed to speak for an intellectual condition drawn to this fortuitous opportunity. The designer revealed the anxiety of one who is immersed in contingent contradictions he intends to commemorate by erecting a monument to "noise" and its inexhaustible richness. Exiled from the metropolis, the fragment was nonetheless charged with an excess of metropolitan values. It served, however, as a mirror reflecting cacophony, a resounding echo chamber. Not coincidentally, Aymonino assigned one of the blocks of the complex to Aldo Rossi. Hieratic and dignified, Rossi's long slab (figure 115) served as silent witness to Aymonino's staging of forms. But it did not ignore typology: the *rue intérieure* that crosses Aymonino's building also penetrates Aldo Rossi's, which appropriates it as the memory of the balconies of ancient Lombard houses, while acknowledging Le Corbusier's *unité*.

The dialogue between Aymonino and Rossi can be seen as one of mutual contamination: the polarities they incarnate prove that each needed the other. Not coincidentally, the two would later collaborate on the competition project for the office district in Florence[8]; similarly, the way Aymonino stripped the campus of Pesaro in 1970 pays homage to the elective affinities linking him to his friend, to the "other."[9]

While Gallaratese called into question the nonlocation of the Milanese agglomeration, Corviale (figure 117), which extended over a kilometer in Rome, was intended to be a magnet that would reorganize a scattered urban site, and integrate residences and services in an exemplary fashion. Gallaratese and Corviale; Aymonino on the one hand, and Fiorentino, Gorio, Michele Valori, and Piero Maria Lugli on the other: occurring twenty years after the Tiburtino, where the same architects had worked with Ridolfi and Quaroni, the examples demonstrate the extent of the differences that made the "Roman school" explode.

A professional who ignored Aymonino's numerous intellectual seductions, Fiorentino soon departed from Ridolfi's "educated" style of his first residential towers on Viale Etiopia and in 1962 consolidated his lexicon in a third group of buildings on Viale Etiopia, also with towers, and in his project, which tied for first place for the competition for the new tribunal offices in Rome in 1959. It may, therefore, be surprising to find him engaged in the above mentioned enterprise of the Asse studio: the structural emphasis suggests that in this project he was also pursuing an essentially aproblematic correctness. On the contrary, in the projects for Roma-Mare and Ostia-Mare in 1970 and for the Flaminio-Tor di Quinto zone in 1971 (figure 116), Fiorentino adhered completely to a fragmentary approach extending to a regional scale and exploiting hypertechnological metaphors all the rage in university centers in those years. In this, at least, he seemed close to Aymonino and to the common "master" Quaroni.[10]

But in Corviale the protection of utopia was no longer the ruling factor (figure 117). Forced to respond to a demand coming from the public sector, Fiorentino completely recovered his capacities as a skillful mediator. Corviale is constituted by a single strip 200 meters wide; it contains new building types and was realized with advanced techniques of prefabrication. Yet as a model, this city compressed into one line remains theoretical and incapable of being reproduced; its value resides in its expression of its own dimensions. Its real accomplishment lay in having convinced the IACP of the validity of its proposal: without resorting to prophecy, this song of praise addressed to the future was proudly built as the limit of the Roman suburb, though its ability to condition development remained unclear.

Fiorentino died suddenly on Christmas, 1982. In spite of his reflections, Corviale remained a "monument to mediation," even though this time Fiorentino made useful not Ridolfi's sanguine research, but the attempt to control the suburban jungle and the anonymous language of technique. He staged a tentative compromise between, on the one hand, the disastrous obstacles created on a gigantic site by fragmented productive cycles and, on the other hand, a management not yet adapted to the newly proposed scale. The camps of those seeking admission to residences completed but not yet assigned were sad reminders of the contradictions inherent in an operation whose main characteristic—sensationalism—was compromised by managerial difficulties.

In spite of this, and because of its didactic character, Corviale remained unique in Rome. Its imperiousness stood out against the surrounding urban zone, its proposal introduced its clients to unusual experimentation, and the link between the long residential structure and its services indicated possible modes of articulation for the complex. Let us reflect upon this further. From San Basilio to Corviale: two "singing" works, the first one renunciatory and crafted, the second one disenchanted but suggestive. And in the middle, an essential "vacuum of values." Nonetheless, neither Aymonino nor Fiorentino were "authors" in Benjamin's sense of the word, and certainly neither of them became as "shrewd as a dove." But the historical project that, *together*, Gallaratese and Corviale defined for the age of reconstruction was telling of the productivity of the ideological *décalage* experienced by Italian culture. The ambiguities of these works reside precisely in their having "experienced" and not directed the crisis. One wonders whether it was a coincidence that, after Corviale, Fiorentino felt the need to return to a neorealist vocabulary—translated, however, into an ascetic language—in his project for residences in upper Lazio of 1979–81 (figures 118–119).

The difficult relationship with the urban entity, which in a different way stood at the base of the solutions of Gallaratese and Corviale, became, in the Gregotti group's project for the Zen complex in Palermo (figure 120), a dialogue with a historically stratified urban fabric and a natural order considered excessively rich in emotional power.[11] Located on the extension of the axis formed by Via Maqueda and Via della Libertà, Gregotti's compact *insulae* solemnly express the stages of a ritual: an act of "founding" is celebrated by the rigorous gate, barely varied at its edges and receiving services in an asymmetrical position relative to the whole. The tall blocks capping the individual *insulae* accentuate this exaltation of the "walled city," functioning from a distance as discrete visual references; the city defends itself mainly from attacks by nature and the foreseeable suburban sprawl. The "overly constructed" quality of the Zen complex is consolidated by its typological unity. The *insula*, peremptory, claims to be whole but is articulated by passageways and incidents. It presents itself as a structure whose antecedents can be found in Michiel Brinkman's superblock in Spangen and in Karl Ehn's Lindenhof, and whose objective is the formation of a "catalogue of statements negating current ideas on the theme of the residence," as a report on the project suggests. Thus, four years after the calibrated distortions of the Rinascente in Turin, Gregotti responded to the examples appearing in a monographic issue of *Edilizia moderna* dedicated to the shape of the region. If Corviale (figure 117) stood like a dike on the threshold of urban development, the Zen quarter was a meteor emerging from urban constellations and condensed under the looming image of menacing forces. The morphologies and modes of production changed; the will to protect oneself from threat remained. The writing that characterized the search for new, balanced relationships between the artificial and the natural became increasingly abstract, as the shadow of Worringer cast itself upon these formal "devices" charged with archaic allusions.

This abstraction was, furthermore, the sign of a will to control the finite fragment: one can legitimately speak of geometrical excess, eloquent reductionism, and estrangement displayed as a rhetorical expedient *malgré soi* in discussing Corviale and the Zen quarter, not to mention the Gregotti group's subsequent projects. Also relevant are the large-scale experiments of Franco Purini and Laura Thermes[12]: the big cross of the office district of Latina of 1972, the long access wall of the project for the organization of the Montericco caves, and the detailed plan for the archaeological harbor area of Terracina of 1975. De Carlo still placed his trust in an architecture capable of taking root in "places" and furnishing "residences"; Aymonino narrated the events that threatened the easy dreams of regeneration, even though he persisted in envisioning an uncertain future; Fiorentino overturned utopia and turned it into realism; Gregotti and Purini accepted the limitations of finite form and of fixed structures that are aware of their own artificiality in geographical space.

Sailing in uncharted waters, the fragments shaping the new ideas tried to come to terms with the historical process looming over them. This was all the more true for the Gregotti associates' last projects: the residential theme was no longer at stake, having given way to that of infrastructures, allowing a discussion of the pathological relationship between architecture and landscape.

One ought to note, however, that Gregotti himself, one of the architects who kept to himself during the brief period of feverish enthusiasm for megastructures, is today executing one of the few regional operations in which size plays an important role: the University of Calabria (figure 121). But Gregotti arrived there after having further explored, with Purini, the Zen quarter themes in a competition project for the new University of Florence in 1971.[13] Once again a system of dikes—five bare blocks constituting the centers for teaching and research—binds the forces of the site. Functioning as a node for the historical nuclei of Florence, Prato, and Pistoia, it presents itself as a mysterious archaeological find. Once again the act of composition assumes ritual garments: the new urban organism is founded in a solemn ceremony. The dialogue with the landscape is charged with hieratic value: architecture reflects intently on itself, and protects itself from external contamination. But in the project that won the competition for the new University of Cosenza, and now being built, the orchestration of signs appears completely muted.[14] Two sets of buildings confront the succession of hills descending toward the Crati valley from the Paolana chain: a series of square blocks for departmental activities is linked to a service bridge 3,200 meters long and placed at a constant height, ignoring all orographical irregularities; the terraced residential fabric is frayed on the northern slope, grafting itself onto nodes where the linear structure parallels the hilltops. The landscape is thus decomposed and recomposed. The ultimate significance of the entire work can be found in the conflict between the artificial passageway—the bridge, taut and secured like a thread—and the natural passageways of the hilltops. Ariadne's thread, suspended in an empty space and indifferent to all incidents, is the only point of reference for an architecture that exhausts itself in a band of pure "relations," and that, as such, "does not live" in its host environment. Gregotti's optimism as a designer—which was also expressed in the project for the Manilva tourist center in Malaga of 1974, designed with Oriol Bohigas, Martorell, and Mackay, and in his Montedison research center in Portici of 1978, rich in quotations from Stirling and Terragni—concealed a fertile anxiety.

8
Architecture as Dialogue and Architecture as "Civil Invective"

The similarity of the paths that some of the most radical Italian "revisionists" of the 1950s followed, despite different means, is cause for reflection. For Gabetti and Isola, as for Gregotti, "neoliberty" represented neither a movement nor a trend. Because they had deep roots in a specific region—in both the provincial and cosmopolitan aspects of the Piedmont—and in specific conditions of production, they were able to pursue confidently and without struggle the path marked by the Bottega d'Erasmo (figure 48). Their brand of realism had an introspective charge strengthened by contact with the *genius loci;* they also had the craftsman's taste for the "good product," which coincided with a lack of formal prejudice springing from a direct rapport with things in the absence of any "desperate existential tension" motivating their work. This work began with a celebration of the object, and managed in Gregotti's case to affect the relationship of the design to the environment. Yet nothing seemed further from this theme than Gabetti and Isola's work in the early 1960s.[1] In the parish church of Montoso in Cuneo of 1963, the two architects combined erudite motives and traditional structures in a homage to the necessity of the clients' participation (the church was built by the parish and the local religious community); a cunning rhythm rules the geometric outbursts of the monument to the Resistance in Prarostino of 1964; a cultivated, refined, and amused realism, attentive to the traditional motifs of rural architecture in the Po valley, as well as to layered memories and literary allusions, informs the residential building on Corso Montevecchio in Turin of 1964, the house-with-hotel Eca in Le Vallette designed with Giorgio Raineri in 1965, the Pinin Farina chapel in Cortanze d'Asti of 1966, the Pero Villa of 1965,[2] and the Furlotti Villa of 1973, as well as his project for the Casa del Gallo in Pinerolo of 1967.

In comparison with these instances of highly professional craftsmanship—sympathetically anchored in the historical centers and in the Piedmont countryside like suggestive ciphers—the residential center built in Ivrea in 1969–70 for the dependents of the Olivetti firm aspired to begin a new chapter (figure 123).[3] The complex was part of a development scheme including a similar intervention on the margins of the historical center of Ivrea, which was designed by Igino Cappai and Piero Mainardis. Two new "architectures for collectors" were thus enriched by Olivetti's eclectic harvest: on the one hand, there was in the city a machinist piece exploring the impact of a muted futurism on the ancient urban fabric; on the other hand, outside the urban center, there was the severe arcadia of the residences that Gabetti and Isola built on wooded terrain near the Castellamonte quarter. Crossing the Dora, and locating itself in the city for the first time, the Olivetti firm—with its center for social and residential uses, by Cappai and Mainardi—presented itself as an astral "machine" with an Anglo-Saxon flavor; facing the countryside, a crescent reminiscent of its eighteenth-century ancestors commented upon the social image of the firm.

The way in which Gabetti and Isola's "crescent in curtain-wall" stood "confidently detached" from nature was significant. The small residential units have only one side facing out, defined by the dense grid of the curved facade; half buried, this refined example of "land architecture" was careful not to interrupt the typology of the site, but inserted itself into the environment with a single confident gesture, and thus made a cogent commentary.

Completed in 1970, the residential center in Ivrea was, for Gabetti and Isola, the prelude to unrealized projects which amplified its themes. These included the competition project for the FIAT office complex in Candiolo near Turin of 1973 (figure

124), and the projects for a residential complex in Volterrano, on the island of Elba of 1975, for a hotel with services for the Club Méditerranée in Sestrière of 1973, and for a residential complex in the mountains of 1975. These projects resembled the Gregotti group's project for the University of Calabria (figure 121) more than those for the Zen quarter (figure 120) or the University of Florence. In them the relationship of the building to the environment remained at the level of a subtle and artistocratic dialogue: the FIAT office complex (figure 124) was reduced to a double escarpment of earth, grass, and inclined glass surfaces describing an enormous circle and dominated at the summit by an enigmatic skylight made of three parallel tubes.

A faint but peremptory sign was thus created in the countryside of the Piedmont, signaling an educated forward thrust propelled by the will for form. This sign was meant to reflect, not to violate; its completeness sought to leave unaltered the site that receives it. Not coincidentally, compared to the nearby Stupinigi complex, it is situated on a barely protected spot, which highlights its quality as an echo of the circular form of the eighteenth-century garden.

It thus became clear that working on a large scale did not necessarily entail utopian or structural emphases for Gabetti and Isola. They too considered the encounter with the landscape as an insertion into early stages of history, and interpreted that history with the same vision that had grasped the intimate quality of the centers of Turin and Pinerolo. Intimism took a leap forward with these projects, demonstrating its capacity to translate memory into forms that transcend the boundaries of the individual object.[4]

The Milanese advocates of neoliberty—Canella, Achilli and Brigidini, and Gae Aulenti—took a rather different path. We have already spoken, with respect to Canella's work, of "angry architecture."[5] The motifs present in the competition project for the office district of Turin and the civic center of Segrate (figure 125) relied on a theory that encompassed an unprecedented commitment to teaching and on the research being done on the role of services in urban structures. For Canella, services and infrastructures were the signs of an intention to oppose the dispersed ambiguity of the actual city and the untying of historical knots that occurs when contextual values are lost.[6] Typological research was thus focused on vital ganglia, affecting their organization and challenging linear models of localization. Canella sought to combine and integrate administrative, educational, commercial, and cultural services: he proposed real networks with multiple functions as compact and evolving structures suited to provocatively triangular urban buildings. The aggressiveness of Canella's images flowed from this programmatic formulation, which was seeking to redefine functions and modes of fruition. In the civic center of the INCIS quarter in Pieve Emanuele of 1968–81—a meteor that crashed into the complex, disrupting its composure —the complexity of functions was formulated in a language that is deliberately "dirty," contaminated, and full of unharmonious juxtapositions. The anxious elegance of neoliberty design was transformed into an *antigraceful* esthetic, providing the inspiration for the big concrete shell mounted on cylinders and crowned with a curved pediment—of Gaudì's *pastiches*—that characterizes the elementary school for the center. The provocation and the exasperated montage, here as in the 1972 project for the secondary school in Saronno, and in the Palazzo Municipale and the lower middle school in Pieve Emanuele of 1979–81 (figure 126), informed the search for a consolidation of functions as well as affecting formal strategies. The impudent eclecticism of Canella, Achilli, and Brigidini distorted closed forms, resorted to lacerated memories, polluted overly defined volumes, and made incompatible images stridently collide. But this was in some way to be expected, given the polemical attitude of the "young men at Casabella" in the late fifties: the message that should have dominated new collective behavior was entrusted to a philosophy of "stoniness," poised between forced dissonance and the loving evocation of classical compositions, as can be seen in the elementary school of Noverasco of 1971–76. Canella's works remind us of Melnikov's formal networks and allude to the pathos of "enlightened" architecture, using both as explicit references to whole universes of related values.

Canella's formal distortions thus assigned a precise task to architecture: its duty was to pronounce "civil invectives," assuming a pathos that harked back to the teachings of the fathers it had previously rejected.

Gae Aulenti's work, on the other hand, reveals none of this anxious evocation; she was the only one in the neoliberty group to pursue a rarefied elegance destined for a specific class with identifiable cultural traits.[7] Aulenti's tired geometry could thus harmonize perfectly with the "pop" objects and images one finds in her Collector's House in Milan of 1968–69 (figure 128), while presenting itself as hermetically monumental in the modular volumes planned for the exhibit on Italian design at the Museum of Modern Art in New York in 1972[8]; that geometry created an ingenious effect of "alienation" for the automobile-object in the FIAT exhibition halls in Turin, Buenos Aires (1967), Brussels, and Zurich (1970), in which artificial galleries evoked an ambiguous suspension of space. Aulenti's design did not intend, however, to remain confined to its specific environment: the objective was to reach the city, whose internal organization it would then compose. This was the direction pursued on different scales in the competition project for the office district of Perugia, designed in 1971 with Sandra Sarfatti and Giovanni Da Rios, in the campus in Cinisello Balsamo of 1973, and in the original proposal for a "global design" for Milan of 1972–74. The operation did not go beyond an elaborated scenography for an improbable city-as-collective theater: not by chance, Aulenti's talents are most evident in the stage designs she executed for the director Luca Ronconi, as well as in the recent, spectacular remodeling of the Gare d'Orsay in Paris, now a museum.[9]

The "Case" of Aldo Rossi

Gabetti and Isola, Canella, and Gae Aulenti thus used different means to induce a state of fatigue in the materials of language, thereby evoking extreme unpleasantness and intellectual *sensi-blerie*. Among the paths left open by the themes discussed in Rogers' arena, there remained the search for the principal elements of the architectural process, a search that led to a liberation from fixed contexts and a movement toward a horizon where private and collected pasts merged. Aldo Rossi was the protagonist of this search: an architect who, beginning in the mid-1960s, presented himself as the most watched and discussed "case" both in Italy and on the international scene, the only "school leader" capable of constantly fueling around his own works and self a controversy and an interest that ended by affecting the very concept of architecture. We have already seen that Rossi was one of Rogers' students, active in the group of writers working for *Casabella continuità*, the designer of one of the most polemical projects presented to the competition for the office district of Turin, and of the "bridge" executed for the 1964 Triennale of Milan. But the complexity and exceptional coherence of his work soon placed him outside of contingent polemics: Rossi did not intend to dirty his hands in controversy; his *poiesis* refused to compromise with reality, since the only way to return to the "ancient house of language" was by maintaining an attitude of surly indifference.[1]

It is undeniable, however, that Rossi's poetics contained a secret reaction to the *desengaño* that Italian architects experienced in the sixties. This too indicated that he was interested in themes and forms that had been swept away by a moralistic gust of wind just after the war.[2] At the twelfth Triennale of Milan, Rossi exhibited a project for the restructuring of the zone around Via Farini: it was an optimistic project, meant to refashion an identity for the suburbs.[3] But the year was 1960, and this optimism soon proved unfounded. In the same year, Rossi's villa in Ronchi, Versilia, hailed the "discovery" of Adolf Loos, whom Rossi celebrated in 1959 in an article in *Casabella*.[4] As he began his search for primary forms, Rossi reflected upon Loos's work as well as that of Max Bill; these forms were exiled from the urban sphere, but spoke of their exile in order to propose a theory of the city as the *locus* of collective memory. There followed in 1964 the competition project for the Teatro Paganini in Parma, in 1965 the monument for the Partisans in Segrate, in 1966 the competition project for a residential complex in San Rocco in Monza, done in collaboration with Giorgio Grassi, and a book, *Architecture of the City*. On the one hand, there was an attempt to redefine urban science through an encounter with the French school's geography; on the other hand, there was the evaporation of the image in search of the pressure point where one can draw from memory a real epiphany of signs. The triangle, the cube, the cone: these obsessive, stripped figures kept reappearing in Rossi's projects. They were not finalized for the sake of an abstract elementarist search, but attempted to circumscribe the source of form in progressively smaller circles. *Desengaño* had become eloquent. It was necessary to turn one's back on the "noise of the world" in order to contemplate places whose alienation had become sacral—the golden suburbs, reminiscent of Sironi's, that appear in Rossi's designs, such as places where life seemed suspended—the project for a new cemetery in Modena of 1971 (figure 129),[5] and also the metaphysical courtyard at the De Amicis school in Broni of 1970. Rossi's projects began to flounder, sinking increasingly into a new realm of images whose source was De Chirico, frozen in spaces abandoned by time, and Böcklin's "unhappy vision." The Gallaratese block, the elementary school in Fagnano Olona of 1972 (figure 130), the projects for the town hall of Muggiò of 1972 and for Villa Bay in Borgo Ticino of 1972, were contrasted with designs, collages, and rallying cries of the seventies. The assembled forms referred to the astonishing fixity of Giorgio Morandi's objects: a hidden eye explored the form-giving act, spying on the hand and mind of the artist, and encountering, in the deepest memories, only words already spoken, but now aligned in sinister fashions or piled in disorderly heaps.

Nor did it matter that the search for a primordial essence was constantly being frustrated. On the contrary, this led to a ceaseless renovation of the game of transformation, played by materials reduced to their zero degree. This was demonstrated in the successive versions of the project for the Modena cemetery, in Rossi's returning to already tested forms in order to make them converse with each other, in the different versions of his "analogous city,"[6] and in the insistent way that the spectral presence of *San Carlo Borromeo* menaced architectural assemblies, with or without "domestic objects." The imagined project concerned a new collective need in a universe that was robbing individual action of its element of fantasy. But whoever immerses himself in imaginary realms today—as Blanchot has warned us—is forced to annul space and time, to send them deep into the nothingness of "literary space." This annulment is indecent and provocative. It has nothing to do with the classical *Entsagung*; it is based on the amoral principle of abstension. Not coincidentally, Rossi's work provoked choruses of indignation, as well as unreflecting love. Yet Rossi had the courage to contemplate this "nothing," to project its impalpable signs onto a magic urn, the mirror of a dream that was being narrated in public. Rossi's *mémoire* was heir to the overwhelming autobiographical trend of the fifties, but it preferred archaic silence to the opulence of Gadda's rhetorical flourishes. For this reason, its introspection was expressed in a humorous and thoughtful work, the Teatrino Scientifico, or little theater of 1978. The Teatrino, which features in its triangular pediment a clock permanently set at five o'clock (in the evening?), is a small temple in the shape of a "little house," the only one appropriate to hold Rossi's architectural works, which are arranged there as permanent and movable sets. The space of representation coincides with the representation of space: Rossi wished to convince himself of this with his metaphysical theater.

But this coincidence had already been announced in the "agitated silence" of the inner courtyard of the school in Fagnano Olona (figure 130) and in the "museum in the shape of a baptistry" that appeared in the competition project for the office district of Florence of 1977. Representation was everything: it was useless to worry about secondary meanings in inaccessible realms. The city—in spite of Rossi's statements to the contrary—revealed itself as a simple pretext. But it was also true that representation presupposed models, archetypes, and figures as points of reference. Rossi's typological research is confined, not coincidentally, to self-description: the type, motionless, does not make history, its repeating and being repeated recall Tessenow's will for *naïveté*. In this way, Rossi's universe may still be experienced as a labyrinthian landscape in which misleading tracks, left by the memory of the artist, confuse the visitor. Architecture is placed fearfully in the balance: its reality, never denied, is perversely bound to the unreal. Lissitzky's Proun changed the course of direction, but continued to fluctuate in an ineffable universe.

Rossi's words assumed the dignity of alchemical signs especially in the projects, designs, and engravings he did in the seventies. In *The Elba Cabins* (1973), in *The Copernican City*, and in *Memories of Florence*, an obstinate magus refuses to look into the Galilean telescope, and instead manipulates an esoteric alphabet. Rossi's rigorism was the condition of his imaginary realm: it sought to demonstrate that alienation can be narrated, that whoever knows how to become a child can escape aphasia. One must be a sublimely irresponsible individual—and this is precisely the point. It explains Rossi's resorting to infantile schemes or to a geometric elementarism reminiscent of Durand's tables: typical, in this regard, were the project for the Palazzo della Regione of Trieste of 1974, homage to an *Aufklärung* without time, and the Teatro del Mondo, which was moored as a poetic and fleeting apparition next to the customs pier in Venice in 1979.[7]

Yet "Dieses ist lange her / Now this is long gone" was the title of an engraving that Rossi did in 1975, in which, as in his watercolor "Architecture Assassinated"—dedicated, perhaps polemically, to this writer—he presented his dreams in a state of collapse. It was, however, a frozen collapse: the fragments dangling or projected into empty space remained immobile. The loss was not painful: the traveler was prepared for it. The "bridge," a supersignifying metaphysical figure that, in projects ranging from the 1964 Triennale to the monument in Segrate and the Gallaratese block, presented itself as connecting inconceivable extremes—memory and history, sign and meaning, the individual and external reality—broke and flew off into space, carrying with it the fragments of a painful will for knowledge.

10
Rigorism and
Abstinence: Toward
the 1980s

It is only possible to decipher Aldo Rossi's alchemical alphabet as a
normal dictionary if one sees his work as tautological. "A rose is a
rose is a rose is rose..." Giorgio Grassi's "logical construction of
architecture" stayed within the boundaries of pure reiteration.[1]
While Rossi represented his heartbroken exploration of "origins"
with a confession of repeated failure, Grassi resigned himself to a
search for "essences" and noumena extracted from a fixed grasp of
primary forms. For him, logic coincided with the classical—not
the classical as exemplified by Goethe's insatiable resignation, but
that of Winckelmann's atemporal perfection, identified with the
spectral reiterations of Weinbrenner's Langestrass in Karlsruhe
and Hilberseimer's laconic images. Grassi's research was initially
tangential to Rossi's, and the two collaborated on a few works: the
hotel at the mountain pass of Monte Croce Comelico of 1963, the
ISES quarter in Naples of 1968, and the San Rocco quarter in
Monza of 1966. But Grassi's work later differentiated itself from
Rossi's by a will for knowledge turned in on itself. His projects for
a laboratory to manufacture equipment for biological research in
Paullo of 1968, for the restoration of the viscount's castle in
Abbiategrasso of 1970, for a residential unit also in Abbiategrasso
of 1972, for riverside residences in Pavia of 1970–73, and for the
secondary school in Tollo (figure 132) all question typologies such
as the courtyard and portico, and compositional strategies such as
symmetry and rhythmic constancy. They aspire to the blank page;

the controversy surrounding what Grassi called "disconnected parody" was resolved in a display of rigorist certainties. It is, moreover, undoubtedly true that the linguistic purification accomplished by Grassi had remarkable consequences. In the plan to salvage the historical center of Teora in Avellino and in the recent project for the reconstruction of the Prinz Albrecht Palais in Berlin, both done with Agostino Renna, the attempt to commemorate Karl Ludwig Schinkel's classical dream was not intended to be pleasurable, and the dessication of forms reached a dignity rich in implications.[2] And with the recent project for the restoration of the Roman theater in Sagunto, Giorgio Grassi's poetics took another qualitative leap forward, demonstrating the fertility of the laconic vocabulary it had chosen.

It is significant that ideas like Grassi's can be evaluated in contrast with the evil contemporary city. Silence can, of course, be resounding when surrounded by noise; it remains to be seen whether that silence can really express something besides the simple will to know, and whether the testimony it offers can have more than the mere value of a symptom.

It should not be surprising that the methods of Rossi and Grassi succeeded in creating a "school." Those who turned to them were in general anxious to find the great mother again, to rest by returning to the womb of Architecture, and to divorce themselves from the miseries of contingency. The didactic success of these two men was a litmus test revealing the anguish and "void of values" pressing in upon the younger generation; that success does not, however, justify the attempt to construct a *tendenza* by putting Rossi's wandering signs on a par with Leon Krier's research, Aymonino's eclecticism, Dardi's eloquence, Ludwig Leo's machinism, or Adolfo Natalini's "continuous monuments," as was done at the fifteenth Triennale of Milan in 1973, under the formula "Rational Architecture."[3] For Rossi, who was responsible for the international sector of architecture at that Triennale, it was a matter of a large collage, which arranged fragments according to a technically organized surrealism. For the facile exegetes, it was a new church in which to burn incense; for the opposing factions, it was an "exhibit on the Starace model" and a return to terms dangerously reminiscent of totalitarian rhetoric.

In reality, Rossi, Grassi, and their immediate circle were not the only ones trying to construct architecture with its own elements and *of those elements only*. If the work of the GRAU members, after the project for the Florence archives (figures 98–99), was disappointing, the work done by Franco Purini (figures 133–136) and Laura Thermes, by the Roman group Labirinto and especially by Paolo Martellotti, and by a few of Quaroni's students revealed itself to be similar, at least in its attempt to define a universe that mirrors itself in the limitations of form.[4] They achieved, in the best cases, an autonomy of language dialectically spoken to the other by the self, and in the worse cases, a segregation presumptuously satisfied with its own immobility.[5]

An insatiable demand for rigor, offset by sudden moments of lyrical abandon, found its way into the stacks of designs produced by these new purists. And, whether they, like Purini, focused on a configuration of events testing the consistency and elusiveness of compositional materials, or whether—as with the Labirinto in reconstructing the Calcografia Nazionale in Rome in 1973–75[6]— they experimented with values inherent in the calculated distortion of visual structures, their program included a self-imposed behavior and approached moralizing. "To take a generation out of the running," Purini and Thermes wrote, "one has only to encourage youth to cultivate the myth of total moral 'integrity': thus they will not know how to accept and practice compromise, certainly not of the petty kind, but of the sort which defines politics as the art of the possible, as the dialectic of the real." Ritual was equated with the obstinate search for the laws determining form. Moreover, an "integrity" without purpose and also without social outlets must eventually be colored with mysticism. The rigor of "words" sets limits to the "frivolous": not coincidentally, it becomes more and more confined to design. The professional abstinence to which, for objective and subjective reasons, that generation seemed condemned, invited reason to travel to the limits of the permissible: in "designed architecture"—the goal and

prison of whoever wanted to claim, "I, too, am Piranesi"—
narcissistic practices abounded, as well as calls for a totality of
values otherwise unobtainable. The Kafkaesque atmospheres
created by these occasionally refined graphic universes have
something coherent about them (perhaps too coherent): in empty
space, they made words resound and set forth superfluous laws.

That all this, moreover, could create a climate suitable for the
reproduction and autonomous life of these rituals was demonstrated by projects like the detailed plan for the new university in
Cagliari of 1977–78, formulated by the group coordinated by M.
Luisa Anversa and Marcello Rebecchini, and by the result of competitions like those for the office district of Florence of 1977 and for
the construction of a piazza on the site of the old military bakery of
Ancona of 1978. The competition in Florence no longer gave rise
to musings on the destiny of the *"terziario"* services sector or to
bodies concerned with encompassing and condensing nuclei to
restructure the national countryside. Marco Porta, working with
Purini, Emilio Battisti, Cesare Macchi Cassia, and collaborators,
tried to make his project harmonize with Gregotti's university
system, adjacent to the new office district, as well as with the
marks that history had left on the region.[7] A sum of themes
emerged: the rotation of axes, the variation of the walled boundary, and the strongholds emerging from an ideal *centuriatio.*
Vocabulary inferred from the work of Rossi, Gregotti, and Purini
formed a lexicon, as was demonstrated by the projects of the
Vernuccio group, the Rosa-Cornoldi-Sajeva-Manlio Savi group, the
Polesello group, and in some ways by the Angelini-Dierna-
Mortola-Orlandi group.

One of the big Italian competitions after the war, for the office
district of Florence—characterized by an announcement that
seemed expressly to recommend abstraction to the competitors[8]—
did not give rise to a debate between diverging ideas, nor to any
significant methodological or formal reflection. The most prestig-
ious competitors stayed within their own "manner": this was true
of Giuseppe and Alberto Samonà, Aymonino and Rossi, Fiorentino
and Anversa, and even of James Stirling, who was associated here
with the Castore group.

In fact, even designed architecture was too limited to contain the universes of the totality of form that constituted the goal of a humanism resulting from the forced acceptance of the marginality of language.[9]

One can take coherence even further in dealing with one's own assumptions; one can turn architectural forms into an imaginary landscape free from the weight of matter. One can, in fact, express with the traditional instruments of engraving, watercolor, and oil paint, the secret aspiration to relive—necessarily as a dream—mythical seasons governed by divine language. And so it happened that Massimo Scolari and Arduino Cantàfora staged their own sublimations with great skill,[10] while a team of younger designers of uneven graphic skill sent a stream of dreamy sketches to private Italian galleries, which accepted them in the hope of forming a new market. In Rome, Bologna, and Milan (as well as New York), exhibits of the designs and engravings of Rossi, Purini, Scolari, Martellotti, and Dario Passi came one after the other, while the "Artistic Encounters" led directly, in 1977–78, to a competition—"Interrupted Rome"—which invited the new international of the imaginary to measure its own fantastic disseminations against places preserved on Nolli's plan.[11] The "need for architecture" thus survived, encouraging skillful collages (such as Nicola Pagliara's architectural works), impatient experimentalism, hymns to "classical" attitudes, songs addressed to the ephemeral, and the "posthumous" violation of inhibitions.[12]

Forced to engage in "parallel actions," the protagonists of this architectural moment thus remained balanced on the ridge separating the *locus solus* of self-reflection from the noisy agora. But they could not partition, consume, and attack the materials of form and history without consequence. The old discipline of "architecture" saw its ruins on a game table surrounded by young players about to make "new techniques" concrete. These players did not, however, despair as they faced the ruins of certainties that had sustained modes of intervention capable only of self-reproduction. The problem was one of controlling differences that were fragmenting the discipline, without imagining them to be precipices in which to sink one's anguish. Faced with a "power" expressing itself in several dialects, no "synthesis" could hold firm; this was also true of the synthesis that began with the theme of form, then aimed at the problem of reform. The golden *domus* of the *Bauen* could therefore be saved without "refounding" and without confounding pleasure with play. It was necessary to proceed "without a home."

At the beginning of the eighties, all that has so far constituted our history appeared to be a "negative prologue" to the new tasks that were taking shape. The "delirious constructions," the story of which we have tried to narrate, were refracted into several languages: urban management, techniques for the reuse of existing structures, construction economics, design on various scales, and formal games. The emphasis initially placed on the "project" had turned into a "criticism of the project," leading to a crisis of models and to the ineffectiveness of passwords: this was the less than negligible result of the intellectual work accomplished by Italian architectural culture during the preceding decades.

Part Two

1980–1985

11
Structural Transformations and New Experiences in Planning

What paths were taken by the proliferating ideas and factions that emerged from the laboratory of the seventies? Is it too early for the "sea of architecture" to yield answers, even tentative ones, to the deep structural transformations that have affected Italian society during the past fifteen years? And, above all, when is it legitimate to ask questions about the problem of the new relations among architecture, urban planning, and social issues? An initial, superficial survey of the current situation suggests that an impassable barrier exists between the world of the planners and that of new collective problems: Italian architects seem to have isolated themselves in ivory towers. But, as noted, this is only a superficial impression. The long labor begun in the mid-1960s was not in vain: the stubborn exploration of the internal structure of languages, though narcissistic and dissipated, had the merit of freeing the very concept of architecture from any grand *récit*—as Lyotard has put it—that is to say, from all large, compact, and collective representations of "general interests." Though the protagonists might favor different formal modes, they increasingly chose the realistic paradigm for design. The potential associated with the idea of abstract projects was lessened by comparison with the possibilities offered by specific commissions. Above all, it consented to a revision of its own criteria for rationality, excluding an immediate relationship between the part, which could be controlled, and the whole, which was placed in parentheses.[1] This did not indicate a defeat. The history we traced above seems to suggest that this antiutopian realism was instead the result of a gradual exhaustion of myths and ideologies originally propounded during the age of reconstruction. It was perhaps true that the frustration experienced in dealing with large-scale solutions, which were as global as they were ineffectual, had accelerated this new realism. Furthermore, the demarcation of experimental fields was accompanied by a progressive reevaluation of local differences and dialects. This process also had distant, prewar roots, and assumed new aspects—after the proliferation of varieties of populism and realism—when forces consolidating the world of mass media and computers *provoked* new needs for self-identification, a new awareness of peripheral identities, and a new desire to remember.

But it is also necessary to consider the other side of the story. The current architectural debate provides less and less stimulus to redefine the rapport between the discipline and politics as it exists on various levels. Not only is it difficult, since the problem is international, to redesign the terms of the conflict in a society that changed greatly during the preceding decades and is now in a period of rapid and continuing change. The crisis experienced by the parties of the left—and it certainly did not begin with the communist losses of 1985 or with the socialists' inability to realize their will for power—reminds us that a new map of boundaries between friends and enemies has yet to be drawn. The problem extends beyond the question of parties, compromising the worn distinctions between left and right, and once again encourages discussion of analytical methods. In such a situation, how can one reunite design needs coming from diverse and mutually uncommunicative systems? Though these systems are now being redefined, they are also being compromised by internal entanglements. Not coincidentally, while the new myths of *deregulation* and neoliberalism are taking root among those intellectuals anxious to be *au courant*, the notion of a reading of reality based on systems theory is being elaborated.[2] Those who long for large synthetic constructions and formulas resolving all the various factors find that these theories are difficult to test; it is nonetheless hard to deny that these theories address contemporary structures.

The "architecture system" should therefore be considered in its particularity: the question that Walter Benjamin addressed to the "author as producer" would be enriched by questioning that system about its ability to "reduce the level of complexity" of the incomplete systems it affects. The question is further complicated by the uncertainty of the institutional picture. Consider the following: on the one hand, the law on the remission of construction, especially with the extension of its application, diminished the credibility of declarations regarding the future management of the cities and regions, while it dramatically revealed the ornamental role relegated to plans and management techniques during the past decades. On the other hand, the Galasso law for the protection of the environment and of national landmarks (approved by Parliament in August 1985) has begun to arrest further ecological damage. But at the same time it shows how the public sector's attempts at planned intervention are inadequate. Moreover, the law on remission has linked—and in a conspicuous way—the issues of taxation to those of natural and manmade resources, making the whole difficult to analyze. As for the new focus on the issues of conservation and cultural artifacts, it has not resolved the problem of conflicting jurisdictions evident in a city like Venice, whose history has been marked by restoration and reuse. And one of the first instances of this conflict led to the cancellation of an intelligent project for the restructuring of the old Saffa areas in Cannaregio, done by Gregotti and his associates[3]: architecture's demarcation of the paradigm of rationality also runs the risk of becoming ineffectual. The case we have cited is typical: the detailed, circumscribed operation is always vulnerable, destined to remain entangled in the web of contradictions resulting when the rules of the game are unclear and contiguous systems "invade the field." How can one specify new rules, moreover, when inflation, the crisis of the socialist state, and the restriction on public spending constantly change shape and meaning? The uncertainty surrounding the future of Italian cities is also linked to the uncertainty of the institutional framework: the demarcation of controllable "games" offers no guarantee, given the vertical interrelationships that may compromise any imposed boundaries.

In such a situation, in which rigidity and uncertainty alternate in striking fashion, nothing is defined, no one asks anything from the "architecture game," nor does anyone wonder how much that "game" is capable of giving to other "games." A few lines of *tendenza*, however, emerge from big business and from the design laboratories, from the decisions made by town councilors, and from public institutions. As we will attempt to demonstrate, there is a discrepancy relative to the demand: architecture as the identifier of formalized programs is being confronted with the absorption of architecture itself into the sphere of computer science (in the field of public relations, in the least noble cases).

A rapid analysis of the transformations affecting Italian urban planning can help specify the new coordinates guiding disciplines and institutions.

One can speak of a real new *tendenza* in Italian urban planning of the 1980s: the one that Bernardo Secchi and Giuseppe Campos Venuti have defined as belonging to the "plans of the third generation,"[4] a *tendenza* that already encompasses studies for the plans of Bologna, Reggio Emila, Florence, and some smaller centers.[5] The motivations behind the new reflections draw on concrete analyses of structural transformations that, in the early seventies, gave new expression to collective needs and their relations to the needs of groups and individual social sectors. These transformations include: the diminished growth of urban populations and the rise in the average age of city dwellers, the processes of decentralization and industrial displacement, the phenomena connected to the reconversion of urban establishments, the dispersal of productive systems, the new demand for services (articulated with particular force in the major cities), the precedence given to the theme of reuse and to refinancing and making functional existing structures, technological innovations in the field of communications and transportation, and the restructuring of the system of political decision making. One of the new themes to become explicit has been the issue of reducing the hardships experienced by minorities, who are as restricted as they are excluded from the system of political exchange[6]: a situation that should have troubled the consciences of the urbanists, before

1968 and after, as scandalous and in need of attention.

We are clearly witnessing a shift in the focus of interest in planning: the new themes are the containment of urban expansion, the restructuring of suburbs and the workplace, and the formation of a new service sector; in short, it is a tendency toward what can be defined as *the quality of urban space.* This analysis of real conditions has, however, taken into account the ingenuous products of urban planning of the age of reconstruction and its center-left. New experiments in planning are overturning many of the dogmas ruling the traditional discipline of urban planning, and it would be unfair to say that these efforts to change course were due to external conditions alone. What is maturing in this sector also has ancient roots: the polemics sustained by De Carlo and Quaroni in 1954, the debates of the early 1960s, and the first project for the Milanese Intercommunal Plan are stages of a history today rounding a bend.

A sign of the matured consciousness of the new problems was a book—*Il racconto urbanistico* by Bernardo Secchi, published in 1984[7]—that now assumes a historical importance worth underlining. Through a harsh scrutiny of the history of urbanism, Secchi proposes a new conception of the problem under discussion, examining systems of expectation, consolidated judgments, and the formation of dominant discourses. Once one realizes that in the past construction and urban planning assumed the forms of a great allegory—one burdened with too many contradictory tasks[8]—urban texts can be read for their narrative structure: as *stories.*[9] The verification of results, relative to stories, is drastic. The great petitions of value and promises, based on the attempt to exchange prevailing signs for their opposites, have been resolved in oversized construction programs, in the inflation of market and land revenues, in wasted housing, infrastructures, and land, in the lack of supervision over production, and in the almost total absence of controls on the quality of physical space. Secchi's text is anything but moralistic; instead, his narration is cold and analytic. He recognizes, however, that the main result of urban planning— which has never had to justify itself through its own results—has been its infiltration into the "structuring of the political system, especially on the local level, and this [has served] to furnish an identity for social actors and agents."[10] Secchi's analysis of "planning styles" gives rise to a historical sequence that includes the embryonic models of the fifties, the successive attempts to stabilize relations between regional plans and political mediation, and more recent experience based on political exchange and the importance of different social practices to each region.[11]

There is also discussion of the schism between the planning and design of physical space. This division was established in the sixties, while the end of the following decade seemed dominated by the "loss of a center." "The new terms are now concession, convention, burden, and contribution. The world no longer seems divided by the ownership of property—not all landlords belong to the upper classes; not all tenants belong to the lower classes. At a time when the housing problems of a few urban minorities contrasts with the most impetuous building 'boom' in the country's history, supply and demand no longer appear as analytic categories standing in banal contrast and needing to be put in equilibrium..."[12] Secchi then acknowledges that the regulated construction of the zoning plans—Corviale, Gratosoglio, Laurentino, and Secondigliano—not only represents the city "as a big warehouse where incongruous objects are deposited," but is also subject to bureaucratic norms that ignore the identity of separate groups, which it forces together in artificially united and strongly determined environmental frameworks.

Secchi thus tries to reshuffle the cards by demonstrating that the old fences between friend and enemy have begun to collapse: he offers a typical historical analysis of the popularization of "quantitative" housing policies.[13] The *urbanist story* does not offer solutions, and therein lies one of its merits. Instead, it expresses the needs of various parties: "to take time,"[14] to shift reflection onto new paths, to redesign the map of problems, and to accept new ideas conditionally, furthermore judging them for their level of realism, and not just on the style of narration. And it is in this spirit that one must consider two experiments in the "new urban planning," embodied in the preliminary projects for Florence and Bologna.

The preliminary project for the new master plan of Florence, drawn up in early 1985 by Astengo, Campos Venuti, Fernando Clemente, Paolo Maretto, Luciano Pontuale, and Giuseppe Stancanelli, not only offered a concise critique of so-called "quantitative urban planning," but also linked the expression of a new theme to the identification of the social actors who would realize the plan itself: this new theme was the modification and transformation of the existing city. The ideological presuppositions of the traditional "plans" thus fell by the wayside. The idea of superimposing a predetermined design—both physical and political—on the existing one was abandoned and the scenario of operators was realistically analyzed, in a move tailoring the proposed strategies to their modalities of action. "General reason" was therefore no longer invoked for the sake of enlightenment, nor was there an attempt to become aligned with a social faction indebted to a totality of social relationships. Conforming to its own premises, the plan was based not on a *model*, but rather on an interpretive analysis of existing urban morphology. A relationship of continuity was established between structures formed by laws of historical stratification, districts unlikely to change, and new interventions. Thus the modes of planning were changed. The abstraction of zoning was replaced by an attempt to introduce a differentiation of many functions into the entire city: large "urban fabrics" are the new building blocks of the urban surface, destined to undergo a *soft* transformation. There has been a consequent boost to social services run by the commune and greater private intervention in housing. Thus homogeneous sections have been designated to be protected from traumatic interventions; on the other hand, the major private and public systems are concentrated in "program areas" located in the heart of each suburban area being regenerated, at least according to the guidelines for development of Sesto and Scandicci, and it is these systems that are emerging as the supporting structures of the general fabric.

The method followed in the elaboration of the preliminary project for Florence deserves our attention: astute and justifiable criticisms have been made regarding a few of its deficiencies,[15] but one must remember that the project was an experiment. In the first place, a new flexibility characterizes the very concept of the plan. The relations between less determined structures and "program areas" seem to allow for an extremely detailed, as well as realistic, management of the urban entity. In the second place, a rapport between analysis and design emerges; the morphological and typological interpretation of existing areas must deal with qualitative themes, and the choices of intervention are made to suit those themes. Furthermore, it is evident from the above discussion that one of the paradigms sustaining the most disinterested research in Italian architecture—the relationship between the long waves of history and *novitas*—also informs those experiments in urban planning tending toward a radical revision of the discipline's methodologies and characteristics.

In this sense, the case of Bologna resembles, with appropriate distinctions, the case of Florence. Bologna, as observed above, had been greeted in the sixties as the *exemplum* of a new way of managing the city. This city, the capital of communist Emilia, had accomplished a complex effort to concentrate public intervention on the recovery of sections of the historical center; this experience proved to be fundamental, for it revealed the limits imposed upon local action when it attempted to interpret social relations, laws, and productive *tendenze*. But there were many issues at play in Bologna, and Pier Luigi Cervellati's action was necessarily interrupted after the 1980 elections.

Some of the serious limitations on the original strategy for the city sectors were opposed by forces that had previously concurred with the administration's policies; the cooperative movement was not interested in the recovery of approximately 150 publicly owned apartments because of high operating costs, and the same Commune seemed unwilling to formulate a management policy in this matter.[16] The plans for low-budget public building have been realized by now, but, hampered by schematic methods, have not addressed the neediest parts of the city. In 1972 an operation began, formalized in 1974 and partially contradicting the plans for recovery for the towers of the Fiera District. The project was entrusted to Kenzo Tange, a choice that barely concealed provincial attitudes while revealing an explicit desire for theatricality. At the beginning of the 1980s, the city, so it has been said,[17] seemed "a group of usable goods the possession of which is *fragmentarily* affirmed," while one of the main conditions of the praised "Emilian model" was missing: a close relationship between producers, the local market, administrators, and cooperatives.[18]

This situation provided the context for the preliminary project for the new master plan of Bologna, which was approved by the Council on July 13, 1984. This project—for which Campos Venuti, Clemente, and Portoghesi served as general consultants[19]—constitutes a critique of quantitative urban planning and the model-plan. It too is founded on articulated intervention into existing structures, especially in the main suburb to the north and east of the historical center; it too assumed *quality* as its objective, historical and morphological analysis as its method, and vacant urban lots as its chosen places for intervention. Thus we have moved from the dogma of indefinite growth in the countryside to a keen interest in transforming the least qualified elements of existing cities. Considerations of an ecological and demographic character have been wedded to ideas concerning the new demand for transformation.[20] Research in planning claims power to "shape a functional and spatial unitary system that is continuous, integrated in the existing city, morphologically specific, and able to contextually blend the majority of identified knots; moreover, it presents itself as an organized reference system and 'organizer' of the urban fabric."[21] There is less of a tendency to trust gigantic "architectural machines" projected onto the countryside, and greater willingness to pay attention to the context, to mix the ancient and the new. The qualitative research has shifted, however, from the pressing theme of the historical center to the decomposition of the disintegrating suburb. The ground covered in Bologna becomes perfectly clear when one compares this strategy with the above mentioned project by Carlo Aymonino and Pier Luigi Giordani for the new northern office district, drafted in the midst of the debate on megastructures.

The project for Bologna introduced another methodological novelty. It proposed a passage from generic zoning to "figured zoning," as exemplified by typological directives of an architectural nature, and a passage from a limiting body of legislation to a methodological one.[22] The content of the "project papers," which exemplify this attempt to enrich the techniques of planning, constitutes the least persuasive element of the proposal. "Quality" is identified with the revival of elements and typologies such as the corridor street, the tree-lined avenue, the portico, and the functional piazza: in short, the relationship with the historical center has become more "figurative" than structural, while the appeal to the "values" of the preindustrial, nineteenth-century city gives the plan an anachronistic flavor. This approach, however, has resumed the now modernized theme of "civic design," and its insertion into an urban plan is interesting. But the concept of quality resulting from the designs presented turns out to be rather flat: familiar images that have been gently "alienated" are proposed in the search for a general consensus about this subjective concept. Significantly, "red Bologna's" notion of quality is that which is in direct relation to social relations of a feudal, absolutist kind, in the tradition of the *ancien régime*. Furthermore, too much is arbitrary in the proposed models. As a result, morphological and typological analysis is lacking; one hopes for a type of urbanization that would forestall indiscriminate saturation, but it remains unclear how this could occur. The theme of "tying and sewing," which has emerged in recent years, risks being stranded on the shoals of ideology.

But let us not be confused by delays caused by the experimental nature of a project that is, on the other hand, seeking realistic interlocutors for its realization. Clearly, the Commune is willing to give priority to business and capital, on the condition that intervention reaps no profit and that it respects dictated strategies.[23]

One therefore wonders: does the new experimentation rest on the premise of negotiated urban planning? A lucid analysis of this question is once again provided by Bernardo Secchi, who is today the most careful interpreter of urban and regional transformations. Realizing that, in the context of negotiations, the plan, like any hypothesis or conjecture, is not something condemned to be executed, but rather the result of a process of decision making destined to falsification and transgression, Secchi writes: "my idea is that the role of 'representation' and the 'bargaining table' entrusted with the plan is typical of societies that continue to reassess their own institutional systems and that consider social conflict capable of effectively questioning those systems; it is typical of societies and economic systems in which the countryside [...] and regional policies are central to the regulation of important social relations."[24] Furthermore, he continues, it is exactly because the market has proved itself incapable of completely reclaiming all the aspects of urban and rural space, that the "reappearance of a focus on the fundamental rules of the physical city and the exceptions to those rules" has acquired significance.[25]

A frame of reference is thus sketched for evaluating of new experimental plans, which will be subject to discussion again later, when it is possible to verify their effects in a concrete manner. In the meantime, two observations are in order. Though the "plans of the third generation" certainly constitute a novelty in comparison to the urban planning of the sixties, they are historically tied to the "turning-point" forecast at the round table of the 1959 INU Convegno in Lecce.[26] On the other hand, the search for new planning techniques—delayed, as was also forecast at that round table—risks overlapping urban planning and architecture in a mechanical way. Without stressing the "project papers" of the Bolognese plan (figure 137), one can consider them to be symptomatic: the danger is that one may ask of architecture something it cannot offer, and thus forgo more careful analyses and interpretations of contexts.

This was the danger that threatened some of the proposals for Rome, a city in which the hopes raised by the council of the left had to be readjusted, until the electoral defeat of June 1985. Making decisions for a large and complex city like Rome, always a process of compromise in previous governments, is certainly not easy. One must recognize the work accomplished, from 1977 on, on the adjustment of services, the review and launching of the new plan for economical public housing, the recovery of historical buildings, and for the planning of museums. But one should also observe that in Rome a different path was taken from that followed in Bologna and Florence. The concept of the plan-program was interpreted in a singular manner, and the quantity of projects and initiatives seemed to follow the logic of the spectacular ephemeral—introduced with success by the town councilor for culture, Renato Nicolini—more than the logic of a program tailored to the reality of its supervision or to concrete analyses of needs. Thus, it was not the issue of suburban transformation—dramatic for the capital—that stood at the center of the debate, nor that of restructuring the service sector. (The eastern office district, pivot of the 1962 plan, was the subject of a feasible scheme, but without theories verifying the congruity of that idea with the new situation.)

In analyzing the management of the town councilor in the historical center of the Commune of Rome, which was strongly marked by the personality of Carlo Aymonino from June 1980 to 1985, one should take into account the symptomatic nature of that experience. Priority was given not to the recovery, for housing, of depressed areas—though the works in Tordinona and San Paolino alla Pergola continued—but to a project to revitalize the entire city, emphasizing its status as capital. On the one hand, there were projects aimed at areas judged suitable for new urban services, and projects for restructuring, organizing, and "embellishing." On the other hand, a vast operation was launched to give scientific and social validity to the area of the Imperial Forums; it would not only restore unity to the great ancient complex, which had been broken up by the Via dell'Impero, but would also seek a formal and functional redefinition of the entire central area of Rome.[27] A long series of projects, assigned by the Special Office for Intervention in the Historic Center or drawn up by the office itself, extended to the central areas: Portoghesi projected a "city of science" for the site of the old slaughterhouse in Testaccio, Maurizio Sacripanti planned a science museum for Via Giuilia, Manieri-Elia took charge of a project for the archaeological organization of the area of Largo Argentina, the *piazzale* opposite the Teatro dell'Opera was entrusted to Quaroni, Maurizio Ranzi designed the "Casa della Città" on Via Francesco Crispi, and Alessandro Anselmi did an admirable building for temporary housing on Via B. Franklin in Testaccio. Projects have also been drafted for the restructuring of the old Centrale del Latte, for the debatable remodeling of Piazza

Colonna, Piazza del Pantheon, and Via Veneto, for the refashioning of Piazza Vittorio Emanuele II, and for the Senior Citizen Center of Piazza Pizzicaria.

In spite of programmatic declarations, there has yet to appear a scheme lending coherence to the various projects. These, for their part, have often been elaborated with the disenchantment of those who do not believe that the requested graphic exercise will be translated into an authentic professional commission and executed. Quaroni's decidedly cynical attitude was typical; he found it convenient to transgress his usual reserve with a scheme imitating neoeclectic modes.[28] Areas in which the foreseen interventions would be disastrous from both historical and functional points of view were identified, as in the case of the science museum on Via Giulia. Apart from the networks that the new architectural objects might create within the city, in the absence of a traffic plan and without selective programs, Rome attempted to imitate IBA's Berlin. A pile of quickly drawn designs is a reminder of the attempt to initiate a new current in design that would revitalize both the architectural climate and professional forces, while at the same time asking architecture to "make a show" to compensate for programmatic weakness.

This, one must understand, has rendered even the project for the Imperial Forums questionable. The project, which the best archaeologists immediately greeted with enthusiasm,[29] soon divided opinion: in partial contrast with Aymonino's intentions, and on the request of the Archaeological Service, a general plan by Leonardo Benevolo and Vittorio Gregotti was presented in 1985 for the organization of the archaeological zones into a vast urban system. There was an urgent need to define short-term and medium-range objectives that would become part of the more complex requirements of the capital. Without a local and comprehensive project for the transportation network—a drastic problem for Rome— without techniques for controlling the speculative effects of the operation on the surrounding zones, without taking into account the great length of time required for stratigraphical excavation, the entire idea risked becoming not only the object of useless polemics, but also a questionable banner, marred by differing intentions.

If Renato Nicolini greeted the situation as an occasion to broaden discussion to include the destiny of the center, for Aymonino it was a matter of the "more important problem of urban science that has existed in Italy from the end of war until today," in that the ancient political and representational complex is an example of urban art resolved "completely in architecture."[30] The unity and articulation of the forums has, therefore, been seen as a moment of reflection for the present and as the point of departure for the recovery of a *principium individuationis* for the capital: motives directly tied to the architectural debate emerged. Immediately afterward, Aymonino did not hesitate to predict a *"ripristino,"* or restoration, of the Imperial Forums to their original "complete form," made legible. He cited, as exemplary points of reference, the "recompositions" completed in the Agora of Athens, in the Knossos Palace in Crete, and at the altar of Pergamon in Berlin. (He also pointed to a temporary reconstruction, the thirteenth-century Piazza San Marco built at Malamocco for the film *Marco Polo.*)[31]

The gap between these hypotheses and the logic of stratigraphical excavation is evident. The concerns of archaeology and urban programming contrasted with those of architecture, with its needs for compensation, its unsatisfied requirements, its impulse to compare itself with the ancient that, moreover, was once again put in the service of spectacle when its own guardians consented to using the Colosseum for the exhibit "Italian Economy Between the Two World Wars" staged in September-November, 1984.

It would be unkind to make Aymonino responsible for the misunderstandings that have plagued the debate on the historical center of Rome. Caught in the vise of bureaucratic difficulties and working without the support of any political strategy equal to the "Roman problem," this architect, who had sublimated uncertainty into an architecture dense with meaning, could only reason as an architect. A mode of relating to the dynamics between politics and architecture was thus exhausted, but the experience was not in vain.

In Rome, one witnessed a double short circuit. The first was triggered by the failed dialectic between sectoral programs and choices made in a politically motivated frame of reference; the second grew out of the emphasis placed on architectural arbitrariness, which was called on to resolve structural problems.

In another context, there have been initiatives in Milan stimulated by the launching of the Railway Passage in 1982 and by the new situation emerging from transformations provoked by the growth of the city's service sector. It is true that the 1953 plan's emphasis on the new office district gradually disappeared, and the exchange centers that the intercommunal plan hoped would link the urban system to metropolitan areas have never materialized; an unplanned service sector was, however, located in or immediately outside of Milan. In the meantime, "urban vacuums" were created: areas that had previously been occupied by manufacturing opened up, creating major problems.[32]

The Railway Passage was launched in this context; it had been proposed about twenty years before by the intercommunal plan, but opposed for a long time. The new subterranean structure was called upon to connect the railway lines coming from the northwest with those coming from the southeast, between the Garibaldi station and the station at Porta Vittoria. Only after the passage was approved, however, did the administration ask itself what sort of significance should be given to the structure, which at the time was seen as a part of the regional system—a logical perspective, given that the third line of the subway system, which heads towards Piazza Duomo, made it necessary to integrate the passage into a communal transportation plan. The issue was immediately broadened: an attempt was made to integrate the passage into plans for restructuring the services sector, which was identified as the lever necessary for intervention in areas affected by the new infrastructure. In 1984 the administration presented a proposal of strategy and area projects for Portello-Fiera and the Garibaldi-Repubblica zone.[33] Given the complex problems resulting from the diffusion of the service sector, the removal of manufacturing, and the fate of urban *vacuums*, these projects—which once wavered halfway between architectural sketches and feasibility studies—were not very relevant. The first, entrusted to Sergio Crotti and collaborators, furnished the Fiera with a convention center and reception facilities, to be consolidated in an interesting and compact complex. The second, the result of the collaboration between Empio Malara and Alessandro Morselli (of the Urban Planning Office of the Milan Commune), mechanically added tall buildings to an unarticulated slab devoid of any features connecting it to the existing fabric: it was a "bureaucratic" model, indifferent to the numerous problems the administration sought to solve.

But the "new way of doing urban planning" submitted to the administration of Milan was lacking in other ways as well. The "Passage Project" was presented along with the "House Project": a sectoral plan coordinating public and private resources for the organic parts of the city, and mainly applied to southern zones. Upon publication of the "Passage Project," there was nevertheless an awareness of the existence, in the built city, of a sizable amount of land suitable for construction: 4 to 6 million square meters were either available or could easily be made so, and a large part of this land was public property. The ideas expressed by the "House Project" were challenged as soon as they were formulated.[34] The result, which also stemmed from the intrinsic difficulties of the execution of the "House Project," was a loss for the first newly negotiated Milanese experiment, while, on a more general level, Guido Canella's criticisms remained valid: he had stigmatized the abstract superimposition of the project-plans onto an urban structure whose morphological structure needed to be understood before any attempt was made to intervene.[35]

A lesson can be drawn from the cases of Rome and Milan. Neither the criticism of the old modes of planning nor the newly visible themes constituted guarantees in themselves. Furthermore, the relationship between program-plans and architectural projects is not mechanical, nor can it be resolved in *escamotages*: a cognitive stage, in which decision making can occur, inserts itself between interpretations of situations and formal solutions; the absence of that cognitive level challenges the credibility of projects and of political mediation. The road toward "new modes of planning" will probably be much longer than it first appeared.

In Naples, unlike the cases we have examined so far, the planning techniques were revised after a catastrophe: the earthquake of November 1980. This southern city, whose decay is due to wild speculation, the spread of illegal practices, a troubled social situation, and urban violence perpetrated by the administrations before 1975, had adopted in 1972 a plan made questionable by oversized provisions. (Among these was an office district entrusted, with a provincialism noted previously, to Kenzo Tange.) First the "suburban plan," launched in the spring of 1980, then the special program for reconstruction—the largest program for public building since the postwar period—led to a healthy inversion of *tendenza*.[36] The rejection of emergency solutions was connected to a program for intervention in the "intermediate zones" making good use of the "suburban plan." The problem of rehabilitating decrepit areas was formulated on a grand scale, using, among others, the plan for economical and public building for the zones of Secondigliano and Ponticelli. The Technical Office of the Commissariat, directed by Vezio De Lucia, used thirteen young architects and directed the rehabilitation programs efficiently; in spite of the schematic methods of some of the projects, reconstruction seemed to be stimulating a new climate of research. Nonetheless, the cultural delays weighed heavily: no recovery was envisioned for the historical center, where the elementary level of the relevant analyses rendered all operations problematic. Furthermore, five years after the earthquake, rural reality is now characterized by the illegal exploitation of millions of lira intended for reconstruction. Meanwhile the tragic situation of the historical center was again brought to the public's attention when a fire broke out in the Spanish quarters on Christmas 1985, causing the death of an entire family. The result was a series of accusatory statements that were brought to the Public Prosecutor's Office: citizens asked the magistrates to force the Commune to do something about the intolerable living conditions of the overcrowded quarter. The Neapolitan situation was an extreme case in Italy, where the significance of sectoral operations was difficult to assess without developing a strategy for radical economic and political restructuring.

This is not to say that one cannot draw partial lessons even from anomalous experiments. If we return to the theme of "modification," of sewing and reuse, our attention is necessarily drawn to two cases, both of which were promoted by big business: the competition of ideas for the reutilization of the FIAT Lingotto in Turin, which closed in 1984, and the competition for the reutilization of the Pirelli Bicocca in Milan, still in process at the time of writing. Both were potential "vaccums" that became cultural issues and posed a problem of recovery for the major Italian industries. These "vacuums," which remained after the existing facilities were remodeled, offered their respective cities a mixed bag of themes that emerged from the specific sites and by implication addressed a broad range of problems. One could say that it was a way to affirm the centrality and primacy of the enterprise, but it was this theme exactly that architects, urban planners, and administrators addressed with increasing urgency, though from different perspectives. Nonetheless, in Turin and Milan the issues of urban connections and rehabilitation were imposed by a circumscribed problem: it is superfluous to remark upon the distance separating similar presuppositions from Adriano Olivetti's utopia of community, which from the factory had influenced the entire country.

For now we can only discuss the results of the competition for Fiat Lingotto, but, from the documents made available so far, it seems evident that the Pirelli building constitutes a critique, based on specific details, of some of the specifications made in the Milanese Intercommunal Plan.[37] An examination of the projects presented to the Turin competition turns out to be complicated. The question of the recovery of the now historical building of Mattè Trucco was compounded by the demand to accommodate new functions, and to establish a connection with the city, made problematic by the station of Porta Nuova and the railway stop, though the latter was intended to be moved.[38] Gregotti, Gae Aulenti and Italo Rota, Gabetti and Isola, Pellegrin, Piero Sartogo, Renzo Piano, and Aldo Loris Rossi, to name only a few of the Italian guests, thus had to deal with an anomalous complex of issues dividing the discipline's traditional areas of competence. They were faced with the idea of a plan starting with a place and a "vacuum" that was, however, marked by historical "richness," and the qualitative proof of that same idea: in order to respond properly, it was necessary to be aware that the competition announcement stretched the limits of the current architectural debate, prefiguring specific new areas of competence. Gabetti and Isola's structure, which was called upon to connect the Lingotto, destined for a university, with the city, was a skillful performance, while the monumental scale chosen by Aulenti and Rota (figure 138) for the complex adapted for residential use tends to memorialize, by way of analogy, one of the characteristics of the original building. As for the historical museum of industrial product design, which was bordered by a park and designed by Gregotti Associates, it ensures continuity with previous functions.[39]

The results, however, have generated a feeling of malaise especially evident in Luigi Pellegrin's project, as well as in the projects of a few foreign competitors. The idea of starting with a group of architectural projects rather than with a traditional urban plan was also new, but the Fiat initiative could only be made concrete by a subsequent careful concentration on the entire area of the Lingotto and the commercial quay, undertaken by the administration.

Architecture was thus entrusted with an unusual task, that of taking a preliminary sounding of formalized hypotheses. This was possible to achieve, but the limits and applicability of the project would have to be evaluated carefully.

12
The Paradigms of Pluralism

To what extent, in fact, does the current architectural debate furnish methods capable of responding to such questions? The most interesting designs of the past fifteen years have given rise to themes revolving around the concepts of place, context, modification, reweaving, the relationship between an intervention and its surrounding conditions, and both typological and morphological continuity. These themes are similar to those that were focal points for the "plans of the third generation." The scale of the analyses and proposals varies—though not in every case—and, most of all, the verification of the ideas is translated into self-verification, as is true of all architecture. (This should be kept in mind by anyone who tends to confuse, thoughtlessly, architecture and urban planning.)

If we accept all these themes and see them as paradigms for the new experiments in design, we obtain two very interesting results. On the one hand, such paradigms, because homogeneous with the new urban themes, lay the groundwork for a dialogue between the two disciplines; and where there is dialogue, there is also the possibility of conflict. On the other hand, these themes are central to the architectural debate: they provide the only focus free of nostalgia and regression, against which the best of Italian culture now seems immunized.

Let us reexamine as a group the above themes: place, context, margins, modification. It is almost too clear that they result from a long, collective gestation, from a prolonged critique of the logocentrism of the previous avant-gardes. In the relationship between site and context, the "pathos of the new" is placed in a critical situation, and language "transforms itself and does not invent." Transformation itself is imbued with meaning, in relation to "the world as I have found it." We use Wittgenstein's phrases intentionally. The themes mentioned above, as they have been translated by the most interesting Italian architects of the last decade, no longer possess the romanticism, the nostalgia for lost totalities, or the anxiety to recover regressive hearths, which characterized those same themes when they first appeared.

Now they are being appropriated as design materials, and are frequently made to react with vocabularies and syntaxes reminiscent of several "modern" currents: those of Gregotti, Purini, Canella, and Aymonino. They are *also* being used as methods of "deconstruction," whether that deconstruction is cold, systematic, or passionate. We will return to this point later on. But, from what has been said, it is evident that the processes mentioned at the end of part one of this book are proliferating in a variegated and articulate fashion: on the one hand, a reunification of paradigms, on the other, a multiplication of ideas. This is no contradiction, but a consequent answer to one of the most urgent problems of our time: the identification of the *orders* in the absence of a *Nomos* or superior Law, of a prefigured *Telos*. But we also have a criticism increasingly conscious of every gesture toward the future, of every instance of secularized eschatology, and of every final model in the name of which the present is sacrificed. What might seem, at a quick glance, an instance of reductionism or the result of "reflux into the private," turns out to be, with more careful reading, an attempt to open new avenues for a restructured discipline. It is a collective attempt—albeit still confused—to shuffle the cards fairly in order to extract from the hybrid that results from a confluence of the new interest in the products of long waves of history with the fragments of the "tradition of the new," a series of experiments emphasizing the problems of time, of permanence and uprooting, and of continuity and discontinuity.

At this point, the Italian experience becomes welded to the international one. We encounter the major ideas that James Stirling began reflecting upon in the sixties, that Louis Kahn had reflected upon previously, and that today interest Rafael Moneo and Alvaro Siza Vieira. But, in our opinion, the Italian contribution has a specific character, evinced by its pluralism.

First of all, there is the confrontation with large-scale planning. Vittorio Gregotti is among one of the few equipped to respond to the problems formulated by the new themes emerging from the changing cities and territories. The scope with which, during the preceding decades, he confronted the question of landscape has today enabled him to re-create disciplinary functions capable of competing with the complex of new duties. The need to control the grand scale with unifying schemes of a high degree of legibility—which characterized the projects for the University of Cosenza and the Zen quarter[1]— characterizes a few of the formally competent proposals he has elaborated in recent years. These include: the projects for the organization of the reception center and the restructuring of the road system of San Marino of 1981, the above mentioned housing project of Sestiere in Cannaregio in Venice, the residential building in the Tiergarten quarter in East Berlin, begun in 1980, the large residential complex in Modena (figure 139), and the schemes for the Garibaldi-Cadorna zone in Milan and for the Olympic stadium in Barcelona (1983).[2] The themes of the urban threshold, of "sewing," and the dialogue with context: Gregotti has demonstrated that these can find hypothetical solutions within an organization of form that recalls the transparency of "grand composing," without leading to arbitrary meanderings (figure 140).

Too many projects, perhaps, have emerged from the Gregotti Associates studio; one inevitably wonders whether the architectural intelligence concentrated here would not be better off engaged by a single, major responsibility with a guarantee of actual construction in the near future. Such conjecture, however, does not begin to express the waste of intellectual resources in Italy caused by public officials, a waste that has nevertheless been compensated for by a multiplication of proposals. To his credit, Gregotti confronted the situation in *Casabella*, whose direction he assumed when Tomás Maldonado's drab reign came to an end: since 1982 *Casabella* has been the organ most intent on collecting the ideas of the moment, and has reflected the prevailing atmosphere accurately. No single issue of the review has been particularly exciting, and a symptomatic *medietas* dominates throughout; but reread in its entirety, it offers a critical catalogue of current problems, none of which, by definition, is "heroic" or cathartic.

And insofar as Gino Valle's work, unlike Gregotti's, has focused mostly on the quality of the object, it is predictable that confrontation with the theme of "modifying and sewing"—as was the case in the skillful project for the offices of the Banca Commerciale Italiana in Manhattan[3]—has provoked a softening of the erudite rigorism of this architect from Udine. Already in designing the scheme for the new public housing behind the Mulino Stucky in Venice, Valle introduced into his repertory a formal flexibility directly related to the context of that urban margin[4]: the project's structure is based upon a careful analysis addressing the flexibility necessary in confronting a dense fabric, and incorporates echoes of an old industrial building. It is evident, however, that in the New York office buildings, in the office district of Pordenone and the project for the new Olivetti offices in Ivrea, and especially in the recent IBM buildings at La Défense in Paris now under construction (figure 141), Valle has displayed a new manner interesting not only in itself, but from a methodological perspective, a manner concerned with large-scale planning, urbanism, the reception of figurative echoes from the context, and a balanced rapport between "big form" and fragments.

Some of the buildings that make good use of the Venetian experiments of Aymonino and the *"gruppo Architettura"* still relate to the themes of transformation, the rehabilitation of the decaying periphery, and the finished fragment. Foremost among these is the IACP housing project in Mestre-Altobello of 1978–83 by Gianni Fabbri and Roberto Sordina (figure 142), constructed on a big V once again reminiscent of Gallaratese, but also controlled, like the raised plaza, by a purism integrating elements of the "cultivated" rural building of the Venetian countryside. Two other complexes are more programmatic, but thematically homogeneous with the work of Fabbri and Sordina. The first is the residential intervention in Cascina del Sole in Bollate by Angelo Villa and Paolo Ferrante[5]—a "boundary" installation, that proposes again an urban block with a typological assembly emulating the complexity of the stratified city; the second is nucleus number six of the PEEP (Plans for Economical Public Construction) in Abano Terme, by Raffaele Panella, Renato Bocchi, Carlo Magnani, Stefano Rocchetto, and Rabio Scasso[6]: a fabric of low buildings intersecting diagonally with a four-story building, and a "terrace house" formed by three terraced blocks placed in a fan relative to a fourth structure. One of the better recent examples of residential building in Rome resembles this kind of work from a cultural point of view, work by Carlo Chiarini, Luigi Cremona, and Italo Melanesi at Tor Sapienza (figure 143), on the margin of a fanciful complex whose gratuitous exhibitionism attempts to give an identity to the suburb. The complex by Chiarini, Cremona, and Melanesi includes a seven-story block 164.25 meters high, with duplexes at the top, exposed on the exterior by cut-aways revealing its inner structures; the lower part is articulated by a group of terraced houses with patios and adjoining gardens. A covered pedestrian space, on the ground level, unifies the two systems: an efficient figurative elementarism is joined with a typological articulation emphasizing the unity of the whole.[7] It is interesting to compare the complex at Tor Sapienza with the one in Corviale: Carlo Chiarini, like Mario Fiorentino, was one of the younger architects who collaborated with Ridolfi and Quaroni on the Tiburtino complex.

Figurative purism, typlogical complexity, morphological unity: it would be erroneous, as well as simplistic, to affix a neorationalist label to these experiments. This is all the more so, given that rigorist *tendenze* in Italy are now being examined in a wide range of interpretations, unified only in the most general way. From Giorgio Grassi's intransigent position (figure 146), to the geometrism of Gianugo Polesello (figure 144)—who designed two very revealing works, the Bibione market in San Michele al Tagliamento, begun in 1980, and designed with F. Panzarin, and the

Montedison office district in Pesaro—to the dignified reserve of architects like Antonio Monestiroli and Franco, one arrives at the stupefied air of Vittorio De Feo's most recent work—as in his competition project for the IRFIS offices in Palermo of 1980—and the ambiguous formulations of Giuseppe Grossi and Bruno Minardi, who ingeniously grafted a two-story addition onto a public building, constructed in Cesena in 1923 and almost entirely preserved. (The contract was submitted in 1978, and execution completed in 1984.) On the theme of modification and "sewing," then, rigorism has generated its own ideas, and facilitated comparison with their alternative.[8]

One might see a reductionism, in the best sense of the term, in the method embraced by the rigorists. A method of design that uses the earliest models of the house and fabric, and that runs contrary to "modern judgment" and belated forms of expressionism, powerfully emerges from Grassi's writings and projects. He has tried to work in conceptual margins, on residues, on the brink of a concept of architecture that substantially weakens the violence inherent in the concept of the project. His position contains aporias, but deserves serious consideration for its potential: it contains the manifestation of a "movement" common to much contemporary thought, intent on "working in the periphery," in the margins of great conceptual constructions changing only gradually because never subject to general criticism.

As we have remarked, moreover, such a "movement" can assume the most varied strategies and languages. It is not by chance that we have contrasted the case of Guido Canella with that of Gabetti and Isola: an obstinate will for form that feels obliged to decompose, violate, and recompose, and proposes new functional stratifications versus a submissive but secure statement tied to the poetics of "let it be." The later works of Canella (figure 147) and of Gabetti and Isola confirm this reading[9]; the works of the Turinese architects also permit additional considerations. In the cheese factory "La Tuminera" in Bagnolo Piemonte of 1980–82, the very refined intervention on Via Sant'Agostino in Turin of 1980–83 (figure 148), the extraordinary project for the judiciary offices of Alba of 1982 (figure 149)—a man-made, terraced, and excavated little mound, with an internal structure in the shape of a palm leaf—and the hermetic "solar house" in Orbassano of 1982–84, the familiarity with the site, the articulation of forms, the extremely skillful use of materials and of techniques constrained to a "soft" rapport with the environment, produce architectural "figures" devoid of hubris, and yet present, acting in their contexts like characters who, in order to demonstrate refined manners, express their strongest opinions in a whisper. The same designs by Gabetti and Isola—often in association with Guido Drocco—are revealing in this regard: the secure images of the upper sections of the designs are almost obliterated at the bottom, as though the project were continually wavering between the will to affirm itself and the will to disappear. Gabetti and Isola's elegiac tone is the opposite of Canella's "invectives" and Grassi's dignified reserve: the comparison of these experiments derives from the conceptual paradigm introduced above. Let the reader be forewarned: while experiments continue to proliferate, the thematic areas where they converge continue, albeit slowly, to become identifiable.

Let us consider, furthermore, that Gregotti, Canella, Gabetti, and Isola are also "masters" capable of training disciples who can articulate their lessons without lapsing into imitation. In Venice, as in Palermo, Gregotti's themes stimulated coherent work,[10] whereas Angelo Torricelli's works (the secondary school in Pieve Lumezzane of 1976–79, and especially the elementary school in Monaca of 1978–81), and the works of Alessandro Christofellis and Giorgio Fiorese testify to the fertility of Canella's teachings.[11] The projects by Guido Drocco and Enrico Moncalvo—see the remarkable competition project for the Opéra on the Place de la Bastille in Paris of 1983— are high in caliber, as are the projects by M. Clara Garcia La Fuente and Mariolina Monge, and by Lorenzo Mamino.[12] In a different way, the faceted poetics of the Turinese masters (Gabetti and Isola, but also Giorgio Raineri) have led to positive developments.

And since we have chosen for our parameters thematic areas, instead of specific issues of form, it is natural to compare the three architects from Piedmont, mentioned above, with Francesco Venezia, one of the most promising architects of the younger generation.[13] Neapolitan, but as detached from local debates as he is from the influence of the official world, Venezia began with a lyrical design from a piazza in Laura in 1973–76: the delicate dialectic between surfaces and passages that connect the Lancellotti castle to the landscape results from an examination of the potential of "marginal piazzas."[14] Venezia demonstrates a high level of thought and the maturity of his design methods at Gibellina, where he installed a fragment of the facade of the Di Lorenzo palazzo, ruined in an earthquake, in a museum in Gibellina Nuova. (The first phase of construction of this project was completed in 1984; figures 151–152.) Venezia set the fragment in a two-color stone support, and placed it in a long hall—a "walled courtyard"—open to the outside only through a single window on the side facing the ruin. The geometrical structure is enclosed by a poetic doubling of the northern boundary, generating a feeling of magical suspension as silent "restfulness" is thus introduced into a calibrated formal game. In 1984, Venezia responded to the initiative of Fiat and Benetton, both of which had invited certain architects to use the theme of industrial archaeology in a project for productive reuse.[15] The idea was to restore valuable silk industries in the eighteenth-century settlement of San Leucio. With a few, careful signs, Venezia created a project truly sensitive to the complexity of this historical site: the project also explored the quality of the real. First one encounters the "reign of water": the Belvedere contains a pool in a hypostile. Then there is confrontation with an important landmark, the Carolino Aqueduct: a discrete "bridge-corridor" that, in its fragmented course, links the fountain of Diana and Acteon to the Belvedere of San Leucio, passing over the street leading into town.

Once again, we must speak of "land architecture" and even more, of "nonviolent" transformation, of a submissive work inhabiting interstices, and as efficient as it is educated and selective.

The judgment passed on the examples of "disciplinary reestablishment" in the seventies grew more severe as these results were reflected upon. A large gap separates the concrete experimentation analyzed so far from the attempts to reconstruct, from the ground up, an epistemology of architecture, generated by an awareness of a crisis of transformation. It is undoubtedly true that all crisis exorcises catastrophe by delaying definitive results as long as possible. It is nonetheless a fact that this "intermezzo" architecture dislocates elements from their frame of reference, accentuating their weakness. But this is a completely positive development. Perhaps because he has acquired a precise understanding of the present historic moment, Adolfo Natalini has been able to complete the long journey that has taken him from the "abstract furors" of "radical" architecture to a series of projects and buildings of notable significance.[16]

The electricity center at Zola Predosa in Bologna of 1978–84, and the offices of the Alzate Brianza branch of the Cassa Rurale e Artigianale near Como, designed in 1978–83 with G. Frassinelli and F. Natalini (figure 153) are the results of a synthesizing reflection on the office building. (A third project, in prestressed concrete, was elaborated at the same time as those just mentioned, but has not yet been executed.) In both cases we find a constancy of type and a variation of its casing: the open levels of the two buildings are screened by gates, brick in the first, stone with intricate weaving in the second. Natalini seems to treat his materials with refinement in order to make his buildings vacillate between monumentality and surreality. The allusions to Louis Kahn in the center of Zola Predosa are matched by more explicit allusions to Le Corbusier in the Cassa in Alzate Brianza. Citation does not assume a primary role. Instead, in Alzate Brianza, the geometrical precision and monumentality of the building are maliciously decomposed by its features: filaments of black neoprene arrayed like a chessboard on reflective crystals; the bands of polished gray granite alternating with light Sardinian granite in the large structural cage; the volumes that emerge from a prism at the base; the diagonal disposition relative to the site; and the veil of water in front of the building. A subtle irony can be detected behind Natalini's knowledge of construction and his compositional skill: it is perhaps an autobiographical element, a reference to the now ancient experiments of the first Superstudio.

Alessandro Anselmi, once involved in the work of the Roman group GRAU, followed a path different from Natalini's and yet analogous to it at points. In the Parabita cemetery designed in 1967–82 with Paola Chiatante, built in an abandoned quarry, the geometrical emphasis was contaminated by anthropomorphic symbols and figurative allusions: the fantasm of a composed capital generates the design of the upper section of the necropolis. Abstraction enters into an ambiguous tension with the will to record lost words; an irresolvable conflict emerges between the architectural "machine" and nature.[17] For Anselmi, too, maturation was the result of the progressive decrease in programmatic intentions. The recourse to history and memory—which Anselmi insists upon[18]—loses its primitive emphatic traits, and makes a "secular" contrast with the compact play of closed forms and distortions in the projects for the churches of Santa Maria delle Grazie and SS. Annunziata in Santomenna, begun in 1981, for the theater of the House of Culture in Chambéry Le Haut of 1982, and for the houses in Testaccio, Rome, mentioned above (figures 154–155). In spite of their common origins and vague assonances, the gap between Anselmi's poetics and the graphic *pastiches* of other GRAU members cannot be bridged.

The recent activity of two important figures, Aldo Rossi and Franco Purini, is more problematic. One is perplexed by the difficulty of fitting their works into the paradigms mentioned above. Both these architects, following very personal paths, seem to be marking time: the first by compromising the greatness of his poetics with mundane phrases, the second by making the products of his graphic *furor* increasingly baroque.

Let us compare the designs that Francesco Venezia presented for San Leucio with those that Franco Purini and Laura Thermes drew up for the same occasion: the figurative extravagance of the latter, approaching Piranesian "excess," cries out.[19] And yet, Purini and Thermes refined and purified their method in the designing of a residential complex in Naples: 65 residential units for Pisciola Marinella, exemplifying Purini's concept of "place"—instead of typology— as a primary value.[20] Isolated nuclei in vertical distribution are surrounded by a network of elements with courtyards—typical of the Neapolitan suburban settlements—that lend meaning to formal "events" and marginal exceptions. But the execution of the "pharmacist's house" in Gibellina is disappointing when compared to the design.[21] Purini needs more time and more opportunities to build, before we can determine whether his contribution is basically one of "architectural narrative," however stimulating. In the meantime, the large molding designed by Purini and Thermes with D. Modigliani for the civic center of Castelforte in Latina (figure 156) indicates a need to renovate completely coherent with the tireless, self-critical labor of a researcher's temperament.[22] Purini practices excess in a rigorist environment: the success of his wager has yet to be tested.

It is, on the other hand, on the level of verification that Aldo Rossi's poetics have generated perplexity. The execution of the Modena cemetery confirms the exceptional quality of that project, in spite of its inferior execution. But Rossi's lack of interest in the execution of his works is thought-provoking. In any case, it was clear from the beginning that Rossi intended to treat the entire thematic range of the discipline according to a highly personal method, which could be identified as a metadiscourse halfway between theorem and autobiographical confession. In his large projects of the sixties and seventies, he had skillfully maintained an equilibrium between the metaphysical pole of his research—the aspiration to return to an *origin*, to recuperate the *arché* or prehistory of architecture—and the need to make his essential signs speak. But, to what degree is such work able to "go down to the city?" Rossi posed the problem in his poetic competition project for the remodeling of the area of the Fiera Catena in Mantua, done with Gianni Braghieri and Coprat Associates, but it became ambiguous in the project he elaborated with Ignazio Gardella and Fabio Reinhart for the reconstruction of the Carlo Felice Theater in Genoa in 1981–82 (figure 157).[23] An architecture of civic relevance and a point of reference for the city: thus the architects characterized their project, in which the reconstruction of Carlo Barabino's building was set in relation to a scenic tower, consistent with the first examples of Rossi's vision. (It is more difficult to determine the continuity with Gardella's preceding works, and even the collaboration between the two men seems circumstantial.) Inside is a pleasant solution—a conical space crossing the entire section beginning with the foyer—and a space in which the *"Genua picta"* is evoked in what has been called a "cruel operation of double mirroring": the outside is brought into the interior, and what could be on the stage is carried into the auditorium. In this novel space, it is the very relationship between the auditorium and the stage that is compromised: Gae Aulenti's criticisms on this point remain relevant.[24]

The difficulty of keeping simultaneously present all the "times" of the architectural object—a difficulty that manifests itself in the project for the Carlo Felice Theater—seems to be even greater in the project for the tall office building designed by Rossi with Gianni Braghieri and with M. Osks, G. Ciocca, and M. Scheurer as collaborators, for Buenos Aires (figure 158).[25] The building, which is tripartite, is constructed on large bands of steel; the lower three quarters of the central tower is covered with gray stone, and its summit is a stepped pyramid in red stone; the roofs of the lateral parts are covered with copper and arched in the shape of a barrel vault. Echoes of Loos are audible here as well as in the fine entrance to the tower, which is punctuated by two squat columns; but the entire object, in spite of the high quality of individual details, hangs together by means of arbitrary artifices and connections.

The pure spaces of the *archai*, once compromised, put Rossi in an uncertain situation, which he has confronted too confidently. Rossi thus seems to have accomplished, at least for now, a trajectory the reverse of Carlo Aymonino's, who in his recent works—in the Benelli office district in Pesaro and especially in the project for the new hospital of Mestre (figure 159)—has reasserted his desire to pursue the stripped-down character masterfully achieved in the Liceo Scientifico of Pesaro.[26]

On the other hand, the tradition of operative urban research introduced at the end of the sixties by Aldo Rossi and Carlo Aymonino had been definitively exhausted, as Massimo Scolari correctly observed.[27] That "refounding," once its contingent function had been carried out, turned out to be—as is natural, in times that preclude "strong" foundations"—a veil to be torn aside so that one could truly read self-verifying poetics. This fact should also be kept in mind in evaluating Aymonino's actions as a member of the leftist Council in Rome.

On the level of the relationship between typological analysis and intervention, however, the works of Grassi, Rossi, Aymonino, and the younger architects are comparable to those of Gianfranco Caniggia, a figure that criticism has so far treated with perplexed reserve, when not busy ostracizing him. We have already mentioned a few examples of Caniggia's design: it is clear that he works, with complete coherence, along lines drawn by Saverio Muratori.[28] After completing a few eclectic projects, [29] he worked on two competition projects—for the Palazzo di Giustizia in Teramo and the one in Brescia—which enabled him in 1964 to formulate the type of the homogeneous building, with alternate rhythmical bays, finished with a continuous veneer. The project for Teramo underwent further revision in two subsequent projects done in 1968 and 1971 (figure 160); the building was finally constructed, though badly, between 1975 and 1981.[30] It is easy to read in the Palazzo di Giustizia of Teramo the memory of reflections that led Muratori to the building he designed for the Democrazia Cristiana in EUR. But now the monumental structure, topped by three tall, turned elements with extradosses, is devoid of pleasing features and stands—dry and dignified—in an isolated area, on the edge of a deep compluvium. The fact remains that Caniggia's work is marked by a profound rigor. The structure of anthropic space is the explicit subject of Caniggia's analyses: that is to say, the formation, in specific places, of ways of life and residential configurations fixed by a prereflective construction, fractured and compromised by an intellectualism drawing upon the Renaissance, the Enlightenment, the nineteenth century, and the contemporary era. Is this, then, a structuralism in which one can glimpse traces of Lukács? Can one draw an analogy with what has happened to other Italian protagonists? Caniggia's work deserves to be read carefully and without prejudice. In reality, his attitude conceals no regressive utopia. What has been shattered cannot be recomposed, but the "critique of the project," implicit in

The Paradigms of Pluralism

the passionate historical reconstruction of urban structures—which are the products of "almost immobile" times—can lead to a paradox: a design contaminated by the roots of a collective *langue*. Once again the results of such an attempt place in question the concepts of "place," "continuity," and even "participation," which had been subjects of reflection for so many of the best Italian architects of the preceding decades. This can be seen in the projects for the recovery of a cluster of buildings in Montecalvario, Naples, of 1981, and for the Abitcoop Liguria quarter in Quinto, Genoa, of 1982, as well as the IACP on the island of Giudecca in Venice of 1985. Caniggia is not interested in the myth of the *new* or in the playful temptations of the *postmodern*[31]: on the contrary, his architecture tries to exorcize the obligation to desecrate every spot, while at the same time remaining highly articulate in its structure and functionally consonant with its contexts.

Caniggia's reflections have led to three recent projects of a high caliber; they were entries in the competitions for a covered pool with annexes in Bagno di Romagna in 1981, for a unifying concept for the railway exit areas and adjacent zones in Pescara in 1982, for the restructuring of the railway connection, and for the new station in Bologna in 1983 (figure 161).[32] This last project, especially—a "bridge" that crosses the tracks diagonally, linking the old station with the northern neighborhoods to be remodeled—constitutes a profound meditation on the representative value of a structure called upon to connect and reorganize two urban poles. Unfortunately, the project has not received the attention it deserves from the evaluating commission of this poorly organized competition.[33]

Moreover, Caniggia has offered clear answers to the questions raised in recent decades. That part of his architecture still linked to a nostalgia for a single imperative *Law* insuring the "speakability" of construction, confronts the rupturing of the "modern" in order to benefit intelligently from its potential. Continuity and discontinuity thus exist in a state of opposition, and new questions, instead of solutions, emerge from this encounter.

So far we have analyzed ideas that are each uniquely exemplary. Their reunification around the table formed by new paradigms is only hypothetical, the result of a wager with the future; it is not something given, not verifiable in concrete situations. The opposite may easily be argued, and is true insofar as it indicates a direction. To enable possible parameters to emerge from this remarkable plurality of experiments, we have suppressed the "evils" afflicting so much recent Italian architecture: its superficiality and desire to be at the center of things, its adherence to the most ephemeral fashions, and the way it is seduced by formulas and sinks into the murkiness of arbitrariness and caricature. We will examine some of these attitudes in analyzing the "postmodern" *vague*. But in the meantime, limiting ourselves to the theme of continuity and modification, we see that the overall picture of the new plan for low-income public housing in Rome is not coherent with our paradigms: even discounting the bureaucratic criteria that determined the various design groups, the new Rome reflects a symptomatic schizophrenia, completely lacking in material for discussion. The objective of an *order without law* is still out of reach, and constitutes a horizon of reference not yet clearly formulated.

At the other end of the scale, we have the increase in average production, the reduction of the cultural distance between "centers" and "suburbs," and the articulation of formal hypotheses.[34] It is undoubtedly true that the decrease, especially for the younger architects, in opportunities to build has contributed to the lack of fertile experimentalism. A fine example of the effects of "artificial occasions" was the third International Architecture Exhibit of the Venice Biennale.

Venice 1985: The Architecture Biennale

The exhibition-competition organized for the summer of 1985 by the Architecture section of the Venice Biennale undoubtedly had its roots in the initiatives of the *Interrupted Rome* (1978) and *10 Images for Venice*.[1] Periodically, architects anxious to place their ephemeral sign on the body—unfortunately idealized—of historical cities in Italy congregate around false problems in order to celebrate an abstract "need for design."

The themes formulated for the competition of the 1985 Biennale were, on the other hand, explicit. None of the most urgent or complex problems of Venetian reality was offered to the competitors, nor were other equally pressing problems such as the terminal on Piazzale Roma, the organization of the Tronchetto, or the recovery of marginal areas. Instead, the themes proposed treated Venice and other nearby places as *pre-texts*, sites where the irrepressible desire for desecration and violence could be concealed under the guises of a "love of the ancient" and a "rediscovered continuity." The competitors were invited to design projects for the completion of the eighteenth-century Palazzo Venier dei Leoni on the Grand Canale, and to produce schemes for the very delicate junction formed by the Rialto, for the Piazza di Este and the Piazza di Badoere, the Rocca di Noale, the Prato della Valle in Padua, and the competition of Palmanova. The only situation that was at all concrete was that of the new bridge at Accademia, which became, not coincidentally, a focal point for the competitors' efforts.[2]

In itself, the ideology upheld at the 1985 Architecture Biennale was conspicuous enough to become a point of reference for many displays of a similar nature. The Venice upon which the competitors were invited to exercise themselves was a city reduced to a characterless vacuum: a Venice devoid of identity, or identified with the reign of the mask and of frivolous discourse, with the goal of libertine "voyages" and arbitrary recompositions. The reference to Canaletto's *Capricci* was not accidental. In this Venice, the realm of the errant "glance" and the play of analogies, a need had been generated: to come to terms with the deep anxiety that Venice itself generates in "modern" sensibilities. The entire history of the *Dominante*, in fact, has made an issue of the "civilization of the project": Venice offers a subtle challenge that affects the very presuppositions of modernity.[3] The response to this challenge was paralysis, hypervenetianism, and uncontrolled hubris struggling to exorcize anxiety. This was the collective response of the projects presented to the 1985 Biennale.

These projects, with a few exceptions—those for the Accademia bridge by Pier Luigi Nicolin (figures 162–163), Monestiroli, Polesello, and by Francesco Cellini and Giovanni Morabito—seem to have been created mainly to join in a most interesting parade. The extent of international participation was certainly impressive: about 1,500 projects. It leads one to reflect upon the professional situations of the more popular younger architects and professionals, as well as on the cultural policies of an organization like the Biennale, which was thus subjected to the wildest and most spectacular formulas.

Almost all the competitors performed at their very worst. The bridges by Canella, Vittorio De Feo, and Leonardo Ricci were mediocre and sloppy, while those of Purini and Dardi were uselessly redundant; a plethora of interchangeable *pastiches* assailed the surviving structures of the Palazzo Venier dei Leoni; gratuitous proposals altered the nature of the Rialto island.

The result of what was intended to be a "festival of architecture" was a kind of banquet around a city treated like a cadaver. Caricature, as well as possibly involuntary mockery, prevailed not only with regard to the context, but also in relation to the architecture itself. This was evident in the projects of Alessandro Mendini and Alessandro Guerriero, Roberto Pirzio Biroli and collaborators, and Giancarlo Leoncilli for the bridge at Accademia, and in the many projects for the Palazzo Venier dei Leoni. Carlo Aymonino seems to have been the only one capable of accepting the exhibition for what it was: he responded with quick and careless graphic games. Venice—as Portoghesi states in the opening of the catalogue—was called upon, in the Biennale, to become a "capital of hope for design."[4] It is hard to say what could be expected to result from a festival of disillusionment like the one organized in the summer of 1985 in the Gardini di Castello. However, at least one fact emerged: the provocation of the most worrisome historical spots of Europe generated, for the majority of architects participating in the event, disorderly dances in search of third-class audiences. As a demonstration of "rediscovered continuities," it was harmless enough: here, even more than in Rome in 1978, the discipline had lost its legitimacy.

The architecture exhibit of the 1985 Biennale was not worthy of its signatory, Aldo Rossi,[5] but was certainly congruent with the cultural strategies of the commission's president, Paolo Portoghesi. The latter, however, with his *Strada Novissima* of 1980, had demonstrated a very different sense of spectacle, confining wood and papier-mâché to the realm of "fiction": a development of a new realm opened to the architectural imagination by more modern circuits of information and consumption.

14
"Gay Errancy": Hypermoderns (Postmoderns)

It is well known that in Italy, Portoghesi launched a style that has been called "postmodern" with his *Strada Novissima* and a dense series of publications, and thus joined an international circuit that includes analogous "opinion-makers" such as Charles Jencks and Robert Stern. Portoghesi was different, though, in that he had a long theoretical and practical interest in the manipulation of historical signs: as we have seen, his first neobaroque experiments began in the late fifties. His more recent "manifestos" are linear.[1] They contain an appeal for a "liberation from ideas" supposedly imposed upon architects and their beneficiaries by the "modern movement," for a joyous rediscovery of the entire repertory of the past, for expressive contaminations of the complexity of historical eras, and for a formal expressiveness linked to the recovery of the concepts of place and continuity. Portoghesi also engaged in a critique of the utopia of the "modern" and of its nihilistic character, which was spiritually grounded in the ideology of progress. "Liberation" is presented as overcoming avant-garde attempts to "reconstruct the universe," and also as canceling incongruous duties, in order to recover the happiness of "rich languages" that have been lost. Echoes of the philosophical writings of Heidegger, Gehlen, Deleuze, and Levinas—listening, simulacrum, *post-histoire*, angel of history—possibly mediated by Mario Perniola and Gianni Vattimo, punctuate Portoghesi's writings, as he travels the seas of contemporary thought, a voyage that, as we shall see, has its own particular significance.

A hedonistic urge and a taste for citation, as well as free association and *pastiche*, counterbalance each other in the proposals of Portoghesi, whose theoretical production has been accompanied by skillful professional and promotional activities. This man and the review *Eupalino* soon became the focal points of a composite school intent on using design and writing to breathe new life into a stringent critique of the "modern," thereby hailing the advent of a new era.

Portoghesi gathers almost all the motifs that have been floating about in the international architectural and philosophical debate of recent decades. His theoretical system accommodates a broad spectrum of issues: a critique of the linear concept of history, a reflection upon memory, the need for a new nonmetaphysical statute for truth, the emergence of new demands for identity and what can be imagined, the demand for peripheral identities, the cult of roots, and the explosion of ephemeral hedonisms. In fact, his cultural project is to make debate a priority once again, focused upon passwords such as the "end of prohibitionism," rediscovered architecture, historical roots, and listening to the site and to history. In this way, the factors characterizing Italian architecture at the present—the multiplication of ideas and the slow formation of parameters of comparison—are flattened in a synthetic attempt, launched with the explicit goal of cultural "management." And that is not all. The reduction of pluralism to a formula includes a study of the true nature of kitsch: there is an answer for everything, and the need for *solutions* predominates.

The superficiality of the "critique of the modern" resulting from such a synthesis is typical. The principal characteristic of the "modern" is constant self-criticism: destructive and gnawing doubts accompanied modernity in its journey, and the critique of the concepts of linear history and progress is intrinsic to both the nineteenth and twentieth centuries. The protagonists of this drama of course include Blanqui, Nietzsche, Freud, Kafka, Rosenzweig, Benjamin, and Heidegger, as well as Loos, Le Corbusier (though certainly not the one of the *vulgata*), Klee, Malevich, and Mies van der Rohe. In order to present the new theoretical proposal as "surpassing" something, a historiographic myth was reinforced: the new research was contrasted with a homogeneous and opaque monolith, an extremely worn historiographic construction: the *modern movement* theorized by Nikolaus Pevsner in 1936.[2] Thus there was an attempt to halt the process of historiographical revision, which has, for some time, thrown light upon the irreducible pluralism of experiments generated since the end of the nineteenth century on: the characteristic features of the labyrinthian map traced by these experiments were falsified implacably. The term *postmodern* as used by Lyotard has rather different coordinates, as he himself remarked during a seminar held in Paris in April 1985, when he opposed the homogeneity of his ideas to those of neoeclectic architecture.[3]

But up to what point is it correct to criticize the postmodern using its own theoretical premises as a starting point? These, in reality, drown in all the myths of the "modern": the cult of *tendenze*, the pathos of the new, and the "surpassing" or "overcoming" of the tragic. Examining Portoghesi's products confirms the "imperfect nihilism" that informs them. The "end of prohibitionism" is translated into montages of allusions and facile effects of "surprise," characterized by a symptomatic ease of composition. This is true of the mosque in Rome and of the following projects: the Unità Sanitaria Locale of Polla, Salerno of 1981, the town hall of Ascea of 1982, the civic center of Padua of 1983, the City of Science in Rome of 1983, the reuse of the Fortezza da Basso in Florence of 1983 (figure 165), the piazza in Latina of 1984 (figure 164), the complex in Rome of 1984, and the restructuring of residences in the historical center of Genoa of 1985.[4] Analogously, an architecture comfortable not only with sadistically deformed caricatures, but also with classical, medieval, and baroque emblems, emerges from the exercises of Riccardo Bichara, Giorgio Blanco, Gianfranco Cundari, and Franz Prati, and approaches comic nuance in the projects of Roberto Pirzio Biroli.[5] The obvious love of history is resolved, in practice, in the game of repeatedly "putting the mustache on the Mona Lisa," now a mass joke thanks to a visual culture more influenced by Disneyland than Duchamp.

It is not clear that this signifies a true turning point. On the contrary, the most superficial characteristics of the "modern" have been taken to extremes. We are left not with a "gay science," but with a "gay errancy" dominated by a perfect equating of form and meaning, by annulling history in reducing it to a field of visual incursions, and by a *choc* technique informed by television: in the end, a *fiction-architecture* comfortably establishes itself in the computer age. There is good reason to label such a mixture of components as *hypermodern*.

Furthermore, Portoghesi revealed how he uses his sources in a singular lapse located at the center of his "The Lights of Lost Paradise," a text introducing a recent anthology of works of "new Italian architects." Evoking the Nietzschean theme of the "eternal return" in order to support—with the help of fragments of Gehlen, Lacan, and Vattimo—the advent of a new sensibility, Portoghesi cites a passage in which the animals who are Zarathustra's friends define the eternal return as the "curved path of Eternity."[6] But the passage, as it is quoted by Portoghesi, cannot be found in the philological edition of *Thus Spake Zarathustra* by Colli and Montinari.[7] Portoghesi took the passage from a text by Löwith, and in so doing landed in a trap[8]: Zarathustra turns to his animal friends soon thereafter—but Löwith, and Portoghesi with him, ignore this—and reproaches them sharply for immediately turning their premonition of the abyss into an "organ grinder's song."[9]

And this is the point: the important themes carelessly assembled by the hypermodern synthesis (those that, in the world of Italian architecture, have been patiently and masterfully explored by Scarpa, by Gabetti and Isola, and by Rossi) have been turned into a "barrel-organ song."

All of this may explain the success of the formula among those on the margins of the profession, seeking a forum and confronting a public eager for eccentric novelties. There are exceptions, of course: a few projects by Francesco Cellini and Nicoletta Cosentino (figure 166) demonstrate a complexity surpassing the limitations cited above, as do a few buildings and projects by Oswald Zoeggler (figure 167). It is nonetheless clear that the hypermodern phenomenon did not arise accidentally. Along with much that is fermenting on the Italian scene, it should be appreciated as a historical symptom. Its character of "imperfect nihilism" does not belong to it exclusively. For this reason we now shift our attention to the question of the relationship between nihilism and the project.

15
The Threshold and
the Problem

Let us examine once again the historical span considered so far, this time shifting our inquiry onto new thematic axes. The multiplication of ideas, in fact, corresponds to the contraction in circumscribed areas of paradigms of verification and falsification; but if merely described, the panorama that emerges risks remaining in the limbo of pure relativism. We should study, instead, what is being conveyed by the composite scenario of the new experiments in Italian urban planning and architecture. Does that scenario reveal a core of issues, not as yet recognized?

Let us consider the effect produced by the repeated grafting of the "new" onto the "mobile" terrain of traditions, and by the continuous compromising of *invention* with memory, by the widespread dismantling of the *ideology of progress* and its correlatives in the field of architecture. Logically, we should leave out the quality of individual works; furthermore, we should place in parentheses the declared intentions, the *tendenze* that serve as points of reference, and the antitheses between languages and attitudes. Our questions, in fact, revolve around the significance of these symptoms, and not the intrinsic value of the works produced. Above all, there appears to have been a cooling of the concept of *novitas*, one of the sustaining values of modernity. This cooling does not imply annulment: on the contrary. What has been taken away is, instead, the *pathos* attributed—first by eighteenth- and nineteenth-century thinking, and then by the historical avant-gardes—to this *novitas;* as a result, its pretense of *absoluteness* is compromised by its cathartic or regenerative effect. The hybrid celebrated in much architecture as well as painting and literature of recent years, in spite of all misunderstandings, implicitly places the project in a critical situation. This makes sense, given that the primary material of these mixtures refers to a nonlinear vison of time. Yet the new poetics of contamination can abandon neither the *new,* nor the *project.* After all, they do not prefigure "happy solutions"— besides, how could they?—and, notwithstanding the declarations of various protagonists, these poetics remain ensnared in nets spread by the traditions that nourish them. This is not to say that the mania for citation, the game of interpretations and fragments, and the incursions into the realms of *déjà vu* do not possess meanings in need of interpretation. We can perhaps take this even further if we consider the Italian case in an international context. With greater depth than the American hypermoderns, the less ephemeral Italian experiments have tended to annul the distance between the assertiveness of the project and the subtle *deconstruction* of its presuppositions: an atmosphere familiar to readers of Derrida (and to readers of Freud). We confront something that is neither pure project, nor pure deconstruction, but rather a tangled web of perspectivism and dissemination, of an *eidos* projected in order to exorcize the unforeseen in the future, and of a freezing of suspended memories. This hybridization increasingly serves as a platform for the new "architectural tales": it is on this conceptual threshold that not only Rossi, Gabetti and Isola, and Caniggia, but also Francesco Venezia and some young "neo-Ridolfian" architects have gathered.

historical?

   The establishment of this threshold is of undeniable significance. Its determination marks the end of the long parabola traveled by European culture, which in Italy has had a rather jumpy history, punctuated by the work of Ridolfi, the BPR, Gardella, Michelucci, and Muratori. As we have seen, totality and an anachronistic *center* have been called forth many times in the course of that parabola. The violence of impulses or "tugs" toward the new, the very acceptance of the ephemeral as material for the imagination, produces—literally *produces*—between anxieties and uncertainties, the same ephemeral attempts to retrieve long-gone centers and hearths. How could that which is true for collective behavior—mass desecration and nostalgic longings for religions, mysticisms, and authority—not hold true for architectural culture as well? Undoubtedly, attitudes critical of prospectivism and *grands récits* also result from collective disillusionment, which, from the 1950s on, has tormented intellectuals by continually compromising their myths. This was effectively demonstrated by François Furet, who analyzed the way French intellectuals of the left treated structuralism.[1] But what is one to make of the current vogue for partial and "feeble truths," of the temptations to give in to mystical "abandon"—perhaps Vattimo's "starting again" is a lay version of Heidegger's *Gelassenheit*—or of the widespread validation of images of the *anciens régimes* occurring even as these thinkers demonstrate their rootedness in the age of computers and equivalences?

It would be almost too easy to identify, in the nostalgia stimulating recent strategies of design, something more than compositional "material." But having said this gets us nowhere, given that such an elementary observation places the reasons for such choices in parentheses. Interpolation and fragmentation: in a very astute essay, Georges Teyssot reads in the architectures of deferral, absence, and fragmentation (a remorse over the end and a cry for new beginnings), and in the architecture of aberrant intensity (the lugubrious), so many metaphors of "funereal discourse."[2] Teyssot's essay introduced a monographic issue of *Lotus* dedicated to cemeteries; but taken out of context, it serves as an interpretation of much recent architecture worldwide. Is it therefore necessary to refer to Hölderlin's verses on the salvation rising on the horizon of maximum peril? An issue fundamental not only to architecture, but to our time as well, would thus continue to escape us.

This problem has been lucidly formulated by Massimo Cacciari in a brief article in *Casabella* that returns to themes he had treated in earlier essays.[3] Cacciari recognizes that the spirit of *completed nihilism* glimpsed by Nietzsche reveals itself so well in no other *techne* as clearly as it does in architecture. But he adds that those who have understood that spirit free of illusions are also those who have spoken in its favor with the greatest "reservations." The very figure of the metropolis with its architectural "speeches" becomes involved in uprooting, in the correlate obsession with overcoming. A question, however, arises within this universe, centered on the very concept of the *project*. The paradox of the modern project lies in the coexistence of its violent will-for-status with the absolute primacy given to the *new*: prefiguration through design effectively annuls the future, as well as the present, for it "*wants* the future to be past."

The apexes of modern thought are nevertheless moving toward a threshold-limit animating a "*profane attention* to difference" with regard to nihilism. "The era of the 'big' project," Cacciari writes, "becomes the 'poor' multiplicity of eras that beat out the rhythm of tradition, custom, environment, and function, both external and internal: *forms of life. Rhythm* between place and space, *rhythm* between the symbolic pregnancy of the work, which does *not* 'surpass' itself in the contemporary project, and this same radical recognition of the aporias of the latter that tests its limits, serves to describe its completion ... . Benjamin's Angel does not 'surpass' the chain of catastrophes that run before his backward glance—but sees the *unicity* of these catastrophes, one by one ... . A promise is perhaps made in this glance: that the architecture of completed nihilism, radically questioned, shall turn itself over into that of its completion."[4]

The situation of contemporary architectural culture is here placed in the context of its epoch: Cacciari's reasoning pursues the problem of architecture to its roots. Identifying nihilism as the motivating force of the *age of technique*, and formulating the idea of its completion, he quickly annuls all attempts at "reintegration" and "return" by labeling them romantic regressions. The form of the modern—of the reduction of values to nothing in the equivalent flux of the metropolis or of the telematic universe—is cogently acknowledged to be a terrain inviting "completion" rather than "surpassing." At the same time, Cacciari implicitly denounces the desire to prolong indefinitely the "state of crisis," a desire, one should add, that has continually threatened the architecture of recent decades. And there is more: directing his analysis between the poles of nihilism and the project, Cacciari identifies the fundamental coordinates for a nonephemeral discourse on the destiny of architecture. The critique of frivolous *dis-course*, of the relativism of meanings, is already contained in the analysis of the *project* as category: the project of which this architectonic is an epiphenomenon. The tradition of thinking that links Nietzsche to Heidegger and beyond is here interpreted *seriously*. The problem is central: how to question *radically*—without entertaining any useless illusions about recomposing what has been shattered or resynthesize the plurality—an era that no longer permits an agreement between wholeness and multiplicity, but also does not oblige one to comply with its most recent victors. We have deliberately defined the figurative hypermodern "dances" as *incomplete nihilism*. Gathered in the limbo of their promises, they obstruct not only radical questioning, but all questioning. There is nothing left to ask about them; everything has already been resolved: we are already *beyond (post)*. Neither the playful, nor the possible in its pure state—the absolute imagined—is a method capable of annulling nihilism. How can we forget that it has always claimed for itself the field of differences between the project and utopia?[5]

   It should be obvious that further subjective inventions will not move us beyond the age of nihilism. To question the will to design is to carry to its limit the *a-rythmos* of the calculating intellect, in order to encompass both differences and unity, and to break the historicist *continuum*. Once the problem has been recognized, the various strategies of Italian (and international) architecture of the recent decades acquire new significance. From the inside of the discipline, after the—tactical?— affirmation of its autonomy, a series of "weak" movements have developed, dislocating, how-ever, the comprehensive scenario. What we have defined as the "paradigms of pluralism" and what we have already recognized as a mixture of project and deconstruction are elements that "weaken" the nihilism of the project, and give life to forms of interrogation having something to do with "differences" and singularity. (These include places, historical periods, traditions, peripheral truths, memories, modifications, expressions of *piétas* for what has been or for what has been vanquished, and transformations avoiding the hubris of the *novum* in favor of "letting be.") One thus discovers that a few of the now mature ideas are approaching—in spite of the atonality of the music they intone—a horizon on the confines of habitual intellectual systems. The threshold we spoke of is perhaps only a point of transition far from such a horizon, but there is ample evidence of movement in that direction. Certainly, it remains difficult to distinguish between symptom-architectures and pioneering work. But what is positive is the formation of a plurality of "possible paths" that can be compared on the basis of the questions, and not the solutions, that they raise. To compose or to design: the alternative does not seem to be an ingenuous choice between the use of prefabricated materials and the "praise of rhetoric." As the "great moderns" have demonstrated in various ways, to compose means to lend a voice to the *tragic*, to make room for "differences" without lapsing into comical *bricolage* or combination. We need, moreover, to realize—after having spoken so much about the architecture of memory—that memory itself does not guarantee the recovery of the homeland of the spirit. On the contrary, memory leads to tragic results: it causes antagonisms to emerge, past and present, and causes conflicts in a composition proceeding by means of "differences." Starting at such thresholds, architecture can question itself in increasingly radical ways. The history traced so far, moreover, is the history of an increasingly intense self-questioning, though one marked by short circuits and prolonged periods of "rest."

As always, however, art has the power to *indicate the problem*, and not to resolve it. (Too many hopes were raised among architects, during this last decade, by the appearance in *Lotus* of the translation of a text by Heidegger, whose metaphorical language is not "translatable" into that of architectural culture.)[6] What the best Italian architects are *indicating* is a question that seems to dominate their reflections only for brief periods of time. This is demonstrated, for instance, by the debate that followed the appearance of Cacciari's essay, a debate in which only philosophers participated, with the exception of Joseph Rykwert, whose response attests to ingenuous interpretations of the theme under discussion.[7]

Massimo Scolari was thus able to draw from that discussion the conclusion that the debate on architecture had lost its center.[8] But his article ends with a call for "good craftsmanship," which is in complete accordance with the tone of Cacciari's essay. It is also through "good craftsmanship" that unforeseen paths have been opened: a reflection to be kept in mind by those who feel obliged to "crown poet" every student at the School of Architecture.

Beyond all of this, there remains a difference between the issues identified by the protagonists of Italian architecture and those now being discussed. One should harbor no arbitrary expectations about the future of this difference: we have no guarantees concerning the destiny of what today appear to be avenues leading toward new forms of consciousness. The impression that some of the "new games," anticipated at the end of part one of this book, are now being defined, is the result of a subjective hypothesis, one easily falsified.

Notes

Chapter 1

1. The historical cycle that we are about to analyze here has not yet been the object of critical constructions of sufficient breadth. Limiting ourselves to texts of a general nature that have appeared since 1978, let us mention, however, V. Gregotti's graceful and focused synthesis, *Orientamenti nuovi nell'architettura italiana* (Milan, 1969); the collection *Il dibattito architettonico in Italia 1945–1975* (Rome, 1977); A. Belluzzi's essay, "Il percorso dell'architettura," in the collection *L'arte in Italia nel secondo dopoguerra* (Bologna, 1979); the catalogue *'28–78 Architettura. 50 Anni di architettura italiana* (Milan, 1979); G. Canella's essay, "Figura e funzione nell'architettura italiana dal dopoguerra agli anni Sessanta," in *Hinterland*, nos. 13–14 (1980), pp. 48ff.; C. De Seta's volume *L'architettura del Novecento* (Turin, 1981). See also the collection *Architettura italiana anni sessanta* (Rome, 1972) and the monographic issue *Italie*

'75 of the review *L'architecture d'aujourd'hui*, no. 181 (1975). There are also summaries and catalogues dealing with individual cities or regions, such as, for Milan, the catalogue *Milan 70/70* (Milan, 1972); M. Grandi and A. Pracchi, *Milano. Guida all'architettura moderna* (Bologna, 1980), and E. Bonfanti and M. Porta's volume, *Città, museo e architettura. Il gruppo BBPR nella cultura architettonica italiana 1932–1970* (Florence, 1973), which, while being a monograph on the Milanese group, constitutes a notable attempt to connect critically the work of the BBPR with the Italian and international scene. For Rome, see G. Accasto, V. Fraticelli and R. Nicolini, *L'architettura di Roma capitale, 1870–1970* (Rome, 1971), and I. De Guittry, *Guida di Roma moderna* (Rome, 1978). On the Tuscan situation, see G. K. König, *Architettura in Toscana 1931–1968* (Turin, 1968), and *Itinerario di Firenze moderna* (Florence, 1976). For Venice, see P. Maretto, *L'architettura a Venezia nel*

XX *secolo* (Genoa, 1969). A history of the debate on urban planning can be found in M. Fabbri's volume, *Le ideologie degli urbanisti nel dopoguerra* (Bari, 1975; new edition: *L'urbanistica italiana dal dopoguerra a oggi. Storia, ideologie, immagini*, Bari, 1983). See also the bibliographical appendix.

2. See "Sistemazione delle Cave Ardeatine," in *Metron*, no. 18 (1974), especially the final project, after the competition held in 1944 and the second level competition; ibid., no. 45 (1952): 17–23, L. Quaroni, "Il mausoleo delle Ardeatine," in *Il cittadino*, April 20, 1949. The entry railing is by Mirko Balsadella, the sculptural group by Francesco Coccia. Regarding the monument by the BPR, see E. Peressutti, "Dedica," in *Casabella*, no. 193 (1946): 3, and Bonfanti-Porta, *Città, museo e architettura*, 109ff. The 1946 monument by the BPR, having deteriorated, was replaced in 1950 by a bronze structure with a base of Carrara marble; in 1955 the monument was restored to its former condition.

3. Ibid.

4. The APAO, the Pagani group of Turin, the MSA of Milan, and the INU were present at the convention held December 14–16, 1945. Among the reports read, let us mention M. Ridolfi, "Appunti sui provvedimenti urgenti per la ricostruzione e sull'orientamento della unificazione e tipizzazione nell'edilizia"; P. L. Nervi, "Per gli studi e la sperimentazione nell'edilizia"; B. Zevi, "L'inseg-

namento delle construzioni di guerra americane per l'Italia," in *Atti*, no. 3. In the same issue appears the response of the Catholic F. Vito, "La demanializzazione delle aree fabbricabili," which advances a hypothesis linked to the elimination of revenue from urban development. See also the volume edited by the INU, *Relazione a cura della Commissione per lo studio dei problemi del piano regionale*, ibid., vol. I, pp. 30 ff. See as well, E. N. Rogers, "Introduzione al tema 'Provvedimenti urgenti per la ricostruzione,'" ibid., 1 ff., reprinted in *Esperienza dell'architettura*, (Turin, 1958), 109 ff.

5. G. De Finetti, "Della proprietà delle aree nei riflessi delle costruzioni," in *Atti*, no. 6, 9 ff. De Finetti remains consistent with the series of reflections on the city and on Milan that he began in the twenties. It was difficult, however, between 1945 and 1950, to follow De Finetti's studies on urban physiology, especially as expressed in the plan for "Lombard Street" (see *La città. Architettura e politica*, no. 2 [1946], no. 2) (figure 4) and in those for the Fair and for the piazzas Beccaria and Fontana in Milan (figure 5), reelaborated several times between 1946 and 1951. (See the collection in the review just cited, from no. 1, 1945, to nos. 3–4, 1946, and G. De Finetti's text, *Milano risorge*, written between 1942 and 1951, reprinted in *Milano. Costruzione di una città*, Milan, 1969.) See the collection *Giuseppe de Finetti. Progetti 1920–1951* (Milan, 1981),

and Renato Airoldi, "'Forma urbis Mediolani:' una illusione aristocratica," in *Casabella*, no. 468 (1981): pp. 34–43. De Finetti, who spared neither Le Corbusier nor Bottoni his ironic comments, does not deserve the accusation, based on his "neoclassical" tastes, that he connived with the past regime. Already antifascist in the thirties, he and his wife belonged to the Partito d'Azione. See, in addition to De Finetti's *Zibaldone* (Archivio De Finetti, Triennale of Milano), Marisa Macchietto's interview with Thelma Hauss of October 29, 1981 (Venice: Dipartimento di Storia dell'Architettura). One should note that among the writings of Loos that De Finetti translated into Italian is *Gli inutili* (in *Paese libero*, June 2, 1947), containing a violent attack against the Werkbund; see also by De Finetti, "La Triennale e l'utilità," in *24 ore*, June 23 and 26, 1951.

6. See A. Della Rocca, S. Muratori, L. Piccinato, M. Ridolfi, P. Rossi De Paoli , S. Tadolini, E. Tedeschi, and M. Zocca, *Aspetti urbanistici ed edilizi della ricostruzione* (Rome, 1944–45).

7. P. Gazzola, "Le vicende urbanistiche di Milano e il piano A. R," in *Costruzioni-Casabella*, no. 194 (1946): pp. 2ff. C. Perelli, " Studi per il nuovo piano regolatore di Milano," in *Metron*, no. 10 (1946): pp. 18–49. See also Bonfanti-Porta, *Città, museo e architettura*, 104–5 and plate 72. Albini, Bottoni, the BPR, Gardella, and Mucchi belonged to the AR group.

8. In 1946 a competition, in which the Italian CIAM group also participated, was advertised for the office district of Milan. See *Metron*, no. 30 (1948), 15ff., with articles by the council clerk for urban planning, M. Venanzi (p. 15), and by L. Piccinato, "Il concorso di idee per il centro direzionale di Milano," 14–17.

9. See *Metron*, nos. 23–24; see also I. Insolera, *Roma moderna*, 3rd ed. (Turin, 1976), 180.

10. See M. Visentini, *Presentazione del Piano Piemontese*, and G. Astengo, M. Bianco, N. Renacco, and A. Rizzotti, *Piano Regionale Piemontese*, both in the monographic issue of *Metron*, no. 14 (1947).

11. See König, *Architettura in Toscana*, 50ff.

12. B. Zevi, *Saper vedere l'architettura* (Turin, 1948). The review *Metron* began publication in August 1945 under the direction of Luigi Piccinato and Mario Ridolfi. In 1945, Piccinato's volume, *Urbanistica*, also appeared in issues of *Metron*, while in 1946, Carlo Pagani, Lina Bò, and Zevi began a popular illustrated magazine, *A-Attualità, Architettura, Abitazione, Arte*. Regarding Zevi's positions in those years, see also his article "L'architettura organica di fronte ai suoi critici," in *Metron*, nos. 23–24 (1947). Regarding the debate between 1943 and 1946, see also D. Borradori and M. Porta, *Architettura e politica italiana 1943–46* (Milan, 1966).

13. See B. Zevi, *Architettura e storiografia,* (Milan, 1951); idem, "Benedetto Croce e la riforma della storia architettonica," in *Metron,* and in *Pretesi di critica architettonica* (Turin, 1960); *Uno storico vitale: Franz Wickhoff,* in *Pretesti;* idem, "Il rinovamento della storiografia architettonica," in *Annali della Scuola Normale Superiore di Pisa,* vol. 22, series 2, nos. 1–2, (1954). See also the autobiographical volume *Zevi su Zevi* (Milan, 1977).

14. Programmatic declaration of the Association for Organic Architecture, in *Metron,* no. 2 (1945): 75–76.

15. The index of Roger's *Domus* (whose chief writer was Marco Zanuso) is significant: one finds there a constant effort to link the actuality of history and architecture to the more complex themes of culture in general. The index features articles by Lionello Venturi on abstract art no. 205 (1946); by Dino Risi on cinema; by Malipiero on music; by Dorfles on contemporary painting, by Ballo, Ragghianti, Elio Vittorini, and Starobinski, "Le rêve architecte, les intérieurs de Franz Kafka," no. 217 (1947), by Roberto Rebora and Sergio Solmi. In 1948, with no. 226, Gio Ponti became editor of the review. Ponti did not neglect the cultural interests of the review, though he proceeded to make it more gossipy.

16. A true history of architectural neorealism in Italy has yet to be written. However, in addition to the separate bibliography on Ridolfi and Quaroni, see L. Quaroni, "Il paese dei barocchi," in *Casabella,* no. 215 (1957), criticizing his own work for the Tiburtino; P. Portoghesi, "Dal neorealismo al neoliberty," in *Comunità* , no. 65 (1958); Idem, "La scuola romana," ibid., no. 75 (1959); M. Manieri-Elia, "Il dibattito architettonico degli ultimi venti anni I: Il primo decennio dalla Liberazione," in *Rassegna dell'Istituto di Architettura e Urbanistica,* no. 1 (1965): 76–96; Accasto-Fraticelli-Nicolini, *L'architettura di Roma capitale,* 523ff.; G. De Giorgi, "Breve profilo del dopoguerra: dagli anni della ricostruzione al 'miracolo economico,'" in the collection *Il dibattito architettonico in Italia,* 23ff.; G. Massobrio and P. Portoghesi, *Album degli anni Cinquanta* (Rome-Bari, 1977) 201ff.; Canella, "Figura e funzione." An attempt to place Italian neorealism within the context of the architectural "realisms" of Europe and the United States of the twentieth century can be found in M. Tafuri, "Architettura e realismo," in the collection *Le avventure delle Idee nell'architettura 1750–1980,* ed. V. Magnago Lampugnani (Milan, 1985), 123–45.

17. On the competition for the Rome station and the Quaroni-Ridolfi project, see Giuseppe Samonà, "I progetti per il completamento frontale della stazione Termini," in *Metron,* no. 21 (1947); L. Piccinato,"La stazione di Roma" ibid.; V. Fasolo, "Il concorso per la nuova stazione di Roma," in *L'Urbe,* no. 2 (1947), interesting as

an exponent of academic culture; S. Muratori, "Concorso per il completamento del fabbricato viaggiatori della nuova stazione di Roma-Termini-Motto: UR," in *Strutture*, nos. 3–4 (1947–48): 56–61. The latter, an analysis of the Quaroni-Ridolfi project, already contains the motifs of a "criticism of the modern" that characterize Muratori's subsequent positions. M. Tafuri, *Ludovico Quaroni e lo sviluppo dell'architettura moderna in Italia* (Milan, 1964), 87–89; Accasto-Fraticelli-Nicolini, *L'architettura di Roma capitale*, 521–23; R. Nicolini, "Il concorso per stazione Termini," in *Controspazio*, no. 1 (1974): 93.

18. See L. Quaroni, "Perché ho progettato questa chiesa," in *Metron*, nos. 31–32 (1949).

19. See Tafuri, *Ludovico Quaroni*, pp. 83–85, and A. De Carlo, "La chiesa di Francavilla a Mare," in *L'architettura—cronache e storia*, no. 52 (1960).

20. The competition (both first and second levels) for the Auditorium on via Flaminia in Rome (see *Metron*, no. 43, 1951, and *Architetti*, nos. 12–13, 1952), constituted a further occasion for a conflict among Italian architects, though with less interesting results than the competition for Stazione Termini. The structural exhibitionism of the projects presented by the Morandi-Carrara-Maruffi group and the Favini-Pallottini group (first level) was superseded by Muratori's design, in which the organicity of the original scheme was muted for the second level of the competition. Note that Muratori's two projects belonged to the same climate of research documented by Quaroni's project for the church of Francavilla: the old collaboration between Quaroni and Muratori once again came to fruition. The projects that Pio Montesi presented are testimony of a scholarly fidelity to elementarist terms.

21. See G. Muratore, "L'esperienza del Manuale," in *Controspazio*, no. 1 (1974): 82–92.

22. This manual was edited by M. Ridolfi, M. Fiorentino, B. Zervi, C. Calcaprina, and A. Cardelli. See also M. Ridolfi, "Il 'Manuale dell'architetto,'" in *Metron*, no. 8 (1946): 35ff.

23. I. Diotallevi and F. Marescotti, *Il Problema sociale costruttivo ed economico dell' abitazione* (Milan, 1948), regarding which see G. Ciucci, "Dalla casa dell'uomo alla casa popolare," in G. Ciucci and M. Casciato, *Franco Marescotti e la casa civile, 1934–1956*, (Rome, 1980), 7–20.

24. C. Ceccucci, I. Diotallevi, and F. Marescotti, "Relazione sui problemi dell'edilizia," in the collection *Il Piano del Lavoro*, (ROME: National Economic Conference of the CGIL, 1950), 3–35.

25. On Marescotti's work, see E. Tadini, "Storia e realtà del primo Centro Sociale Cooperativo 'Grandi e Bertacchi,'" in *L'architettura—cronache e storia*, no. 13 (1956): 482–89; the *Quaderno 9*

(1979), of the Departmental Institute of Architecture and Urban Planning at the University of Catania; Ciucci-Casciato, *Franco Marescotti*, cited in the preceding bibliography. See also the account of the meeting with Marescotti held in May 1976 at the Politecnico of Milan, in *Hinterland*, no. 13–14 (1980): 10–19.

26. The initial idea for the QT8 was already contained in a project of 1934 by Bottoni, Pagano, and Pucci for an experimental complex for the sixth Triennale of Milan. The entire history of the QT8 was traced by *Metron*; see "QT8: un quartiere modello," ibid., no. 6 (1946): 76–79; ibid., the special issue of nos. 26–27 (1948); "Il quartiere sperimentale della Triennale di Milano," ibid., no. 43 (1951): 56–61. See also E. N. Rogers, "Esperienza dell' ottava Triennale," in *Domus*, no. 221 (1947). See as well the articles by G. Canella and V. Vercelloni, "Cronache di 10 Triennali," in *Comunità*, no. 38 (1956): 44–52, and by F. Buzzi Ceriani and V. Gregotti, "Contributo alla storia delle Triennali, 2: Dall'VIII Triennale del 1947 alla XI del 1957," in *Casabella*, no. 216 (1957): 7–12. On the work of Piero Bottoni see the monographic issue of *Controspazio*, no. 4 (1973).

27. In order to understand INA-Casa's politics of urban planning and construction, it is important to go back to the two publications, *Ina-Casa. Suggerimenti, norme e schemi per la elaborazione e presentazione dei progetti. Bandi di concorso*, (Rome, 1949), and *Ina-Casa. Suggerimenti, esempi e norme per la progettazione urbanistica. Progetti tipo*, (Rome, 1950). The editorial influence of Arnaldo Foschini, the president of the agency, was decisive. Foschini's works after the war—projects for the central offices of the Banca d'Italia in Naples of 1949–55 (figure 15), for the church of the Immacolata in EUR of 1955, etc.—remained tied to academic formulas, but a determining factor in his management of INA-Casa was the paternalist ideology that redeemed itself by using the popular etymons upheld by neorealism. (See the collection, *Arnaldo Foschini. Didattica e gestione dell'architettura in Italia nella prima metà del Novecento*, Faenza, 1979.) Adalberto Libera directed the technical office of INA-Casa, and Foschini charged Mario De Renzi, Cesare Ligini, and Ridolfi with the elaboration of typical projects based on selected schemas. The Italia complex in Terni of 1948–49, by Ridolfi and Frankl, was one of the first models executed. On INA-Casa see L. Beretta Anguissola, *I 14 anni del piano Ina-Casa*, (Rome, 1963); *Ina-Casa*, in *Per l'Italia. Atti e documenti della ricostruzione italiana*, vol. 4: *Politica sociale*, edited by the Democrazia cristiana, (Rome, 1953), 87–118; F. Gorio, "Un parere sul Piano Fanfani," in *Urbanistica*, no. 3 (1950), reprinted in *Il mestiere del architetto*, (Rome, 1968); F. Tentori, "Dieci anni della gestione Ina-Casa: necessità di un dibattito costruttivo," in *Casabella*, no. 248 (1961): 52ff., reprinted in

L'architettura delle città nell'Italia contemporanea, (Bari, 1968).

28. On the work of Quaroni, from the thirties until 1964, see Tafuri, *Ludovico Quaroni,* which examines projects done with Ridolfi; see also A. Bandera, S. Benedetti, E. Crispolti, and P. Portoghesi, *Omaggio a Cagli. Omaggio a Fontana. Omaggio a Quaroni,* an exhibition catalogue (Rome: l'Aquila, 1962). Quaroni's writings have been gathered in the volume *La città fisica,* ed. A. Terranova, (Rome-Bari, 1981). On Fiorentino's activities in the forties and fifties, see F. Gorio, "Dieci anni di produzione coerente: opere dell'architetto romano Mario Fiorentino," in *L'architettura— cronache e storia,* no. 45 (1959). On Ridolfi, see nos. 1 and 3 (1974), of the review *Controspazio,* and the catalogue *Le architetture di Ridolfi e Frankl,* ed. Francesco Cellini, Claudio D'Amato, and Enrico Valeriani, (Rome, 1979). See also G. Canella and A. Rossi, "Architetti italiani: Mario Ridolfi," in *Comunità,* no. 41 (1956): 50–55; G. De Carlo, "Architetture italiane," in *Casabella,* no. 199 (1957): 19–33; Portoghesi, "Dal neorealismo;" "Una mostra e un convegno su Ridolfi e Frankl" (papers given at the conference in November 1979), in *Controspazio,* nos. 5–6 (1979): 63ff.; F. Cellini and C. D'Amato, "Il mestiere di Ridolfi," in *La presenza del passato,* (Milan: La Biennale di Venezia,1980): 68–71. Interest in Ridolfi's work has revived only recently, and to the point that he

has been counted among the "fathers" of postmodernism in the exhibit organized for the Venice Biennale in 1980 at the Corderie dell'Arsenale. Articles dedicated to his more recent production are cited below. On Ridolfi's work on the Tiburtino, see G. Muratore, "Gli anni della ricostruzione," in *Controspazio,* no. 3 (1974): 6–25, and G. Monti, "Le palazzine romane," ibid.: 26–35. On the Tiburtino, besides Quaroni's article, "Il paese dei barocchi," see C. Aymonino, "Storia e cronaca del quartiere Tiburtino" in *Casabella* no. 215 (1957); C. Chiarini, "Aspetti urbanistici del quartiere Tiburtino;" F. Gorio, "Esperienze d'architettura al Tiburtino." See also, for the consequences of that work, M. Girelli, "Dal Tiburtino a Matera," ibid., no. 231 (1959), and C. Conforti, *Carlo Aymonino: l'architettura non è un mito,* (Rome, 1980): 15ff.

29. It is important to remember that Ridolfi and Frankl had planned that every block in the Viale Etiopia would have, halfway up, facilities for the care and schooling of children. The continuous loggia interrupting the first three towers constitutes the only trace of this intention.

30. See De Giorgi, "Breve profilo del dopoguerra," 33.

31. See V. Gregotti, "Alcune opere di Mario Ridolfi: case Ina a Cerignola, case Ina a Terni, casa di città a Terni, palazzina in via Vetulonia a Roma," in *Casabella,* no. 210 (1956).

32. See M. Coppa, "Il piano regolatore di Terni: parte seconda," in *Urbanistica*, no. 35 (1962): 59 ff.; V. Fraticelli, "Terni: progetto e città," in *Controspazio*, no. 3 (1974): 74–79.

33. See G. Muratore, "Le nuove carceri di Nuoro," *Controspazio*, no. 3 (1974): 44–49.

34. Carlo Mollino's career undoubtedly constitutes a unique "case" in Italian architecture. An acrobatic aviator, a designer of planes and automobiles, a lover of car racing and photography, a creator of patented "inventions," as well as an architect, Mollino continually crossfertilized his various interests, enjoying his role as the enfant terrible of architecture. In his ornaments, furnishings, objects and photographs, he experimented with a language that absorbed surrealism—that of Man Ray as well as that of Mirò—along with the suggestions of Gaudí, Mackintosh, and Eames. As an architect, after the Sled-lift Station, he designed the Teatro Regio, the Chamber of Commerce, and the Lutrario ballroom in Turin, where his homage to the imaginary was not above an encounter with kitsch. On Mollino, in the fifties, see Massobrio-Portoghesi, *Album degli anni Cinquanta*, and C. Borngräber, *Stilnovo. Design in den 50er Jahren. Phantasie unt Phantastik*, (Frankfurt): 14ff. A brief excursus on the Mollino archive can be found in the articles by G. Brino, "Architettura a tempo perso. Hobby a tempo pieno," in *Modo*, no. 4 (1977): 43ff., and "Carlo Mollino," in *Lotus*, no. 16 (1977): 122ff.

35. The career of Edoardo Gellner (b. 1909) forms another singular case in Italian architecture of the fifties. After having studied in Vienna and Venice, Gellner worked in Cortina d'Ampezzo, demonstrating a remarkable sensitivity to the specific qualities of the environment and the mountain landscape. In Cortina, he executed the Palazzo della Telve between 1953 and 1954, the Post Office from 1953 to 1955, the Giavi house from 1954 to 1955, and the "Residence Palace" condominium, which revealed—besides an attention to materials—a particular interpretation of Wright's geometry. The years from 1955 to 1958 saw the construction of his Villaggio Eni in Corte di Cadore, with its detached houses set in nature, and enriched by a service building and a colony of pavilions; Gellner's uninhibited language is detectable in the connecting ramps, whose infinite rhythm of openings recall Le Corbusier's solutions, united with the geometric distortion provoked by their oblique movement. See L. Ronchi,"Opere dell'architetto Edoardo Gellner: cinque edifici nel centro di Cortina d'Ampezzo," in *L'architettura—cronache e storia*, vol. 5, no. 44 (1959): 82–121.

36. G. C. Argan, *Progetto e destino*, (Milan,1965), 90.

37. See Tafuri, *Ludovico Quaroni*, 100ff. Before joining the *Comunità*

movement, Quaroni collaborated with organizations like the Movement for Civic Collaboration and the School for Social Assistance, with the objective of integrating sociology and urban analysis. See L. Quaroni, "Le indagini urbanistiche del centro di ricerche sociali," a paper given at the first national convention of socialist technicians in Milan in June 1947 (unpublished). On the negative attitude of the Italian left regarding sociology, at least until the convention of "Marxism and sociology" organized in 1959 by the Gramsci Institute, see L. Balbo and V. Rieser, "La sinistra e lo sviluppo della sociologia," in *Problemi del socialismo*, no. 3 (1962). See also L. Quaroni, M. L. Anversa and others, "Indagine edilizia su Grassano," in *Inchiesta parlamentare sulla miseria*, vo. 13 (Rome, 1954). Symptomatic of Quaroni's positions in those years are his writings, "L'urbanistica per l'unità della cultura," in *Comunità*, no. 13 (1952); "La città," ibid., no. 26 (1954); "L'architetto e l'urbanistica," in the collection *L'architetto d'oggi*, (Florence, 1954).

38. On the relationship between Olivetti's ideologies and architecture, see Fabbri, *Le ideologie degli urbanisti nel dopoguerra*; *Politique industrielle et architecture*, monographic issue of *L'architecture aujourd'hui*, no. 188 (1976). See also B. Caizzi, *Gli Olivetti*, (Turin, 1962), and the two testimonies, given sixteen years apart, by C. L. Ragghianti, "Adriano Olivetti," in *Zodiac*, no. 6 (1960), and L. Quaroni, "L'expérience de la Martella," in *Politique industrielle*: 46–47. See also G. Berta, *Le idee al potere. Adriano Olivetti tra la fabbrica e la Comunità* (Milan, 1980), and U. Serafini, *Adriana Olivetti e il Movimento Comunità*, (Rome, 1982).

39. See A. Restucci,"La dynastie Olivetti," ibid., 2–6; Idem, "Un rêve américain dans le Mezzogiorno," ibid., 42–45. See also, as a document of ideas on the south that were similar to Olivetti's, R. Musatti, *La via del Sud*, (Milan, 1955).

40. See F. G. Friedmann, "Osservazioni sul mondo contadino nell'Italia meridionale," in *Quaderni di sociologia*, no. 3 (1952) and *Un incontro: Matera*, (Rome: UNRRA-Casas, 1953), as well as the publications of the Commissione per lo studio della città e dell'Agro di Matera (1956), ed. UNRRA-Casas: F. Friedmann, R. Musatti, and G. Isnardi, *Saggi introduttivi*; T. Tentori, *Il sistema di vita nella comunità materana*; F. Nitti, *Una città del Sud*.

41. G. Baglieri, "La controriforma fondiaria," in *Comunità*, no. 60 (1959).

42. On the "case" of the Sassi of Matera, see N. Mazzocchi Alemanni and E. Calia, "Il problema dei Sassi di Matera," a report given to the consortium of the middle valley of Bradano (1950); F. Aiello, "Dai Sassi alla borgata," in *Nord e Sud*, no. 5 (1955): 62–88; R. Giura Longo, *Sassi*

e secoli, (Matera, 1966); M. Fabbri, *Matera, dal sottosviluppo alla nuova città,* (Matera, 1971); Group "Il Politecnico," *Rapporto su Matera. Una città meridionale fra sviluppo e sottosviluppo,* (Matera, 1971); M. Tafuri and A. Restucci, *Un contributo alla comprensione della vicenda storica dei Sassi* (Matera: Ministero dei Lavori Pubblici, 1974); A. Restucci, "Città e Mezzogiorno: Matera dagli anni '50 al concorso sui 'Sassi,'" in *Casabella,* no. 428 (1977): 36–43; idem "Gli intricati destini di Matera," in *Spazio e Società,* no. 4 (1978): 93ff.; the monographic issue of *Storia della città,* no. 6 (1978).

43. On Martella, see G. De Carlo, "A proposito di La Martella," in *Casabella,* no. 200 (1954); F. Gorio, "Il villagio La Martella, autocritica," ibid.; Tafuri, *Ludovico Quaroni,* 105–16; Quaroni, "L'expérience de la Martella."

44. See L. Piccinato, "Matera: i Sassi, i nuovi borghi e il piano regolatore," in *Urbanistica,* nos. 15–16 (1955). On the projects for Matera's new complexes, which in their own way adhered to the neorealist line, see L. Quaroni, "I concorsi nazionali per il quartiere Piccianello a Matera e per il Borgo di Torre Spagnola," in *L'architettura— cronache e storia,* no. 2 (1955). The complex of Spine Bianche, executed in 1954–57 by Aymonino, Chiarini, Girelli, Lenci, and M. Ottolenghi, represented an attempt to rationalize a populist vocabulary, which would have consequences for Aymonino's work: along with other

contemporary works of the "Roman school," it was the sign of a style that was broadly diffused in the fifties. See also Conforti, *Carlo Aymonino,* 19–22.

45. On the theme of the Roman "palazzina," see I. Insolera, "Lo spazio sociale della periferia romana," in *Centro sociale,* nos. 30–31(1959–60): 33–34; idem, *Roma moderna,* 98–99; P. Portoghesi, "Palazzina romana," in *Casabella,* no. 407 (1975).

46. On the work of Ugo Luccichenti, which exemplified an entire era of Roman professionalism, see M. Manieri-Elia, *Ugo Luccichenti architetto,* (Rome, 1980).

47. On Moretti, see G. Ungaretti, *50 immagini di architettura di Luigi Moretti* (Rome, 1968); R. Bonelli, *Moretti* (Rome, 1975). It is no coincidence that Moretti's work is today being reevaluated in the United States by more intellectual minds oriented toward Europe. See T. Stevens, "Introduction" to L. Moretti, "The Values of Profiles" and "Structures and Sequences of Spaces," in *Oppositions,* no. 4 (1974): 110–111 (with a translation of the two texts by Moretti on molding and spatial structure originally published in *Spazio,* no. 6 (1951–52), and no. 7 (1952–53).

48. See G. C. Argan, *Gardella,* (Milan, 1956), reprinted in *Progetto e destino,* 353–73, and A. Samonà, *Ignazio Gardella e il professionismo italiano* (Rome, 1981). On Samonà's work in the 1940s and 1950s see G. Ciucci, "La ricerca impaziente:

1945–1960," in the collection, *Giuseppe Samonà. Cinquant'anni di architetture*, 2nd ed. (Rome, 1980), 57ff.

49. On the INA building in Parma, see E. Gentili, "La sede dell'Ina a Parma," in *Casabella*, no. 200 (1954), and Gio Ponti, "Lezione di una architettura," in *Domus*, no. 266 (1952). On Albini's work in general, see E. Gentili, "Franco Albini," in *Comunità*, no. 28 (1954); G. Samonà, "Franco Albini e la cultura architettonica in Italia," in *Zodiac*, no. 3 (1958): 83–115; V. Viganò, "Franco Albini. Trente ans d'architecture italienne," in *Aujourd'hui*, no. 13 (1961); F. Menna, "Albini o l'architettura della memoria," in *La regola e il caso* (Rome, 1970); M. Fagiolo, "L'astrattismo magico di Albini," in *Ottagono*, no. 37 (1975): 20–53; "Testimonianza su Franco Albini," ed. F. Helg, in *L'architettura—cronache e storia*, no. 288 (1979): 551ff.; the collection, *Franco Albini. Architettura e design 1930–1970* (Florence, 1979), with a complete bibliography.

50. The bibliography on the work of Michelucci is vast. Considering only postwar works of a general nature, let us mention E. Detti, "Giovanni Michelucci," in *Comunità*, no. 23 (1954): 38–42; L. Ricci, "L'uomo Michelucci, dalla casa Valiani alla chiesa dell'autostrada," in *L'architettura—cronache e storia*, no. 76 (1962): 664–89; *Giovanni Michelucci*, ed. Franco Borsi (Florence, 1966); L. Lugli, *Giovanni Michelucci. Il pensiero e le opere*,

with an introduction by Fernando Clemente and a selection of writings (Florence, 1966); M. Cerasi, *Michelucci* (Rome, 1968); König, *Architettura in Toscana; Quaderni dell'Istituto di Elementi di Architettura*, no. 2 (Genoa: Facoltà di Architettura, 1969); *Michelucci, il linguaggio dell'architettura*, ed. M. C. Buscioni (Rome, 1979), with texts by Michelucci, a register, and bibliography. In addition to the anthologies of Michelucci's writings cited, see G. Michelucci, *La nuova città*, ed. R. Risaloti (Pistoia, 1975). See also the collection, *La città di Michelucci*, an exhibition catalogue (Fiesole, 1976), and G. Michelucci, *Intervista sulla nuova città*, ed. F. Brunetti (Rome-Bari, 1981). A complete monograph on Michelucci is being written by Amedeo Belluzzi and Claudia Conforti.

51. In this connection it is interesting to look at the articles published by Michelucci in 1946 in *La nuova città*: "Architettura vivente," nos. 1–2: 4–8; "Architettura vivente. Della collaborazione," no. 3: 5–13; "Architettura vivente. Della città," nos. 4–5: 4–12; "La nuova città?", no. 8: 1–4; "Troppa arte," nos. 9–10: 5–9.

52. Idem, "Come ho progettato la chiesa della Vergine," in *L'architettura—cronache e storia*, no. 16 (1957): 709–13, and L. Lugli, "La chiesa della Vergine (SS. Maria e Tecla) a Pistoia nel quadro della tradizione creativa di Giovanni Michelucci," ibid.: 704ff.

53. See G. Michelucci, "Considerazioni sull'architettura. La nuova sede della Cassa di Risparmio di Firenze," in *Il Ponte*, no. 11 (1957): 1663–73, and L. Lugli, "La Cassa di Risparmio a Firenze," in *L'architettura—cronache e storia*, no. 31 (1958): 8–16.

54. See F. Dal Co, *Abitare nel moderno* (Rome-Bari, 1982), and *Teorie del moderno. Architettura Germania 1880–1920* (Rome-Bari, 1982).

55. See G. Samonà, "Premesse alla nuova urbanistica," in *Accademia*, no. 1 (1945): 35–38, in which the project for the Lavinaio quarter was published, and Ciucci, "La ricerca impaziente," 59–60.

56. See *Casabella*, no. 216 (1957): 16–35, and R. Bonelli, "Edilizia economica: politica dei quartieri," in *Comunità*, no. 70 (1959): 52–54, for a primarily negative critique.

57. See G. Astengo, "Falchera," in *Metron*, nos. 53–54 (1954): 13–63.

58. Regarding these two complexes, see E. Gentili, "Unità residenziale 'Villa Bernabò Brea' a Genova," in *Casabella*, no. 204 (1955): 49ff; M. Zanuso, "Unità d'abitazione orizzontale nel quartiere Tuscolano a Roma," ibid., no. 207: 30; A. Libera, "Il quartiere Tuscolano a Roma," in *Comunità*, no. 31 (1955): 46–49.

Chapter 2

1. See the articles already cited by A. Restucci; Tafuri, *Ludovico Quaroni*, 116ff.; R. Olivetti, "La Società Olivetti nel Canavese," *Urbanistica*, no. 33 (1961); E. N. Rogers, "L'unità di Adriano Olivetti," *Casabella*, no. 270 (1962): 1–9; G. Ciucci, "Ivrea ou la communauté des clercs," *L'architecture d'aujourd'hui*, no. 18 (1976): 7–12; Berta, *Le idee al potere*.

2. On the work of Figini and Pollini, see E. Gentili Tedeschi, *Figini e Pollini* (Milan,1959); C. Blasi, *Figini e Pollini* (Milan, 1963); J. Rykwert, "Figini and Polini," *Architectural Design*, no. 7 (1967): 369–78; *Luigi Figini e Gino Pollini/ architetti*, ed. Vittorio Savi (Milan, 1980), with the preceding bibliography. On the two architects at Ivrea, see also Ciucci, "Ivrea ou la communauté des clercs," and L. Quaroni, "Due opere di Luigi Figini e Gino Pollini," *L'architettura—cronache e storia*, no. 48 (1959): 390ff.

3. See Tafuri, *Ludovico Quaroni*, 150–151.

4. See G. Accasto, "L'asilo di Canton Vesco," *Controspazio*, no. 3 (1974): 51–52.

5. On Adriano Olivetti's program, see Aldo Garosci's testimony in *Ricordo di Adriano Olivetti* (Milan, 1960), and Restucci, "Un rêve américain." On Cosenza's factory and residential quarter, see M. Labò, "Lo stabilimento e il quartiere Olivetti a Pozzuoli dell'ing. L. Cosenza," *Casabella*, no. 206 (1955);

R. Guiducci, "Appunti dal giornale del direttore dei lavori," ibid.; and Ciucci, "Ivrea ou la communauté des clercs," 12.

6. P. Fossati, "Les transformations de l'image du produit," *L'architecture d'aujourd'hui*, no. 188 (1976): 50.

7. B. Huet, "Des magasins pour ne rien vendre," ibid.: 54.

8. Note that the Olivetti branch in Barcelona of 1959–62 was entrusted to the BPR, who took the opportunity to create a building that had its own symbolic presence, whereas for the industrial buildings in Argentina (Buenos Aires, 1954–62) and in Brazil (São Paolo, 1954–59) the firm relied on Marco Zanuso's certain competence. Zanuso and Edoardo Vittoria later on also took charge of Olivetti's shops in Marcianise in 1969 and Crema in 1970. See M. Zanuso, "Les machines à travailler," ibid.: 66.

9. Only six of the twelve programmatic publications have been published by the technical group for the urbanistic coordination of the Canavese. On the plan for Ivrea see N. Renacco, "Il piano regolatore generale di Ivrea," *Urbanistica*, nos. 15–16 (1955); Olivetti, "La Società Olivetti;" C. Doglio, "Il piano della vita," *Comunità*, no. 109 (1963); Tafuri, *Ludovico Quaroni*, 116ff.

10. It was produced by La Meridiana Film. Three short films were by G. De Carlo, C. Doglio, M. Gandin, M. L. Pedroni, L. Quaroni, and E. Vittorini.

11. G. De Carlo, "Intenzioni e risultati della mostra di urbanistica," *Casabella*, no. 203 (1954): 24.

Chapter 3

1. See Fabbri, *Le ideologie degli urbanisti nel dopoguerra*, 64ff., and M. Allione, "L'esperienza italiana di pianificazione," in "Atti del Seminario sulla programmazione economica e l'assetto territoriale," *Quaderni dell'Istituto di Architettura e Urbanistica* (Bologna: Facoltà di Ingegneria,1968).

2. For Quaroni's housing quarter, see R. Bonelli, "Quartiere residenziale di S. Giusto presso Prato," *L'architettura—cronache e storia*, no. 3 (1958), and Tafuri, *Ludovico Quaroni*, 152–54. See as well, L. Quaroni, "Politica del quartiere," *La casa*, no. 4. (1957). Note that this self-critical essay is contemporaneous with another, "Il paese dei barocchi."

3. See Quaroni., "Due chiese per Genova," *Architettura cantiere*, no. 15 (1957); E. N. Rogers, "Architetti laici per le chiese," *Casabella*, no. 238 (1960); Tafuri, *Ludovico Quaroni*, 138–142.

4. See F. Gorio, "Idee in margine a via Cavedone," *Casabella*, no. 267 (1962): 24ff., reprinted in *Il mestiere di architetto*, 59ff., and M. Vittorini, "Produttività edilizia nello studio del progetto," *Casabella*, no. 267 (1962). For Benevolo's attitude, see Benevolo, "L'architettura dell'Ina-Casa."

5. See H. Selem, "Opere dell'architetto Luigi Carlo Daneri: 1931–1960," *L'architettura—cronache e storia*, no. 56 (1960), in which, in addition to the Villa Bernabò and Forte di Quezzi quarters, Daneri's other major works are published, and their continuity with prewar works is demonstrated. Among these, the most remarkable for their formal rigor are the terraced houses on the hill of Quinto of 1952, the condominium complex on the Lido of 1952, the La Foce complex of 1934 58, and the Palazzo Fassio—all of them in Genoa.

Chapter 4

1. Having already appropriated in 1949 the themes John Dewey had expressed in *Art as Experience*, Argan indicated that the path to take was one that would lead to museums and the world of production. See G. C. Argan, "Il museo come scuola," *Comunità*, no. 3 (1949). See, on the same subject, Bonfanti-Porta, *Città, museo e architettura*, 150ff. See also, A. Piva, *La fabbrica di cultura. La questione dei musei in Italia dal 1945 ad oggi* (Milan, 1978).

2. See G. C. Argan, "La Galleria di Palazzo Bianco a Genova," *Metron*, no. 45: 25ff.; C. Marcenaro, "The Museum Concept and the Restoration of the Palazzo Bianco, Genova," *Museum*, no. 4 (1954).

3. M. Labò, "Il Museo del Tesoro di San Lorenzo in Genova," *Casabella*,

no. 213 (1956):6; G. C. Argan, "Il Museo del Tesoro di S. Lorenzo a Genova," *L'architettura—cronache e storia*, no. 14 (1956): 557ff.; P. A. Chessa, "Il Museo del Tesoro di S. Lorenzo," *Comunità*, no. 47 (1957); B. Zevi, "Museo di S. Lorenzo a Genova. Quattro tholos moderne per un tesoro antico," *Cronache di architettura* vol. 2, no. 109 (Bari, 1971); *Franco Albini, architettura per un museo* (Rome, 1980).

4. See Fagiolo, *L'astrattismo magico di Albini*, 52.

5. See F. Calandra, "Uffici comunali a Genova," *L'architettura—cronache e storia* no. 11 (1956); R. Viviani and G. K. König, "Gli uffici comunali di Genova di Franco Albini," *Comunità*, no. 64 (1958). One of Albini's small masterpieces of composition was realized in Genoa by his assistant Cambiaso in 1955–61, while the competition project done in collaboration with Mario Labò for the Genovese Palazzo dell'Arte in 1957 seemed more mannered.

6. See G. Mariacher, "Il nuovo allestimento del Museo Correr," *Comunità*, no. 21 (1953):62ff., which underscores the provocative character of Scarpa and G. Mazzariol's composition, and "Opere di Carlo Scarpa," in *L'architettura—cronache e storia*, no. 3 (1955): 340ff., which reproached Scarpa for his excessive refinement at the Correr.

7. Among the articles favoring the BPR's work at Castello are M. Labò, "A favore del Museo,"

L'architettura—cronache e storia, no. 33 (1958): 154, and G. Samonà, "Un contributo alla museografia," *Casabella*, no. 211 (1956): 51–53. More critical is the article by R. Pane, "Riserve sul Museo," *L'architettura—cronache e storia* no. 33 (1958): 162–63, and the violently polemical A. Cederna, "Il regista invadente," *Il Mondo*, 9 October 1956. See, for the designers' intentions, Belgiojoso, Peressutti, and Rogers, "Carattere stilistico del Museo del Castello," *Casabella*, 63ff. See also the astute criticism by Bonfanti-Porta, *Città, museo e architettura*, op. cit., pp. 150 ff.

8. E. N. Rogers, "Le preesistenze ambientali e i temi pratici contemporanei," *Casabella*, no. 204 (1954), reprinted in *Esperienza dell'architettura*, 304ff.; idem, "Il problema del costruire nelle preesistenze ambientali," a report given to the Comitato nazionale di studi dell'Inu, March 1957, ibid.

9. Regarding the Torre Velasca, see G. Samonà, "Il grattacielo piú discusso d'Europa, la Torre Velasca," *L'architettura—cronache e storia*, no. 40 (1959): 659–74; P. C. Santini, "Deux gratte-ciel à Milan," *Zodiac*, no. 1 (1957): 200–5; G. M. Kallmann, "Modern Tower in Old Milan," *Architectural Forum*, no. 2 (1958): 109–11; R. Gardner-Medwin, "A Flight from Functionalism," *The Journal of the Riba*, no. 12 (1958): 408–14; *CIAM '59 in Otterlo*, ed. O. Newman (Stuttgart, 1961), 92–97, for Rogers' presentation of the tower at Otterlo and the controversy it caused;

Bonfanti-Porta, *Città, museo e architettura*, pp. 156ff. On the work of the BPR, also see L. Belgiojoso, *Intervista sul mestiere d'architetto*, ed. C. De Seta (Rome-Bari, 1978).

10. One should mention here the Italian pavilion at the Brussels Expo in 1958, for which the BPR collaborated with Quaroni, A. De Carlo, Gardella, and Perugini: in it the theme of the "village" was rationalized in an interpretation that was both controversial and critical regarding the elements of the International Style popular in Brussels at the time. The work was important because it signaled a moment of convergence among Italian architects, just before their different avenues of research diverged irrevocably. On the Brussels pavilion, see "Inchiesta sul Padiglione italiano a Bruxelles," *L'architettura—cronache e storia*, no. 36 (1958): 399ff.; R. Pedio, "La crisi del linguaggio moderno all'Esposizione Universale di Bruxelles," ibid.: 384–95; B. Zevi, "Successo dell'ultimo minuto," *L'Espresso*, 1 June 1958; Tafuri, *Ludovico Quaroni*, 154–58.

11. Rogers' devotion to Scotellaro is clear in his editorial, "Le responsabilità verso la tradizione," *Casabella*, no. 202 (1954): 2–3. There he states that it is a "duty" to weld popular (spontaneous) culture and the culture of the elite together in a single tradition: only then can authenticity and critical capacity be fused. The article was crucial in that it explained *tendenze* already alive in Italian architecture by

giving them theoretical foundations, and indicated the ways in which northern culture experienced populist afflatus. Within such a perspective—populism guaranteeing authenticity for a language intent on critical interpretation—works like those of Gardella, the BPR, and G. De Carlo of the fifties became more comprehensible.

12. See G. Samonà, "Una casa di Gardella a Venezia," *Casabella*, no. 220 (1958): 7; G. Mazzariol, "Umanesimo di Gardella," *Zodiac*, no. 2 (1958): 91–110; R. Pedio, "Due nuove opere di Ignazio Gardella," *L'architettura—cronache e storia*, no. 29 (1958): 729–41.

13. Argan, *Progetto e destino*, 370.

14. E. N. Rogers, "Continuità o crisi," *Casabella*, no. 215 (1957). In the same issue, along with a letter to Gregotti accompanying the drawings and photograph of the Bottega d'Erasmo (R. Gabetti and A. Isola, "L'impegno della tradizione"), there appeared V. Greggoti's article in response, "L'impegno della tradizione." Gabetti and Isola responded with a letter to the editor (*Casabella*, no. 217, 1957), which Rogers answered in the same review. His response ("Risposte ai giovani") proposed a "modesty vigil" and "a clear delimitation of our acts," though he kept his distance from the champions of "modernistic formalism." All these texts have been reprinted in *Controspazio*, nos. 4–5 (1977): 84ff., along with the articles by C. D'Amato, "La 'ritirata'

italiana dal Movimento Moderno: memoria, storia e questioni di stile nell'esperienza del neoliberty:" 50–51, and by F. Cellini, "La polemica sul neoliberty:" 52–53. For the work of the Turinese group, until 1971, see *Gabetti, Isola, Raineri* (Chiasso, 1971).

15. In this connection, the article by M. Bellini, R. Orefice, and L. Zanon Dal Bo is still interesting: "I baroni rampanti del movimento moderno. 3 generazioni di architetti nel dopoguerra italiano," *Superfici*, n.s. (1960): 23–30; also ibid., no. 1 (1961): 7–9. Both the article and the review wavered between Adorno's thought, phenomenology, and progressive Catholicism; they were signs of the new climate influencing young Milanese designers, as well as of an impatient attitude toward the clique at *Casabella*. It is, however, interesting that this essay speaks of the "tonality of usurpation" and "inimitable *perfidy*" of the recent experiments in Milan, Novara, and Turin.

16. E. N. Rogers, "Ortodossia dell'eterodossia," *Casabella* no. 216 (1957): 2ff.

17. See A. Rossi, "Il passato e il presente della nuova architettura," ibid., no. 219 (1958), with illustrations of the house in Superga by Giorgio Raineri, the residence with stables in Milan by Gae Aulenti, and the duplex houses in Cameri by Gregotti, Meneghetti, and Stoppino.

18. See E. N. Rogers, *Auguste Perret* (Milan, 1955), and V. Gregotti,

"Classicità e razionalismo di Auguste Perret," *Casabella*, no. 229 (1959): 6–11.

19. It should be noted, however, that a first reading of Muzio's contribution is to be found in Canella-Rossi's essay, "Architetti italiani: Mario Ridolfi." Muzio's postwar production never again attained the results he had obtained in the twenties and thirties: the master who had executed the *Ca' brüta* outlived himself in the Basilica dell'Annunciazione in Nazareth (1959–69) and in the Albergo Casa Nova in Betleme of 1980. But the building for the Banca Commerciale on Via Borgonuovo in Milan of 1959–69 represents a singular exploit. In the addition on the Via dei Giardini, a light metallic structure, superimposed on the stone facade, is modulated by solutions that invert Ridolfi's motifs. See *Giovanni Muzio, opere e scritti*, ed. G. Gambirasio and B. Minardi (Milan, 1982). One of Muzio's most interesting postwar works is "Ricostruzione e architettura" (inaugural lecture given 5 November 1947 at the Politecnico of Turin), reprinted in *Giovanni Muzio*, 261–81.

20. R. Banham, "Neoliberty: The Retreat from Modern Architecture," *The Architectural Review*, no. 747 (1959). Rogers rose up against Banham with his editorial "L'evoluzione dell'architettura, riposta al custode dei frigidaires," *Casabella*, no. 228 (1959), while Zevi commented several times on the work of the new northern sphere. See Zevi's editorial "L'andropausa degli architetti moderni italiani," *L'architettura—cronache e storia*, no. 46 (1959), and his "Torniamo al Liberty," *L'Espresso*, 24 May 1959. Responses to Banham also came from Portoghesi in *Comunità*, no. 72 (1959), and from the younger writers of the review *Superfici*. See M. Bellini, R. Orefice, and L. Zanon Dal Bo, "Cavalieri, libertini e Frères Maçons sulla scena milanese," ibid., no. 1 (1961): 39–40; R. Orefice, "Parabola di intermezzo su Cavalieri e Baroni," ibid.: 40–41; idem, "Trucchi e galateo di un 'Aufklärung' milanese," ibid.: 41–46. The three articles cited were gathered under a single, significant title: *Un inquisitore da passegio*. See also, on the neoliberty phenomenon, the debate published in *Casabella*, no. 318 (1967).

21. See *Nuovi disegni per il mobile italiano*, an exhibition catalogue, (Milan, 1960), with articles by Gregotti, Rossi, Gabetti, Isola, and Canella. The most significant is by G. Canella, "La prova del nove," defending the power to "browse in the poetic world of the *novecentisti*" and observing that the "fathers" who criticized atheism had themselves followed the path of representation, in this only "overtaken" by "amorous, grateful, and sympathetic sons."

22. Portoghesi, "Dal neorealismo al neoliberty." See also, idem, "L'impegno delle nuove generazioni," in *Aspetti dell'arte contempora-*

nea, catalogo della mostra (Rome: L'Aquila, 1963). A response to Portoghesi's 1958 article was C. Melograni, "Dal neoliberty al neopiacentinismo?" *Il Contemporaneo*, no. 13 (1959). See also F. Tentori, "D'où venons nous? qui sommes nous, où allons nous?" *Aspetti dell'arte contemporanea*.

23. See P. Portoghesi, "Architettura e ambiente tecnico," *Zodiac*, no. 7 (1960).

24. See P. Portoghesi's autobiographical volume, *Le inibizioni dell'architettura moderna* (Rome-Bari, 1979). Portoghesi's architecture, which explored geometric modulations in various combinations, aimed at a semantics of redundancy reaching its peak in his Casa Papanice in Rome of 1964–67, his Chiesa della Sacra Famiglia in Salerno of 1968–73 (figure 52), and his library and cultural center in Avezzano of 1970. It was finally wedded to kitsch in his project for the Mosque and Islamic Center in Rome of 1977. Portoghesi collaborated with Vittorio Gigliotti for all of these works except the mosque, where he worked with Sami Mousawi. Portoghesi's work is neobaroque insofar as it expresses a taste for excess devoid of tension. But the presence of vortexes in his architecture marks the remains of vaunted historicism, and is resolved in a controlled and captivating labyrinth of signs that are reified despite themselves. Portoghesi's works have been gathered in a volume by C. Norberg-Schulz that contains many

careless echoes of Heidegger, *Alla ricerca dell'architettura perduta. Le opere di Paolo Portoghesi e Vittorio Gigliotti, 1959–1975* (Rome, 1975), and in the catalogue *Paolo Portoghesi. Progetti e disegni 1962–1979* (Florence, 1979).

25. See S. Muratori, *Architettura e civiltà in crisi* (Rome, 1963).

26. See S. Muratori, *Studi per un'operante storia urbana di Venezia* (Rome, 1960); S. Muratori, R. and S. Bollati, and G. Marinucci, *Studi per un'operante storia urbana di Roma* (Rome, 1963); S. Muratori, *Civiltà e territorio* (Rome, 1967). See also the bibliographical appendix and the projects of Muratori's school: the monument to the Trinità dei Pellegrini in Rome by Gianfranco Caniggia and the projects by Caniggia and the Bollati group for the new offices of the Chamber of Deputies in Rome. For the latter, see M. Tafuri, *Il concorso per i nuovi uffici della Camera dei Deputati* (Venice, 1968), 69–72. Muratori's analytic method has been explored in G. Caniggia's, *Lettura di una città: Como* (Rome, 1963) and *Strutture dello spazio antropico* (Florence, 1976). See also G. Caniggia and G. L. Maffei, *Composizione architettonica e tipologia edilizia*, vol. 1 (Venice, 1979). On Caniggia's later work, see the second part of this volume. Compared to Muratori's work, that of Luigi Vagnetti, which was for some time tangential to his, reveals less depth. First, Vagnetti executed near Foschini in Livorno the Palazzo Grande of 1949, which Reyner Banham would define as

"Italian Eclectic" (*Architectural Review*, October 1952). As Muratori's assistant when he moved from Venice to the chair of Architectural Composition in Rome in 1954, Vagnetti realized works of faint *ambientismo*, like his new center for the Banca d'Italia in Cremoni of 1954 and Casa della Sposa in Rome of 1959.

27. See *I piano regionali. Criteri di indirizzo per lo studio dei piani territoriali di coordinamento in Italia* (Rome: Ministero dei lavori pubblici, 1952), and *La pianificazione regionale* (Venice: INU, 1952). See also Fabbri, *Le ideologie degli urbanisti nel dopoguerra*, 55ff.

28. The history of the master plan for Rome has been charted in great detail in *Urbanistica*, nos. 28–29 (1959), especially in the following essays: L. Benevolo, "Le discussioni e gli studi preparatori al nuovo Piano Regolatore"; L. Piccinato, "L'esperienza del Piano di Roma"; M. Valori, "Fare del proprio peggio." In addition, see L. Benevolo, "Osservazioni sui lavori per il P. R. G. di Roma," *Casabella*, no. 210 (1958), and Insolera, "Roma moderna." An anthology of reports given by the communist group to the communal council can be found in P. Della Seta, C. Melograni, and A. Natoli, *Il piano regolatore di Roma* (Rome, 1963). Regarding events that occurred between 1959 and 1963, see *Urbanistica*, no. 40 (1964), especially the following articles: M. Coppa, "La lunga strada per il piano di Roma;" I. Insolera and M. Manieri-Elia, "Tre anni di cronaca romana;" by

M. Girelli, "Il piano per l'attuazione della 167 a Roma."

29. The CET was formed by E. Lenti, R. Marino, L. Piccinato, V. Monaco, L. Quaroni, S. Muratori, G. Nicolosi, and E. Del Debbio.

30. In *Urbanistica,* no. 27 (1959). Reprinted in L. Quaroni, *Immagine di Roma* (Bari, 1969).

31. See I. Insolera, "Il concorso per la Biblioteca Nazionale di Roma," *Casabella,* no. 239 (1960):35-36; T. Giura Longo, "Una biblioteca per Roma," *Il Contemporaneo,* no. 23 (1960); B. Zevi, "Biblioteca Nazionale a Roma. Tutti hanno superato tutto," *L'Espresso,* 6 March 1960, reprinted in *Cronache di architettura*, vol. 3, no. 304: 486–89.

32. See V. Gregotti, "La nuova sede dell'Inail a Venezia," *Casabella,* no. 244 (1960): 4–13.

33. See Conforti, *Carlo Aymonino*, 30ff.

34. See R. Pedio, "'Brutalismo' in forma di libertà: il nuovo Istituto Marchiondi a Milano," *L'architettura—cronache e storia,* no. 40 (1959), and *The Architectural Review*, no. 771 (1961): 304ff. A brief profile of Viganò can be found in P. C. Santini, "Incontro con i protagonisti: Vittoriano Viganò," *Ottagono,* no. 39 (1975): 72–77.

35. See P.L. Santini, "L'architettura 'milanese' di Caccia-Dominioni," *Ottagono,* no. 6 (1967): 91–94.

36. Regarding Zanuso's work before 1957 see V. Gregotti, "Marco Zanuso un architetto della seconda generazione," *Casabella,* no. 216

(1957): 59ff., and R. Guiducci, "Appunti sulla fabbrica di São Paolo in Brasile," ibid.: 66ff., which analyzes one of the most remarkable projects by Zanuso for Olivetti. On Mangiarotti, see E. D. Bona, *Angelo Mangiarotti: il processo del costruire* (Milan, 1980), which gives a broad survey of his works, from the Chiesa di Baranzate of 1957 to the Snaidero restaurant in Majano of 1978.

37. See J. Rykwert, "The Work of Gino Valle," *Architectural Design*, no. 3 (1964):112ff.; F. Dal Co, "Gino Valle, la necessità dell'architettura," *Lotus*, no. 11 (1976): 172ff.; *Gino Valle architetto, 1950–1978* (Milan, 1979), with bibliography.

38. Libera's postwar work remained consistent with premises traced in the years preceding the war and was marked by a tendency toward "magical abstraction": for example, the Airone cinema in Rome, the competition project for the Christian-Democrat offices in EUR, and the Palazzo della Regione in Trento, designed in collaboration with Sergio Musmeci. Libera's purism preserved, however, something outdated, balanced between detached refinement and excessive simplicity. Not coincidentally, Libera and De Renzi remained in the 1950s among the Roman masters least heeded by the new generation; only recently has their work attracted interest. On Libera's work see "Adalberto Libera (1903–1963)," ed. A. Alieri,

M. Clerici, F. Palpacelli, and G. Vaccaro, in *Architettura—cronache e storia*, nos. 123–26 and 128–33 (1966); G. C. Argan, *Libera* (Rome, 1975); V. Quilici, *Adalberto Libera. L'architettura come ideale* (Rome, 1981).

39. The role played by Pier Luigi Nervi in Italian architectural culture is only partially included in the historical outline given here. Analysis of his structuralism should take into account the modes of production conditioned by the concrete and steel monopolies, and the connections between the technological exhibition of "exceptions" in public services and the political use of technological backwardness and mass housing. However, one should stress Nervi's inventiveness in his large structures: his technological intuition prevailed over any pretense of objectivity. His salons in the Palazzo delle Esposizioni of Turin of 1948–50, the Lanificio Gatti in Rome of 1951–53, the elevated Via Olimpica of 1959, and the Palazzo del Lavoro in Turin of 1960 (figure 66) brought "invention" to a static condition that remained mute in his collaborations with other architects, such as his Pirelli skyscraper, Palazzetto dello Sport of 1956–57, designed with Annibale Vitellozzi, and Palazzo dello Sport in EUR of 1958–59, designed with Piacentini. See, by P. L. Nervi, *Arte o scienza del costruire?* (Rome, 1954); idem, *Costruire correttamente* (Milan, 1955); idem, *Nuove strutture* (Milan, 1963). See

also, G. C. Argan, *P. L. Nervi* (Milan, 1955); J. Joedicke, *P. L. Nervi* (Milan, 1957); A. L. Huxtable, *P. L. Nervi* (New York, 1968; Milan, 1960); *Pier Luigi Nervi*, ed. P. Desideri, P. L. Nervi, Jr., and G. Positano (Bologna, 1980). Italian structuralism has furthermore, in the works of Riccardo Morandi, offered a contribution of exceptional interest (figure 67), particularly in application of precompressed concrete, which, in works like the garages and cinemas of Rome, the hangars in Fiumicino, and especially the series of bridges and overpasses, reached notable levels of formal suggestiveness. See G. Boaga and B. Goni, *Riccardo Morandi* (Milan, 1962); L. Vinca Masini *Riccardo Morandi* (Rome, 1974).

40. See M. Manieri-Elia, "Roma: Olimpiadi e miliardi," *Urbanistica*, no. 32 (1960): 105–19.

41. See SAU, *Una discussione sui problemi di architettura e di urbanistica* (Rome, 1960), which collects many pieces written by members of the association.

42. See B. Zevi, "La morte del Ciam e la nascita dell'Istituto Nazionale di Architettura," *L'architettura— cronache e storia*, no. 51 (1960); idem, "Prospettive In/Arch anno II," ibid., no. 58 (1960); idem, "Sul 'corporativismo' dell'In/Arch," ibid., no. 72 (1961).

43. The first project for Rome's Rinascente was published in *Casabella*, no. 233 (1959). Regarding E. N. Rogers's building, see "Un grande magazzino a Roma," *Casabella*, no. 257 (1961); P. Portoghesi, "La Rinascente in piazza Fiume a Roma," *L'architettura— cronache e storia*, no. 75 (1962): 602–18; B. Zevi, "La Rinascente romana di Albini," *Cronache di architettura*, vol. 4, no. 386; R. Banham, *The Architecture of the Well-Tempered Environment* (Chicago, 1969; London, 1969); F. Menna, "La Rinascente di piazza Fiume," *Palatino*, nos. 1–4 (1963), reprinted in *La regola e il caso*, 101–12.

44. See the texts from the round table held at the Lecce convention in *Urbanistica*, no. 32 (1960): 6–8.

45. See B. Zevi, "La figlia di Venezia," *L'Espresso*, 17 April 1960; idem, "Viatico alle psicopatie lagunari," *L'architettura—cronache e storia*, no. 57 (1960); L. Benevolo, "Un consuntivo delle recenti esperienze urbanistiche italiane," *Casabella*, no. 242 (1960); F. Tentori, "Un piano urbanistico per Mestre," *Il Contemporaneo*, nos. 27–28 (1960): 124–37. On Quaroni's project—his own report on it can be found in *L'architettura—cronache e storia*, no. 57 (1960)—see Tafuri, *Ludovico Quaroni*, 158–69. See also I. Insolera, "L'insegnamento delle città: la periferia di Venezia," *Comunità*, no. 83 (1960). The three projects presented by the Muratori group formed an alternative to the Quaroni group's project (figure 72). The two former collaborators now found themselves in conflict. Yet Muratori and Quaroni both called for interpretations of the urban

structure of Venice: Muratori for synchronic cuts, Quaroni for a diachronic synthesis. Tentori was one of the few who gave the Muratori group's project serious consideration: see "Un piano urbanistico per Mestre," 132ff.

46. See ILSES, *Nuova dimensione della città. La città-regione,* conference proceedings of the Stresa convention (Milan, 1962). A picture of urban culture was provided by the ninth national congress of the INU (Milan, 1962), especially in papers given by G. De Carlo and S. Lombardini. See G. De Carlo, "Proposte operative," *Urbanistica,* no. 38 (1963) (which also contains other papers) and *Casabella,* no. 270 (1962). See also L. Semerani, "Il IX Congresso Inu a Milano," ibid. Among commentaries on and reactions to the Stresa convention, see B. Zevi, "Neotecnico a posteriori o progetto dinamico?" *L'Espresso* (1961), reprinted in *Cronache di architettura,* vol. 4, no. 405: 363–65; F. Tentori, "Stasi e dinamica nel panorama italiano 1962," *Casabella,* no. 268 (1962); Portoghesi, "L'impegno delle nuove generazioni"; G. Piccinato, V. Quilici, and M. Tafuri, "La città-territorio, verso una nuova dimensione," *Casabella,* no. 270 (1962).

47. See *Casabella,* no. 232 (1963), with articles by S. Tintori, "Lo stato attuale degli studi," and by G. De Carlo, "Realtà e prospettive del primo schema;" idem, *La pianificazione territoriale urbanistica*

nell'area milanese (Padua, 1966); V. Vercelloni, "Dal piano del '53 al piano intercomunale," *Casabella,* nos. 451–52 (1979): 52–55.

48. See *La città territorio. Un esperimento didattico sul Centro direzionale di Centocelle in Roma,* ed. C. Aymonino (Bari, 1964), and F. Tentori's review in *Casabella,* no. 289 (1964). For the climate of those years, see A. Samonà, "Alla ricerca di un metodo per la nuova dimensione," *Casabella,* no. 277 (1963); idem, "Il dibattito architettonico-urbanistico oggi in Italia," *Comunità,* no. 115 (1963): 68ff; *Edilizia moderna,* nos. 82–83 (1964), entitled *Architettura italiana 1963;* and *Casabella,* nos. 289 and 291 (1964), dedicated to the *tendenze* of the new generation. The appeal to the head council of the INARCH (April 15, 1962) stands as testimony of the hope that characterized the early sixties, as do B. Zevi's two articles, "L'alienazione e la politica di centro-sinistra," *L'architettura—cronache e storia,* no. 81 (1962): 146–47, and "Gli architetti e la programmazione economica," ibid., no. 86 (1962): 505–7. On the theme of office districts, see also *Casabella,* no. 264 (1962), with the articles by A. Rossi, G. Amorosi, C. Aymonino, M. Tafuri, L. Calcagni, and C. Carozzi; and G. Canella, "Vecchie e nuove ipotesi per i Centri Direzionali," ibid., no. 275 (1963).

49. P. Ceccarelli, "Urbanistica opulenta," *Casabella,* no. 278: 5ff. The same issue contains the competition projects for the office

district of Turin.

50. See C. Aymonino and P. L. Giordani, *I centri direzionali* (Bari, 1967), and M. De Michelis and M. Venturi, "Il centro direzionale di Bologna: la gestione del problema urbano nel PCI," *Contropiano*, no. 3 (1968).

51. See R. Banham, *Megastructures. Urban futures of the recent past* (London, 1976).

52. See, in addition to the general bibliography given in chapter 1, note 50, the collection *La Chiesa dell'Autostrada del Sole* (Rome, 1964); P. Portoghesi, "La chiesa dell'Autostrade del Sole," *L'architettura—cronache e storia*, no. 101 (1964): 798–809; J. M. Fitch, "Church of the Autostrada," *Architectural Forum*, no. 1 (1964): 101–9; B. Zevi, "Un compromesso tra Medioevo e Wright," *L'Espresso*, 5 April 1964; *Chiesa e quartiere*, nos. 30–31 (1964), with articles by L. Figini, G. Trebbi, G. Gresleri, and G. Michelucci.

53. For Michelucci's last works, see the collection, *La chiesa di Longarone* (Florence, 1978), and *Michelucci, il linguaggio dell'architettura*.

54. See König, *Architettura in Toscana*.

55. See B. Zevi, "Michelangiolo in prosa," *L'architettura—cronache e storia*, no. 99 (1964): 651; P. Portoghesi, "Mostra critica delle opere michelangiolesche al Palazzo delle Esposizioni in Roma," ibid., no. 104 (1964): 90–91; R. Bonelli, "La mostra delle opere michelangiolesche," *Comunità*, no.

122 (1964): 22ff; the collection "Michelangelo Pop," *Marcatré*, nos. 6–7: 125ff. On the significance and limitations of "operative criticism," see M. Tafuri, *Teorie e storia dell'architettura*, 5th ed. (Rome-Bari, 1980), 161ff.

56. B. Zevi, "Architettura e comunicazione," *L'architettura—cronache e storia*, no. 122 (1965): 493, and R. Pedio, "Edificio per abitazioni, uffici e negozi in via Campania a Roma," ibid.: 496–522.

57. The five experts nominated in November 1961 were M. Fiorentino, P. M. Lugli, V. Passarelli, L. Piccinato, and M. Valori.

58. In the early 1960s G. Piccinato gave an interesting analysis of EUR in two articles, "Luci e ombre dell'Eur," *Superfici*, no. 6 (1963): 30–41, and "L'Eur: una struttura direzionale in una vecchia dimensione," *La città territorio*, 34–38.

59. See L. Moretti, "Nuovo quartiere Incis, nella zone Eur," *La Casa*, no. 7 (1962):109–22.

60. See M. Petrignani, "Le cento città d'Italia: Roma, 2: Gli edifici pubblici: la lunga attesa del compromesso," *Controspazio*, nos. 1–2 (1970): 27–33.

61. The studies and papers of the Asse studio were collected in *L'architettura—cronache e storia*, nos. 4–5 (1975), with essays by L. Quaroni, L. Passarelli, and G. Scimemi, and an "Itinerario cronologico urbanistico dal 1962 al 1975," by Edgardo Tonca, in

addition to technical and descriptive reports.

62. An historical synthesis of these events can be found in L. Bortolotti, *Storia della politica edilizia in Italia. Proprietà, imprese edili e lavori pubblici dal primo dopoguerra ad oggi (1919–1970)* (Rome, 1978). See also A. Acocella, *L'edilizia residenziale pubblica in Italia dal 1945 ad oggi* (Padua, 1980).

63. The Vigne Nuove quarter (zoning plan no. 7, IACP) of 1972–80, directed by Luci Passarelli with the help of Fausto and Vincenzo Passarelli, Alfredo Lambertucci, Paolo Cercato, Enrico Censon, Valerio Moretti, Emilio Labianca, and Claudio Saratti, was one of the most successful complexes of the "new Rome," even though it contained facile figurative solutions. One should also note the mannerist complex of Vigna Murata in Rome, by Gianfranco Moneta and collaborators, based on a primitive idea of the AUA studio. On the implementation of the "167" in Rome, see P. Samperi, "Il piano per l'attuazione della legge 167 a Roma," *Urbanistica*, no. 40 (1964); also see chapter 2, note 28. Also see "Il problema edilizio a Roma," *Parametro*, nos. 76–77 (1979): 16ff., and, in the same issue, the paper on the Laurentino quarter by Pietro Barucci, Alessandro De Rossi, Luciano Giovannini, Camillo Nucci, and Americo Sostegni, pp. 36ff.

64. Bonfanti-Porta, *Città, museo e architettura*, 177.

65. M. Tafuri, "Les 'muses inquiétantes', ou le destin d'une génération de 'Maîtres'," *L'architecture d'aujourd'hui*, no. 181 (1975): 14–33.

66. Gardella's works in the late sixties and seventies try to recover the grand scale of his "revisions" in the Olivetti refectory, in order to confront the languages of constructivism and surrealism. In this regard, even more significant than the buildings for the Kartell in Binasco of 1971–75, were the competition project for the new theater of Vicenza of 1968 (figure 86) and the technical offices of Alfa Romea in Arese of 1968–72 (figure 85) in which Gardella elegantly engaged a further pre-text, the language of geometric absolutism. The mastery of typological organization and the refinement of detail remain, along with the attention paid to memory, the "materials" employed by Gardella. He was also involved in a project for the restructuring of the ancient Genovese fabric, including a detailed plan for the new university buildings. See I. Gardella and S. Larini, "Genova: un progetto per la città antica," *Controspazio*, no. 2 (1974): 5ff.; P. C. Santini, "Incontri con i protagonisti: Ignazio Gardella," *Ottagono*, no. 46 (1977): 42–49; G. C. Argan, "Il teatro di Gardella. Un progetto monumentale per Vicenza," *Lotus*, no. 25 (1979): 92ff; "Gardella" (the text of a meeting held in 1976 at the Politecnico di Milano), *Hinterland*, nos. 13–14 (1980): 20ff.; P. Farina, "Il fascino del presente," in the

collection *La presenza del passata*, 50–57; Samonà, *Ignazio Gardella*.

67. See R. Pedio, "Edificio in piazza Meda a Milano," *L'architettura— cronache e storia*, no. 176 (1970): 76–85. Regarding the Milanese climate, see also V. Vercelloni, "L'autoritratto di una classa dirigente: Milano 1860–1970," *Controspazio*, nos. 2–3 (1969): 11–28.

68. See the pertinent commentary in P. Portoghesi's article, "Presenza di Ridolfi," *Controspazio*, no. 1 (1974): 6–8. Ridolfi maintained that a spiral column in the Temple of Solomon had inspired him for this project. It is interesting to compare Ridolfi's experiences in Terni with the fascinating history of that city, as narrated by several voices in A. Portelli, *Biografia di una città. Storia e racconto: Terni 1830–1985* (Turin, 1985).

69. The works that Ridolfi executed after his car accident in 1961, which provided him with an opportunity to withdraw to Terni, drew renewed attention from Italian critics. Thus began, albeit in a different way, the recuperation of this master. See V. Vercelloni, "L'occasione di una ricerca: l'ultimo lavoro di Mario Ridolfi," *Controspazio*, no. 1 (1969): 38–43 (Casa Lina alle Marmore); the monographic issues of *Controspazio* (1974); A. Anselmi, "Logos ed Eros," ibid., no. 3 (1977): 16 (see also the letter from Ridolfi, p. 2 of the same issue, and his project for the house in Norcia, pp. 3–15); *Le architetture di Ridolfi e Frankl*; Cellini-D'Amato, "Il mestiere di Ridolfi"; "Ridolfi" (text of a meeting held in February 1977 at the Politecnico di Milano), *Hinterland*, nos. 13–14 (1980): 30–35. See also G. Polin, "Nuovo palazzo per uffici del Comune di Terni," *Casabella* 47, no. 489 (1983): 48–61; N. Cosentino, "Casa Luccioni a Terni, 1977–79," *Controspazio* 14, special issue, nos. 1–2 (1983): 63–69; the essay by F. Cellini, "Su Mario Ridolfi. Geometria e costruzione della pianta centrale," and the one by C. D'Amato, "Il ciclo delle Marmore," *Lotus international*, no. 37 (1983): 15–24 and 25–33, both of which illustrate the new generation's way of reading the architecture of Ridolfi and Frankl. The obituary referred to in the text is that of L. Benevolo, "Ricordo di Mario Ridolfi," *Casabella* 48, no. 508 (1984): 30.

70. See Ciucci, "La ricerca impaziente."

71. On Costantino Dardi's work, see the volume *Semplice, lineare, complesso* (Rome, 1967). See also Dardi's essay, *Il gioco sapiente. Tendenze della nuova architettura* (Padua, 1971).

72. See M. Sacripanti, "Il Totalteatro," *I problemi di Ulisse*, July 1969: 32–34. For an evaluation of Sacripanti's theater in the context of contemporary theatrical poetics, see *Architettura e teatro*, a monographical issue of *Sipario*, no. 242 (1966), and M. Manieri-Elia, "Il teatro moderno," *Bolletino del Cisa Andrea Palladio* (1975): 379–89.

73. See *Casabella*, no. 290 (1964), which includes the following

articles: E. N. Rogers, "La Triennale uscita dal coma": 1; G. Dorfles, "La XIII Triennale": 2–17; G. U. Polesello, "Questa Triennale e l'architettura discoperta": 33–42; G. Canella, E. Mantero, and L. Semerani, "La Triennale dei giovani e 'L'ora della verità'": 45–56; F. Tentori, "Unità delle arti": 48–50.

74. Polesello, "Questa Triennale": 40–42.

75. The theme of the INU convention in Trieste was "City and terrritory in the functional and figurative aspects of continuous planning" ("Città e territorio negli aspetti funzionali e figurativi della pianificazione continua"). *Ediliza moderna*, nos. 87–88 (1966) was dedicated to the "shape of the countryside," with essays by V. Gregotti, P. Caruso, R. Orefice, P. L. Crosta, E. Battisti and S. Crotti, C. Norberg-Schulz, C. Guarda, D. Borradori, C. Pellegrini, V. Di Battista, S. Bisogni and A. Renna, and G. Piccinato. Many of the themes discussed there were later gathered in V. Gregotti's volume, *Il territorio dell'architettura* (Milan, 1966).

76. Semerani and Tamara's work includes very interesting projects, such as the Ospedale Generale of Trieste (figure 145), begun in 1965 by Luciano Semerani and Gigetta Tamaro, with Carlo and Luciano Celli and Dario Tognon (final project by Semerani and Tamaro), and the residential complex in the hills of Trieste of 1969–1970. See C. Aymonino, "Progetti dello studio Semerani-Tamaro 1965–1971," *Controspazio*, nos. 7–8 (1971): 18ff. See also, L. Semerani, *Progetti per una città* (Milan, 1980).

77. See G. K. König, "Montecitorio valle di lacrime," *Casabella*, no. 301 (1967); B. Zevi, "Dodici Parlamenti per una Repubblica," *L'Espresso*, no. 33 (1967): 29ff.; Tafuri, *Il concorso per i nuovi uffici della Camera dei Deputati*; L. Benevolo, "Una linea piú precisa nella ricerca architettonica," *Rinascita*, 26 April 1968.

78. See G. Chiari, "Il grattacielo Peugeot, architetto Maurizio Sacripanti," *L'architettura—cronache e storia*, no. 87 (1963): 602–7.

79. Among Sacripanti's most recent projects, note the new theater in Forlí (figure 95), which won the 1977 national competition: a changing object functioning as a hermetic forum for the city. See also the project for the secondary school in Sant'Arcangelo di Romagna, which finished third in the 1980 competition. See M. Tafuri, "Un teatro per Forlí," *Paese Sera/Arte*, 5 February 1978: 20, and R. Pedio, "Scuola a Sant'Arcangelo di Romagna, *L'architettura— cronache e storia*, no. 302 (1980), 678–89. Among Sacripanti's writings, see "Città di frontiera," *L'architettura—cronace e storia*, no. 187 (1971). See also M. Garimberti and G. Susani, *Sacripanti-architettura* (Venice, 1967).

80. See GRAU, "'Isti Mirant Stella'. Un progetto per il Concorso Nazionale per l'Archivio di Stato di Firenze," *Controspazio*, no. 2 (1974):

52–61.

81. A summary of Italian architecture competitions, including the one for the new offices of Parliament, can be found in V. De Feo's article, "Les concours d'Architecture. L'arme ultime de l'intellectuel?" *L'architecture d'aujourd'hui*, no. 181 (1975): 57–62.

Chapter 5

1. See P. Navone and B. Orlandoni, *Architettura radicale* (Segrate, 1974).

2. See V. De Feo, *Il piacere dell'architettura* (Rome, 1976).

3. An astute critique of the *Progetto 80* and of the political and economic projects of the 1970s in the essay by A. Asor Rosa, "La felicità e la politica," *Laboratorio politico*, no. 2 (1981): 5ff.

4. See E. Salzano, "Potere politico e tecno-struttura nella politica della casa," *Servizio sociale*, no. 3 (1972): 74–84.

5. The literature on construction and the problem of housing in Italy is vast and specialized. See F. Sullo, *Lo scandalo urbanistico* (Florence, 1964); A. Carrassi, "Casa e urbanistica, bilancio e prospettive," *Critica marxista*, no. 1 (1971); the collection *Lo spreco edilizio*, ed. F. Indovina (Padua, 1972); P. Cacciari and S. Potenza, *Il ciclo edilizio* (Rome, 1973); B. Secchi, "Il settore edilizio e fondiario in una prospettiva storica," *Archivio di studi urbani e regionali*, nos. 1–2 (1975); P. Ceri, *Casa, città e struttura*

sociale (Rome, 1975); R. Stefanelli, *La questione delle abitazioni in Italia* (Florence, 1976); *Il secondo ciclo edilizio*, ed. A. Barp (Milan, 1976); the collection *La situazione della casa in Italia* (Milan, 1976); Bortolotti, *Storia della politica edilizia in Italia*; Acocella, *L'edilizia residenziale pubblica*.

6. See B. Cillo, "L'uso capitalistico del territorio e la nuova città nolana," *Parametro*, nos. 12–13 (1972); and R. Pedio's interview with F. Di Salvo, "La 'città nolana' nell'area metropolitana di Napoli," *L'architettura—cronache e storia*, no. 190 (1971).

7. See M. De Michelis and A. Restucci, "Le Bâtiment: hypothèses sur la transformation de la commande," *L'architecture d'aujourd'hui*, no. 181 (1975): 7–10.

8. See S. Bracco, "Les coopératives et la destruction de logements en Italie," ibid.: 11–13.

Chapter 6

1. No satisfactory monograph or catalogue exists for Scarpa's designs, which are among the most singularly significant in the history of contemporary Italian architecture. One should at least consult, regarding Scarpa, Mazzariol, *Opere dell'architetto Carlo Scarpa*; F. Tentori, "Progetti di Carlo Scarpa," *Casabella*, no. 222 (1958): 9–14; C. C. Ragghianti, "La 'Crosera de Piazza' di Carlo Scarpa," *Zodiac*, no. 84 (1959): 128–50; S. Bettini, "L'architettura di Carlo Scarpa," ibid., no. 6 (1960): 140–87; M.

Bottero, "Carlo Scarpa il veneziano," *The Architectural Review*, no. 2 (1965); S. Los, *Carlo Scarpa architetto poeta* (Venice, 1967); M. Brusatin, "Carlo Scarpa architetto veneziano," *Controspazio*, nos. 3–4 (1972): 2–85; S. Cantacuzino, *Carlo Scarpa architetto poeta*, the catalogue for the RIBA exhibit (London, 1974); *Carlo Scarpa*, catalogue for the Vicenza exhibit (1974); the monographic issue of *SD*, no. 153 (Tokyo, 1977); the monographic issue of the review *Architecture, mouvement, continuité*, no. 50 (1979); P. Portoghesi, "In ricordo di Carlo Scarpa," *Controspazio*, no. 3 (1979): 1–5; the monographic issue of *Rassegna*, no. 7 (1981), ed. A. Rudi. See also the bibliographical appendix of this book.

2. See P. C. Santini, "Il nuovo negozio di Carlo Scarpa a Bologna," *Zodiac*, no. 10 (1962).

3. See G. Mazzariol, "Un'opera di Carlo Scarpa: il riordino di un antico palazzo veneziano," *Zodiac*, no. 13 (1964).

4. See L. Magagnato, "La nuova sistemazione del Museo di Castelvecchio," *Marmo*, no. 4 (1965); P. C. Santini, "Il restauro di Castelvecchio a Verona," *Comunità*, no. 126 (1965): 70–78.

5. See P. Bucarelli, "Mostra di Piet Mondrian a Roma," *L'architettura—cronache e storia*, no. 17 (1957).

6. See the volume by G. Samonà, *L'unità architettura urbanistica. Scritti e progetti 1929–1973*, ed. P. Lovero (Milan, 1975).

7. On Samonà's more recent activity, see P. Lovero, "Progetti dello studio Giuseppe e Alberto Samonà 1968–72," *Controspazio*, no. 2 (1973): 43-53; F. Dal Co, "Il gioco della memoria: 1961–1975," in the collection *Giuseppe Samonà*, 105ff.; Tafuri, "Les muses inquiétantes."

Chapter 7

1. See A. Quistelli, "Progetti dello studio Quaroni: dieci anni di esperienze didattiche e professionali," *Controspazio*, no. 2 (1973): 8ff. Quaroni gathered his recent reflections not only in *La città fisica*, but also in the two volumes, *La torre di Babele* (Padua, 1967) and *Progettare un edificio. Otto lezioni di architettura* (Milan, 1977). However, his most significant essay of the seventies remains "Le muse inquietanti: riflessioni su trenta anni di architettura in Italia," *Parametro*, nos. 64–65 (1978): 44–57, which constitutes, in its own way, a history of architecture from the Middle Ages to the present, a self-critical confession, a "memento" for subsequent generations, and a naive plan for the future.

2. On De Carlo's work, see the collection *Giancarlo de Carlo* (Milan, 1964); the monographic issue of *Forum*, no. 1 (1972); "G. De Carlo. La Réconciliation de l'architecture et de la politique," *L'architecture d'aujourd'hui*, no. 177 (1975): 32ff. (issue dedicated to Team X). On De Carlo's work as a member of Team X, see K. Frampton, "Les

62ff. Regarding the Urbino plan, see G. De Carlo, *Urbino* (Padua, 1970); on the Rimini plan, see *Parametro,* nos. 39–40 (1975). In addition, see F. Brunetti and F. Gesi, *Giancarlo De Carlo* (Florence, 1981) with bibliography. One should consult, besides De Carlo's volumes *Questioni di architettura e urbanistica,* 2nd ed. (Urbino, 1965) and *La piramide rovesciata* (Bari, 1968), his recent essay, "Corpo, memoria e fiasco," *Spazio e società,* no. 4 (1978): 3–16, as the most representative of his thinking. One should also note the course of the review *Spazio e società,* directed by De Carlo, which in 1978 began a series of unusually coherent publications. In 1977, G. Canella began to direct the review *Hinterland*; meanwhile *Controspazio,* directed by Portoghesi from 1969 on, began to publish less frequently.

3. See G. De Carlo, *An Architecture of Participation* (Melbourne, 1972) and "L'architettura della partecipazione," *L'architettura degli anni '70* (Milan, 1973).

4. See S. Bracco, "Un banco di prova nella conduzione della città," *Casabella,* no. 421 (1977): 13–16, and G. De Carlo, "Alla ricerca di un diverso modo di progettare," ibid.: 17–19.

5. Among Aymonino's many publications on this theme, at least see *La città di Padova,* ed. C. Aymonino (Rome, 1970); *Origini e sviluppo della città moderna* (Padua, 1971); *L'abitazione razionale. Atti dei congressi Ciam 1929–1930* (Padua,

1971); *Il significato delle città* (Bari, 1975); *Lo studio dei fenomeni urbani* (Rome, 1977).

6. Regarding this phase of Aymonino's career, see Conforti, *C. Aymonino,* 41ff.

7. See C. Dardi, "Abitazioni nel quartiere Gallaratese a Milano," *L'architettura—cronache e storia,* no. 226 (1974); "Monte Amiata Housing," *A + U,* no 7 (1974); C. Conforti, *Il Gallaratese di Aymonino e Rossi* (Rome, 1981).

8. See *1977: Un progetto per Firenze* (Rome, 1978); C. Conforti, "1977: un progetto per Firenze," *Casabella* (1979): p. 444, and the texts cited in chapter 10, note 8.

9. See C. Aymonino, "Materia e materiali," *Lotus,* no. 15 (1977), and *Campus scolastico a Persaro,* ed. F. Moschini (Rome, 1980). Also see F. Moschini, "Tra continuità e rottura. Due interventi di Carlo Aymonino," *L'industria delle construzioni* (November 1977).

10. Fiorentino collaborated in these projects with Gabriele De Giorgi, who was also his collaborator in the Asse studio: not coincidentally, these projects bear some resemblance to those of the Roman group Metamorph. In the group's projects—for the competitions for the AGIP motel of 1968 and for the universities of Florence and Cosenza—the "machinist picturesque" celebrated technique, invoking it as *daimon.* See C. Conforto, G. De Giorgi, A. Muntoni, and M. Pazzaglini, *Città come sistema di servizi* (Rome, 1976),

Notes   **231**

with an introduction by C. Dardi. On Fiorentino's work before 1970, see L. Quaroni, "Itinerario dell'architetto Mario Fiorentino, 1958–1970," *L'architettura—cronache e storia*, no. 182 (1970). See also V. Gregotti, "Un ricordo. Mario Fiorentino 1918–1982," *Casabella*, no. 489 (1983): 31. Two essays that analyze Corviale, Vigne Nuove, and other complexes in the new Roman suburbs in the context of contemporary building policies are V. Fraticelli's "I piani di zona: 1964–1978," *Casabella*, no. 438 (1978): 22–24, and G. Rebecchini's "La progettazione dei piani di zona," ibid.: 25ff., which presents astute criticism.

11. See V. Gregotti, "Quartiere Zen a Palermo," *Lotus*, no. 9 (1975). On Gregotti's recent work, see M. Scolari, "Tre progetti di Vittorio Gregotti," *Controspazio*, no. 3 (1971): 2–6; O. Bohigas, "Vittorio Gregotti," *Once Arquitectos* (Barcelona, 1976), 67–82; the monographical issue of *A + U*, no. 77 (1978); M. Tafuri, "Le avventure dell'oggetto: architetture e progetti di Vittorio Gregotti," and E. Battisti, "Architettura come problema," both in *Il progetto per l'Università della Calabria e altre architetture di Vittorio Gregotti* (Milan, 1979). Among Gregotti's theoretical writings, let us mention "Avanguardia come professione" (written with Oriol Bohigas and Gae Aulenti), *Lotus*, no. 25 (1980). But one should also see the editorials that Gregotti wrote for *Casabella* from 1982 on: they form,

for the most part, a coherent corpus of reflections on the present state and future prospects of the discipline.

12. Franco Purini's work is among the most interesting and promising of the younger generation, though so far limited to theory. On Purini, see P. Melis, "Il 'timore' e il 'bisogno' dell'architettura. Una nota sulle incisioni di Franco Purini," *Controspazio*, nos. 4–5 (1977): 61–63, and M. Tafuri, "Natural-Artificial. The Architecture of Franco Purini," *A + U*, no. 8 (1980): 35–40. Purini's texts are among the most lucid of those produced by architects active in the past decade. See the volumes *Luogo e progetto* (Rome, 1976) and the recent *L'architettura didattica* (Reggio Calabria, 1980). The latter, which collects reflections and lectures from 1977 on, demonstrates an exemplary balance in its distinction of the motives of *poiesis* and the analysis of architecture's historical corpus; the two are later unified in the author's drawings and theoretical writings.

13. Regarding the competition and problems surrounding the placement of the University of Florence, see A. Montemagni and P. Sica, "La politica urbanistica fiorentina e il concorso internazionale per la nuova Università," *Urbanistica*, no. 62 (1974).

14. See J. Rykwert, "La nuova università della Calabria," *Domus*, no. 540 (1974): 13ff., and *Il progetto per l'Università delle Calabrie*.

Chapter 8

1. Gabetti and Isola did not enjoy favorable criticism after the controversy surrounding the "neoliberty" movement: the coy attitude of the two architects from Milan met with critics often distracted by other work. Only Zevi's "chronicles" *(Cronache di architettura,* nos. 451, 481, 610, 780, 933) did them justice, aided by occasional presentations of their work. In fact, in 1977 Portoghesi drew attention to Gabetti and Isola in an issue of *Controspazio* (nos. 4–5) that documented their work from 1965 to 1976. See P. Portoghesi, "Dentro la storia e fuori delle 'storie,'" ibid.: 16ff., and G. Accasto, "La complessità dell'essenziale: riflessioni sugli ultimi lavori di Gabetti e Isola," ibid.: 34ff., which led to dissatisfaction of a different kind. In the same issue, see R. Gabetti and A. Isola, "Sulla schiena del drago," 2, and the articles by D'Amato and Cellini on the neoliberty phenomenon cited above. See also, *Gabetti, Isola, Raineri.*

2. See P. Portoghesi, "Oggettività e contradizione: una casa sulla collina torinese," *Controspazio,* no. 3 (1969): 30.

3. See Zevi, *Cronache di architettura,* no. 933; R. Pedio, "Residenziale ovest a Ivrea," *L'architettura— cronache e storia,* nos. 212–13 (1973); Accasto, "La complessità dell'essenziale."

4. Similar to Gabetti and Isola's poetics was that of Giorgio Raineri who, as we have seen, collaborated with them on a few works. Raineri also extracted a confident syntax from a polished "trade" and from careful exploration of the historical context of the Piedmont landscape. He integrated a refined treatment of material with an equally refined manipulation of geometry, with the result that he turned "polite speech" into a linguistic pretext infinitely rich in developments. Works like the nursery school in Mondoví designed with Lorenzo Mamino in 1969–72, the house on the hill of Turin of 1968–72, the restoration and remodeling of the neogothic castle of Miradolo of 1975–78, and the nursery school of Collegno of 1975–77 all stand as proof of impressive formal competence, proportional to the attention that Raineri dedicated to the "detail." See, in addition to *Gabetti, Isola, Raineri,* R. Gabetti, "Intimismo, dieci opere in dieci anni," *Casabella* no. 338 (1969): 7–21; V. Gregotti, "1954–1979: Architetture di Giorgio Raineri. La strategia dell'invenzione e la poesia del mestiere," *Controspazio,* no. 3 (1979): 26–30, and R. Gabetti, "Una lettera a Giorgio Raineri," ibid.: 46.

5. Criticism has still not given Canella the serious attention he deserves. The relevant bibliography thus lacks articles presenting his work: see B. Zevi, *L'Espresso,* no. 50 (1967); L. Berni, *Panorama,* nos. 561 and 606 (1977) and no. 668 (1979); A. Christofellis, "Scuole materne come case del popolo," *L'architettura—cronache e storia* no.

252 (1976): 294–307.

6. Among Canella's works of typological research, see the volumes *Il sistema teatrale a Milano* (Bari, 1966); *Il carcere come modello di decongestione* (Milan, 1967); *Università. Ragione, contesto, tipo*, written with Lucio D'Angiolini (Bari, 1975). See also, by G. Canella, "Dal laboratorio della composizione," in the collection *Teoria della progettazione architettonica* (Bari, 1958), and "Critica di alcune correnti ideologiche," *Controspazio*, nos. 1–2 (1970): 34–41.

7. On Gae Aulenti, see G. Drudi, "The Design of Gae Aulenti," *Craft Horizons* (February 1976); P. C. Santini, "Gae Aulenti: Architettura, scene, design," *Ottagono*, no. 47 (1977); *Gae Aulenti*, the catalogue of the exhibit at the PAC (Milan, 1979), with an introduction by V. Gregotti, an essay by E. Battisti, "Architettura è donna," 7–11, an essay by F. Quadri, "Teatro come trasgressione," 12, and fragments of a conversation between Aulenti and Quadri, published in *Il Patalogo uno* (Milan, 1979), 317–330.

8. See *Italy: The New Domestic Landscape*, ed. E. Ambasz (New York, 1972), 150–59.

9. See G. Aulenti, "Teatro e Territorio. Il laboratorio di Prato," *Lotus*, no. 17 (1977): 4ff.; idem, "Il progetto per il museo di Orsay: l'architettura come integrazione delle scelte," *Urbanistica*, no. 81 (1985): 30–34.

Chapter 9

1. The bibliography on Aldo Rossi is vast: there has been an attempt to turn this master of the restrained sign, of boundaries and "laconic eloquence" into a fashionable item for easy consumption. See, however, E. Bonfanti, "Elementi e costruzione. Note sull'architettura di Aldo Rossi," *Controspazio*, no. 10 (1970): 19ff.; M. Steinmann, "Architektur," *Aldo Rossi, Bauten Projekte* (Zürich, 1973), 3–5; R. Nicolini, "Note su Aldo Rossi," *Controspazio*, no. 4 (1974): 48–49; the monograph issue of *Construcción de la ciudad 2c*, no. 2 (1975); V. Savi, *L'architettura di Aldo Rossi* (Milan, 1976); *A + U*, no. 65 (1976): 55ff. (a monographical issue); F. Dal Co, "Criticism and Design. For Vittorio Savi and Aldo Rossi," *Oppositions*, no. 13 (1978): 2–16; *Aldo Rossi progetti e disegni 1962–1979* (Florence, 1979); P. Eisenman, "Preface" and "The House of the Dead as the City of Survival," *Aldo Rossi in America: 1976 to 1979*, cat. 2, IAUS (New York, 1979); the monographical issue of *Construcción de la ciudad 2c*, no. 4 (1979); M. Tafuri, *La sfera e il labirinto. Avanguardie e architettura da Piranesi agli anni '70* (Turin, 1980), 330ff.; D. Vitale, "Ritrovamenti, traslazioni, analogie. Progetti e frammenti di Aldo Rossi," *Lotus* no. 25 (1980): 55–58; P. Portoghesi, *Dopo l'architettura moderna* (Rome-Bari, 1980), 182ff. For a dissenting voice, see B. Zevi, "Con Piacentini in nome di Lenin," *L'Espresso*, 14 October 1973.

Among Rossi's writings, note *L'architettura della città*, 3rd ed. (Padua, 1973), and *Scritti scelti sull'architettura e la città 1965–1972*, ed. R. Bonicalzi, 2nd ed. (Milan, 1975).

2. And it would be a matter of "metaphysics" indebted to Max Klinger and Arnold Böcklin, of *novecentismo*, of Lombard neoclassicism, of Giovanni Muzio, of Loos, and even of a few aspects of Marcello Piacentini: all the themes, essentially, that had been censored by the "progressive" culture of the forties and fifties, from which also follows the appreciation of so-called "Stalinist" architecture and the Stalinallee in Berlin. This appreciation was expressed in an unpublished article by Rossi and Canella: there was no leftist review that cared to print it at the beginning of destalinization.

3. See G. U. Polesello, A. Rossi, and F. Tentori, "Il problema della periferia nella città moderna," *Casabella*, no. 241 (1960): 39–55.

4. A. Rossi, "Adolf Loos 1870–1933," ibid., no. 233 (1959): 5–12.

5. See idem, "L'azzurro del cielo," ibid., no. 372 (1972), and in *Controspazio*, no. 10 (1972); R. Moneo, "Aldo Rossi: the idea of architecture and the Modena cemetery," *Oppositions*, no. 15 (1976): 1–30, and Vitale, "Ritrovamenti, traslazioni, analogie."

6. See A. Rossi, "La arquitectura análoga," *Construcción de la ciudad 2c*, no. 2 (1975): 8–11, and M.

Tafuri, "Ceci n'est pas une ville," *Lotus*, no. 13 (1976): 10–13.

7. See idem, "L'éphémère est éternel. Aldo Rossi a Venezia," *Domus*, no. 602 (1980): 7–8; F. Dal Co, "Ora questo è perduto," *Lotus*, no. 25 (1980), 66ff.; P. Portoghesi, "Il teatro del mondo," *Controspazio*, nos. 5–6 (1979) 2 and 9–10; S. Planas, "El Teatro del Mondo de Aldo Rossi, o el 'lenguaje de las cosas mudas,'" *Carrer de la Ciudat*, no. 12 (1980) 5–15; J. J. Lahuerta, "Personajes de Aldo Rossi," ibid.: 16–27.

Chapter 10

1. On Grassi, see A. Monestiroli, "Teoria e progetto. Considerazioni sull'architettura di Giorgio Grassi," *Controspazio*, no. 2 (1974): 72–91. Also see G. Grassi, *La construzione logica dell'architettura* (Padua, 1967), and *L'architettura come mestiere e altri scritti* (Milan, 1980).

2. See "Il quartiere, il castello, la chiesa, la via. Piano di recupero del centro storico di Teora (Avellino), *Lotus international*, no. 36 (1982): 77–93; J. P. Kleihues, "Un non-luogo. I progetti di concorso per il Prinz Albrecht Palais a Berlino," ibid., no. 42 (1984): 101–10 (on 111–19, see Grassi and Renna's project, designed with N. Di Battista, F. Collotti, and G. Zanella). On Giorgio Grassi's project (designed with A. Renna, A. Del Bo, and E. Guazzoni) for the Lützowplatz in Berlin (figure 146), see "Edificio unico," ibid., no. 33 (1981): 26–31. On Grassi's work,

also see J. J. Lahuerta, *Arquitectura de Giorgio Grassi* (Barcelona, 1985).

3. The collection *Architettura razionale. XV Triennale di Milano. Sezione internazionale di architettura* (Milan, 1973). Two of the articles most critical of the initiative were G. Gresleri, "Alla XV Triennale di Milano," *Parametro*, nos. 21–22 (1973): 6ff., and J. Rykwert, "XV Triennale," *Domus*, no. 530 (1974): 1–15. Favoring the initiative was R. Nicolini, "Per un nuovo realismo in architettura," *Controspazio*, no. 6 (1973): 12–15. The exhibit did, however, make the mistake of artificially uniting under the unfortunate term of *tendenza* architectures of opposing *tendenze*: in this respect, the exhibit was in perfect agreement with Portoghesi's exhibit for the Biennale of Venezia of 1980. Let us mention, therefore, for the benefit of those who are still fond of the term *tendenza*, that Massimo Scolari, who was responsible for it, when recently questioned, said that in 1973 he was making an ironic Dadaist "gesture."

4. On the GRAU group, see P. Portoghesi, "Architettura del Grau," *Controspazio*, nos. 1–2 (1979): 2 and 96; C. D'Amato, "1964–78: Storia e logica nella progettazione del Grau," ibid.: 4ff.; GRAU, *Isti mirant stella. Architetture 1964–1980* (Rome, 1981).

5. On the research done by the young Romans, see G. Muratore, "I gruppi romani tra neoavanguardia e neomanierismo," *Casabella*, no.

449 (1979): 10–17, and "Architetti romani: un dibattito," ibid.: 18ff.

6. See "Progetti dello studio Labirinto," *Controspazio*, no. 4 (1975): 80ff.; Studio Labirinto, *La città di carta*, with papers by C. Bertelli, F. Menna, and F. Moschini (Rome, 1978).

7. F. Purini and L. Thermes, "La ricerca dei giovani architetti italiani. Una generazione ritrovata," *Controspazio*, nos. 5–6 (1978): 8.

8. See M. Mattei, "Crisi dell'urbanistica, urbanistica della crisi. Note in margine al concorso per l'area direzionale di Firenze," ibid., no. 6 (1977): 23–28, which deals with the lack of choices of location and functional ideas. On the results of the competition, see, in the same issue, the note by P. Portoghesi, "Ancora paura dell'architettura," 2. See G. Gresleri, "Depressione su un concorso di architettura moderna," *Parametro*, no. 63 (1978): 11–12 (on 15ff., see the projects and excerpts from papers given).

9. In this context, attempts to define *tendenze* on the basis of formulas are bound to be more confusing than enlightening. This is what happened at the exhibit organized in 1977–78 in Bologna under the title—shaped by Renato Barilli's critical program as inspired by Heidegger—"*Assenza-Presenza*," in which the neo-avant-garde "radicals" were contrasted with heterogeneous "absent" figures such as Dardi, Isozaki, Moore, Scolari, Purini, Rossi,

Sartogo, and Hedjuk. See the catalogue *Assenza/Presenza, un'ipotesi di lettura per l'architettura* (Ascoli Piceno, 1979), and the critical article by L. Thermes, "Bologna: una mostra e un convegno," *Controspazio*, no. 6 (1977): 58.

10. See M. Gandelsonas, "Massimo Scolari. Paesaggi teorici," *Lotus*, no. 11 (1976): 57–63; M. Tafuri, "The Watercolors of Massimo Scolari," *Massimo Scolari: Architecture between Memory and Hope* (New York: IAUS, 1980), 2ff.; *Massimo Scolari, acquarelli e disegni 1965–1980*, ed. F. Moschini (Florence, 1981); A. Cantàfora, *Architetture* (Milan, 1984).

11. See the catalogue *Roma interrotta* (Rome, 1978); L. Thermes, "Il Nolli, dodici architetti e una città," *Controspazio*, no. 4 (1978): 4–24; P. Ceccarelli, "La Messa per Moro, la Pianta del Nolli e l'immaginazione ibernata," *Spazio e società*, no. 4 (1978): 89–92.

12. See N. Pagliara, "Architetture e progetti, 1960–1979," *Controspazio*, no. 3 (1979): 6ff., with a commentary by P. Portoghesi, "Materia e spazio: il lavoro di Nicola Pagliara," ibid.: 19, and G. K. König, "Italian eclecticism, quant'è wunderbar," *Modo*, no. 17 (1979): 29–33. An interesting testimony of the attitude in the sixties toward the "paternal languages" is the little volume by N. Pagliara, *Appunti su Otto Wagner* (Naples, 1968). It is not surprising that Pagliara's subsequent work—which moved from the exasperated constructivism of his first projects to the exuberant materiality of his Chiesa di Tursi of 1967, to the ironic montages of the Casa Crispino in Melito of 1978 and of more recent projects—was anything but influenced by the Venetian formal masters of language. It was instead marked by the "perversity" with which many of those born into architecture in the sixties looked at their predecessors. The ferment in the new *tendenze* was not, however, praised in the promotion initiated by Portoghesi in organizing the exhibit for the Venice Biennale of 1980, *Presenza del passato* (see the catalogue, and, for its theoretical base, the volume by Portoghesi, *Dopo l'architettura moderna*). Not coincidentally, Purini gave an astute critique of "postmodern" ideology at the Venice exhibit (see Purini, *L'architettura didattica*, 41, n. 14, and 93 and 120).

Chapter 11

1. See, for example, how this is expressed as the central thesis of L. Benevolo's book, *L'ultimo capitolo dell'architettura moderna* (Rome-Bari, 1985), especially in the last chapter, 233–51. Such theses relate to ideas expressed in the editorials by V. Gregotti, "Modificazione," *Casabella*, nos. 498–99 (1984): 1–7; idem "Orizzonti perduti," ibid., no. 505: 2–3; idem "Moderno e non moderno," ibid. no. 513 (1985): pp. 2–3; "Il luogo definito dell'esperimento," ibid., no. 519 (1985): 2–3.

Also see the many articles on urban planning published in recent years by Bernardo Secchi in the same review. One ought to note that Italian architectural culture did not need, in order to dismantle its own *grands récits*, the appearance of the volume by J.-F. Lyotard, *La condition postmoderne* (Paris, 1979; Italian trans. Milan, 1981): what we have called the ideological *décalage* of Italian architecture began in the late 1950s. It was in order to accelerate its course (and in a moment of artificial expansion) that, in 1973, I published *Progetto e utopia* , 4th ed. (Rome-Bari, 1984): a work that many have found convenient to misinterpret, leveling accusations of necrophilic *tendenze*. See my response in a letter to the editor published in *Op. Cit.*, no. 51 (1981): 83–85.

2. See, for example, the recent volumes by G. Marramao, *Potere e secolarizzazione. Le categorie del tempo* (Rome, 1983); idem, *L'ordine disincantato* (Rome, 1985).

3. See M. Tafuri, *Vittorio Gregotti. Progetti e architetture* (Milan, 1982), 81–88.

4. See B. Secchi, "Piani della terza generazione," *Casabella*, no. 516 (1985): 14–15; G. Campos Venuti, "Ancora sui piani della terza generazione," ibid., no. 518: 22–23; idem, "Un piano della terza generazione," *Urbanistica*, no. 81 (1985): 50–58 (an analysis of the preliminary project for Florence).

5. See, for Bologna, G. Mattioli, R. Matulli, R. Scannavini, and P.

Capponcelli (ed.), *Bologna, una città per gli anni '90. Il progetto del nuovo piano regolatore generale* (Venice, 1985), and *Urbanistica*, no. 78 (1985), with articles by: P. Gabellini (ed.), "Il progetto preliminare del Prg di Bologna": 44–53; G. Campos Venuti, "Innovazioni e continuità nell'urbanistica bolognese": 54–58; P. Portoghesi, "Urbanistica e storia della città": 59–62; P. di Biagi, "Qualità e periferia": 63–66; R. Matulli (interviewed), "Il tema, i destinatari, le procedure": 67–69; G. Mattioli, "Il contesto del piano": 70–71; R. Scannavini, "La novità del piano": 71–72; P. G., "Uno schema interpretativo": 73–75. Also see V. Quilici and A. Sichenze, *Costruttori di architetture. Bologna 1960–1980* (Bologna, 1985), and R. Mazzanti, "Intervista sull'urbanistica bolognese," eds. M. Pinardi and I. Juliano, *Parametro*, no. 140 (1985): 60–63. Regarding Florence, see no. 81 of the same review, with articles by: P. Gabellini, "Il Progetto preliminare del Piano regolatore di Firenze": 46–49; Campus Venuti, "Un Piano"; B. Secchi, "Le condizioni del progetto urbanistico": 59–65. The plan for Florence was to replace the plan drawn up in 1962 by Edoardo Detti, which had been subjected to successive vicissitudes. On Detti's experience and, in general, the Florentine urban experience, see M. Zoppi, *Firenze e l'urbanistica: la ricerca del piano* (Rome, 1983).

6. B. Secchi, "Una nuova prospettiva," *Urbanistica*, no. 78 (1985): 8–9.

7. Idem, *Il racconto urbanistico. La politica della casa e del territorio in Italia* (Turin, 1984).

8. Ibid., xviii-xix.

9. Ibid., xxi.

10. Ibid., 7–8.

11. "The more recent plans, in the end, can be understood if one realizes that their conceptual extension has been ... increased: the vast experimental field of social practices that are heterogeneous among themselves, of their crossing with political and administrative action and with the situations of the territory are not conceptualized as a process, that is to say as a judiciary cause, as a voyage, as production ... Using yet other words, in each of the periods to which I am summarily referring there is above all one strata of experience that seems particularly resistant and opaque, which prevents the texts written and designed by urbanists from adhering completely to things, to the city or to the territory, giving them a meaning immediately comprehensible to everyone. In the sixties it was the stratum of the political decision-making system; in the following years it was primarily that of scattered social practices" (ibid., 61–62).

12. Ibid., 84–85.

13. The second part of the book cited is dedicated to this theme, pp. 88ff., and analyzes the behavior of the left during the fifties. The left at that time favored the expansion of production and increased employment, and the boosting of construction, public and private (the latter under the Aldisio law), relying on phenomena of "filtering" previously denied. Secchi's analysis is very precise regarding the rapport between centrist politics and the importance given to the middle classes, also in consideration of Minister Sullo's utopian attitude in this sphere (128). Secchi sees the reason for the approval of law 1179 in 1965, and of law 291 in 1971, to be the lack of discussion of the axiom according to which the main purpose of construction policy is to sustain the expansion of the number of residences. Pages 159ff. are dedicated to the differences between quantitative theory—for which the plan is an instrument of social compensation for the modern welfare state—and distributive theory, for which the plan is an institution that regulates social relations and various group behaviors.

14. This is the title of a single "microhistory" published by Einaudi whose content is symptomatic of the new atmosphere of the eighties. See P. Marcenaro and V. Foa, *Riprendere tempo. Un dialogo con postilla* (Turin, 1982).

15. Secchi, "Le condizioni del progetto urbanistico," especially 63–65. Secchi remarks that the recognition of urban morphologies is, in the preliminary project for Florence, still schematic and limited to large historical transformations, while a detailed analysis

of the nature and specificity of places is lacking, though this would have given substance to the notion of a service sector spreading out in veins over the countryside. Furthermore, he notes that the proposed rise in urban standards conflicts with the restrictions on public spending. This last argument recalls the interdependence of local and general systems: one of the most problematic issues at present.

16. See the interview with Pier Luigi Cervellati, in Quilici and Sichenze, *Costruttori di architettura*, 188–89.

17. See V. Quilici, "Le evoluzioni dell'intreccio," ibid., 13ff., especially 20.

18. Ibid.

19. The complete organization chart of the designers of the preliminary plan for Bologna and of the guidelines for the Intercomunale urban plan is in *Urbanistica*, no. 78 (1985): 75.

20. On these themes, see P. L. Cervellati, *La città post-industriale* (Bologna, 1984), which lends cohesion to the reflections of the seventies and early eighties on the transformation of production systems, ecological and environmental decay, the prejudices of quantitative urban planning, and the programmatic recovery of urban "empty spaces" and historical centers, with a synthetic history of the successes and failures of the Bologna experience. Between Cervellati's theses and those of the designers of the preliminary plan for Bologna, there exist notable differences, in spite of the many declarations of continuity with past experiments. See Mazzanti, "Intervista," with a critique of the idea of housing placed along the axis of the ancient Canale Navile. I also agree with Mazzanti's critique of the "Cassarini-Pallotti" houses, an intervention that falsifies the concept of "recovery" with mediocre and cunning environmental mimicry.

21. "Relazione tecnica," p. 11, quoted in Gabellini, *Il progetto preliminare*, 50.

22. See Campos Venuti, "Innovazioni e continuità," 56; Di Biagi, "Qualità e periferia," 65–66; Scannavini, "La novità del piano," 71–72; Portoghesi, "Urbanistica e storia della città," 60–62.

23. See, for example, the interview with Matulli, "Il tema, i destinatari," 69.

24. B. Secchi, "Il piano," *Urbanistica*, no. 78 (1985): 2–5, quotation on 5.

25. Ibid.

26. See, in this volume, chapter 4 of part one.

27. Among the many programmatic writings on this subject, particularly significant are those of C. Aymonino, "Archeologia e disegno urbano," *Casabella*, no. 482 (1982): 36; idem and R. Panella, "Roma una città a parte. Utilizzare il ritardo storico per costruire una capitale diversa," ibid., nos. 487–88

(1983): 90–97; C. Aymonino, "La città storica e la città politica," in the collection *Roma: continuità dell'antico. I Fori Imperiali nel progetto della città* (Milan, 1981), 29–32 (here also see the writings therein by Adriano La Regina and Renato Nicolini); idem, "Un centro storico per una città moderna," *Controspazio* 25, no. 4 (n.s.) (1984): 26–28 (and see the entire issue of the review dedicated to *Roma: i problemi di una metropoli. La nuova architettura*). See also the catalogue *Roma, archeologia e progetto* (Rome, 1983); I. Insolera and F. Perego, *Archeologia e città. Storia moderna dei Fori di Roma* (Roma-Bari, 1983); C. Pavolini, "Fori Imperiali: le ragioni dell'archeologia," *Parametro* 16, no. 138 (1985): 43–49, and the many articles on the theme in *Parametro*, no. 139 (1985).

28. The specific character of Ludovico Quaroni's project for the expansion of the Teatro dell'Opera—an expression of skepticism not unusual in Quaroni's work—has not been grasped by commentators, who have created around this chance event a debate disproportionate to its significance. See, in this context, F. Moschini, "Dal dubbio alla certezza. Un progetto di Ludovico Quaroni," *Lotus International*, no. 40 (1983): 23–28; F. Purini, "Osservazioni sul complesso dell'Opera di Roma di Ludovico Quaroni," ibid.: 29–35; L. Benevolo, "Buona e cattiva accademia," *Casabella*, no. 503 (1984): 42–43; P. Melis, "Lo 'strappo' dal moderno," *Domus*, no.

652 (1984) 18–25; P. Portoghesi, "Ritorno alla città. L'ampliamento del teatro dell'Opera di Roma," *Eupalino*, no. 2 (1984): 16–26; the collection *Ludovico Quaroni. Architetture per cinquant'anni*, ed. A. Terranova (Rome-Reggio Calabria, 1985), 106–14. In fact, Quaroni had already adopted pseudostylized ciphers in his project for the office and apartment building on Via Maqueda in Palermo of 1982, commissioned by the Curia Vescovile, drawn up in Turin while he was working in an "international vocabulary" for the FIAT office building in Borgo Saõ Paulo, designed with L. Passarelli in 1979–84: it was yet another sign of Quaroni's deep disillusionment. A much more interesting project was the one by Quaroni and collaborators, which won the first prize in the competition for the urban park of Porto Navile and the Manifattura Tabacchi in Bologna of 1984.

29. See A. La Regina, "Rome: continuità dell'antico," in *Roma: continuità dell'antico*, 11–18; Pavolini, *Fori Imperiali*, and the bibliography assembled in the notes.

30. See, in this regard, C. Aymonino, *La città storica*, 30, and "Intervista a Italo Insolera," ed. Enrico Valeriani, *Controspazio*, no. 4 (1984): 22–25.

31. C. Aymonino, *Archeologia*; idem, *La città storica*, 31.

32. See A. Cagnardi, "Documento direttore e progetti d'area," *Casabella*, no. 508 (1984): 20–21.

33. See the precise criticism of the Passage in G. Zambrini, "Il Passante: un 'progetto' per Milano," *Casabella*, no. 485 (1982): 38. For the urban projects, see V. Gregotti, "Milano: schemi di progetto urbano," ibid., no. 507 (1984): 2; and "I progetti e il piano per Milano," ibid., no. 508 (1984): 18–29. (Writings by Augusto Cagnardi, Riccardo Cappellin, Maurizio Mottini, Achille Cutrera, Sergio Crotti, Empio Malara and Alessandro Morselli, Giancarlo Polo, and Guido Canella.)

34. See G. Polo, "Progetto Casa e Progetto Passante: discordanze e analogie," *Casabella*, 27–28. Also see the letter from town councillor Maurizio Mottini, which takes issue with the article by Polo cited above, and the latter's response in *Casabella*, no. 512 (1985): 35–56.

35. G. Canella, "Passato e passante nell'architettura milanese," *Casabella*, no. 508 (1984): 28–29. Also see the project for the Cadorna-Pagano zone drawn up by Gregotti and collaborators, which contrasts methodologically with the area project for the Garibaldi-Repubblica zone, in S. Brandolini and P.-A. Croset, "Gregotti associati, G 14 Progettazione, Studio GPI. Cadorna-Pagano: un progetto per il centro di Milano," *Casabella*, no. 513 (1984): 52–63.

36. See C. De Seta, *Dopo il terremoto la ricostruzione* (Rome-Bari, 1983), which gathers a series of articles on the history of urbanism in Naples and Campania, from 1945 to the present, with an ample bibliography in the notes, and "Il caso Napoli," ed. Giancarlo Cosenza, in *Casabella*, nos. 487–488 (1983): 30–43, which includes Salvatore Bisogni's project for the housing project of Via Aquileia, the project by Pietro Barucci, Vittorio De Feo, and collaborators for Barra San Giovanni, and the project by Riccardo Dalisi and collaborators for Ponticelli. Another case, also determined by two natural disasters—the earthquake of 1972 and the landslide of 1982—was that of Ancona, which in 1973 entrusted its own plan to Giuseppe Campos Venuti, Romeo Ballardini, Giovanni Zani, and Silvano Tintori, establishing guidelines that favored inland expansion. In Ancona too the historical center—70 percent of which was damaged—has remained unaffected by reconstruction programs. Nonetheless, it was right in the central district of Guasco San Pietro that, starting in 1974, an interesting residential structure was built by Sergio Lenci, Arnaldo Bruschi, Gianni and Piero Gandolfi, Andrea Reichlin, and Franco Zagari. On the other hand the Q. 1 and Q. 2 projects, in the zones projected in the plan, were disappointing, whereas Giancarlo De Carlo envisioned for the Q. 3 a unifying backbone of services with a pedestrian walkway, capable of lending a distinct identity to the intervention. See S. Brandolini, "Ancona: dal terremoto a Ralph Erskine," *Casabella*, no. 519 (1985):

20–27; G. Petti and G. Mascino, "Sviluppo urbano e attuazione dei piani," ibid. : 22–23. Ancona, like Bologna and Naples, called upon a foreign architect—the Anglo-Swedish Ralph Erskine—to resolve a delicate problem of urban identity: the restructuring of the Guasco quarter. Erskine's project, with its diverting montages of artifacts and "picturesque" recompositions, envisioned—as Brandolini has aptly put it—a "townscape," and one "that recalls, a little dangerously, the false image of itself that Mediterranean Europe has projected in Northern Europe" (Brandolini, "Ancona," p. 26). James Stirling—or so his project for the public library in Latina seems to suggest—has been the only foreigner capable of entering into a dialogue with the Italian context. See M. Zardini, "James Stirling, Michael Wilford and Associates. Progetto per una biblioteca pubblica a Latina," *Casabella* no. 507 (1984): 4–13.

37. See *Progetto Bicocca. Invito alla progettazione urbanistica e architettonica di un centro tecnologico integrato* (Pirelli, Milan: 1985).

38. See M. Zardini, ed., *Venti idee per il Lingotto*; B. Secchi, "Il Lingotto 'vuoto'; Una visita al nuovo Lingotto. Intervista con Mario Botta," *Casabella*, no. 502 (1984): 16–31; the collection, *Venti progetti per il futuro del Lingotto* (Milan, 1984). Also see F. Corsico, L. Falco, and P. De Rossi, "Lingotto: un problema di ristrutturazione urbana," *Casabella*, no. 486

(1982): 12–23; R. Banham, "Lingotto: un punto di vista transatlantico," ibid., no. 501 (1984): 304–5.

39. On the themes of continuity and discontinuity, in the specific case of the Lingotto building, see Secchi, "Il Lingotto 'vuoto'," especially 19.

Chapter 12

1. On the execution of the Zen quarter, see P. Lovero, "La generazione dello Z.E.N. Evora, Vitoria, Palermo: tre quartieri a confronto," *Lotus International*, no. 36 (1982): 27–45, in which the quarter by Gregotti is compared with the Matteotti Village in Terni by Giancarlo De Carlo, with the Actur di Lacua quarter in Vitoria in Spain of 1977 by Rafael Moneo and Manuel Solá Morales, with the Quinta de Malagueira quarter by Siza in Evora in Portogallo, and with the San Polo quarter in Bescia of 1972–79 by Leonardo Benevolo and communal technical offices. On the latter—in which Benevolo inaugurated a direct relationship with the administration of Brescia, attempting a nonbureaucratic coordination of urban and construction policies—see L. Benevolo, *Brescia, San Polo. Un quartiere ad iniziativa pubblica* (Brescia, 1978). Unfortunately, the builders of the San Polo quarter thwarted Benevolo's commitment with shoddy construction.

2. For projects before 1982, see Tafuri, *Vittorio Gregotti*. See also Brandolini and Croset, "Gregotti

associati"; O. Bohigas, "I progetti per l'anello olimpico di Barcellona," *Casabella*, no. 501 (1984): 4–15 (the project appears on 14–15); G. Polin, "Nuovi uffici Bossi a Cameri," ibid., no. 493 (1983): 2–9.

3. See S. Marpillero, "Grattacielo a metà. Gino Valle: uffici della Banca Commerciale Italiana a Manhattan," *Lotus International*, no. 37 (1983): 96–119. Pierre-Alain Croset is preparing a complete monograph on the works of Gino Valle. In the meantime, see P.-A. Croset, "Gino Valle. Edificio per uffici alla Défense a Parigi," *Casabella*, no. 519 (1985): 4–15, followed by "Una conversazione con Gino Valle": 16–17.

4. See G. Polin, "Nuove abitazioni popolari a Venezia," *Casabella*, no. 478 (1982): 50–61.

5. See "Venezia. Mestre-Altobello," in M. Casciato and G. Muratore, eds., *AA 1984. Annali dell'Architettura contemporanea* (Rome, 1985), 95–99; G. Polin, "Gianni Fabbri e Roberto Sordina. 74 abitazioni popolari a Mestre," *Casabella*, no. 496 (1983): 2. (Also, on 8–9, "Gianni Fabbri e il 'Gruppo Architettura.'") Also see "Bollate. Cascina del Sole," in Casciato and Muratore, *AA 1984*, 87–94; M. Prusicki, "Case popolari a Cascina del Sole di Bollate," *Casabella*, no. 516 (1985): 56–63. See, finally, J. Manuel Palerm Salazar, "Como introducción a dos proyectos," *Periferia*, no. 2 (1984):37–38. On 39–47, see the complexes of Mestre-Altobello and Cascina del Sole.

6. See "Abano Terme. PEEP nucleo sei," in.Casciato and Muratore, *AA 1984*, 101–6.

7. See "Edificio residenziale a Tor Sapienza," *Controspazio* 25, n.s., no. 4 (1984): 118–21.

8. This attitude was exemplified by some of Leonardo Savioli's last works (he died in 1982), as well as by the works of D. Santi and collaborators, in spite of the increased formal control compared to some of their projects of the preceding decades: for example, the IACP residential complex Le Fornaci in Pistoia, begun in 1980, the new flower market in Pescia of 1970–1981, and the new cemetery in Montecatini. The works of Aldo Rossi derive from another cultural sphere, and those of Michele Capobianco also belong to the Neapolitan environment—the new university of Salerno of 1972–76, the technical institute of Pomigliano d'Arco of 1972–78, and the "G. Galilei" high school in Naples, of 1978–1984—and are increasingly intent, moreover, on the recovery of organizing geometries as points of departure. Expressionist temptations, moreover, characterize a few of the later works of Luciano Semerani and Gigetta Tamaro, like the town hall of Osoppo, done in 1979 with Adalberto Burelli, while in the monolith of the new Hospital of Trieste at Cattinara done in 1965–1983 with Carlo and Luciano Celli and Dario Tognon (figure 145), in the Institute of Pathological Anatomy at the University of Trieste of 1979–1983,

in the project for the School of Medicine, Surgery and Pharmacy at the same university, done in 1982 with M. Cosmini, G. Foti, and C. Pagliaro, a language of severe signs is called upon to control large-scale building, heir to the lesson of Giuseppe Samonà. See G. Rosa, ed., *Semerani + Tamaro. La città e i progetti* (Rome, 1983). Regarding Guido Canella's expressionism, see chapter 8 in part one of this volume.

9. On Canella's recent production, which has confirmed his status as one of the most interesting northern architects, see K. Suzuki, *Guido Canella* (Bologna, 1983), and V. Savi, ed., *Guido Canella. Opere recenti*, exhibition catalogue (Modena, 1984). On Gabetti and Isola, see the recent monograph by F. Cellini and C. D'Amato, *Gabetti and Isola. Progetti e architettura 1950–1985* (Milan, 1985), a balanced account containing a list of works and a complete bibliography.

10. See, for example, C. Magnani, "Un corso di progettazione sulla laguna," *Casabella*, no. 465 (1981): 59–60 (and the projects on 47–58); P.-A. Croset, "Un progetto per la gronda lagunare di Venezia," ibid., nos. 487–88 (1983): 102–11 (graduate thesis of 1980–81 by Michele Reginaldi, Daniela Saviola, and Mario Tassoni).

11. See G. Canella, "Gusto della falsificazione e gusto della realtà," *Controspazio* 16, n.s., nos. 1–2 (1985): 28. The projects and buildings presented in the article appear on 29–39.

12. See R. Gabetti and A. Isola, "Orientamenti nuovi, consolidate tradizioni nelle giovani opere di alcuni architetti torinesi," ibid., 4–5; illustrations of the projects are on pp. 6–19. Also see S. Giriodi, "Una lettera a Roberto Gabetti e Aimaro Isola," ibid., 20; on 21–27, see works by Giriodi, Luciano Re, Edoardo Ceretto, Andrea Mascardi, and Walter Mazzella.

13. On Francesco Venezia's work, see F. Venezia, "Piazze marginali," *Lotus International*, no. 22 (1979): 71–78 (regarding the piazza in Lauro); idem, "La costruzione del limite: un piano per Laura," *Casabella*, nos. 498–99 (1984): 100–5; L. Ortelli, "Architettura di muri. Il museo di Gibellina di Francesco Venezia," *Lotus International*, no. 42 (1984): 121–25 (in the appendix, F. Venezia, "Note sulla construzione," 126); "San Leucio: cinque proposte per un territorio," *Casabella*, no. 505 (1984): 4ff. (F. Venezia's project, with Rosaria Gargiulo, Riccardo Lopes, Bruno Messina, Filippo Morelli, Gabriele Petrusch, and Michele Di Natale, on 16–19; F. Venezia, "La medaglia e il suo rovescio. Progetto per il Municipio di Taurano, 1979," *Lotus International*, no. 28 (1981): 111–15.

14. Venezia, "Piazze marginali."

15. See "San Leucio."

16. See B. Minardi, "Edificio a doppia maniera. Involucro tradizionale e contenuto sofisticato," *Lotus International*, no. 37 (1983): 52–60; A. Natalini, "Edificio con rivestimento in

pietra. Sede della Cassa Rurale ed Artigiana di Alzate Brianza, Como," *Lotus International*, no. 40 (1983): 4–18; V. Savi, "Storia di un progetto. Adolfo Natalini e una sua architettura," ibid., 19–20; F. Irace, "Basilica suburbana," *Domus*, no. 648 (1984): 5–12; A. Natalini, *Figure di pietra* (Milan, 1984); A. Belluzzi and C. Conforti, *Architettura italiana 1944–84* (Rome-Bari, 1985), 53, 89, 155–58. Also see G. Pettena, ed., *Superstudio, 1966–1982. Storie, figure, architettura* (Florence, 1982), and "Confessioni. Intervista-dialogo con Adolfo Natalini," an interview-dialogue conducted by M. Petranza and D. Schiesari in *L'architettura—cronache e storia*, no. 362 (1985): 900–4.

17 .See P. Portoghesi, "Sulle fertili ceneri dell'ideologia. I cimiteri di Alessandro Anselmi," *Lotus International* no. 38 (1983): 18–29, which provides good documentation of the projects and buildings of the cemeteries of Parabita and Attilia (by Anselmi with G. Patanè and G. Angotti).

18. See A. Anselmi, "Due chiese," in Casciato and Muratore, *AA 1984*, 235–37. The projects for the churches of Santomenna, in Sardinia, were elaborated in collaboration with Giulio Figurelli.

19. See "San Leucio," op. cit.: 120–22, with the essay by F. Purini, "San Leucio 1984: l'officina totale." Purini and Laura Thermes collaborated on the San Leucio project with G. Dupasquier, F. Ghersi, G. Neri, and C. Columba.

20. See F. Dal Co, "Franco Purini e la coerenza della nostalgia," *Casabella*, no. 494 (1983): 2–4 (the project is on 6–11).

21. See G. Accasto, "Le case nella casa. Considerazioni su un'architettura di Franco Purini e Laura Thermes," *Lotus International*, no. 40 (1983): 70–79; F. Purini, "Casa del farmacista di Gibellina (Sicilia): un cantiere nel sud," ibid.: 80, with photos of the building on 81–89.

22. See "La grande modanatura. Progetto per il centro civico di Castelforte, Latina," *Lotus International*, no. 43 (1984):101–8.

23. See "Concorso di prove. Progetti per l'area di Fiera Catena a Mantova," ed. P.-A. Croset and M. Zardini, *Casabella*, no. 493 (1983):12–21. On 16–18, see the project by the Rossi group; on 19–21, see the winning project, also remarkable, by Emilio Battisti, Carlo Malnati, Gigi Piantanida, and collaborators. See also I. Gardella, A. Rossi, F. Reinhart, and A. Sibilla, "Dalla storia all'immaginazione. Progetto per il teatro Carlo Felice in Genova," *Lotus International*, no. 42 (1984): 12–23; P.-A. Croset and G. Polin, "Progetto per la ricostruzione del teatro Carlo Felice in Genova," *Casabella*, no. 502 (1984): 52–53; G. Aulenti, "Un punto di vista sull'architettura del teatro," ibid.: 60–62.

24. G. Aulenti, "Un punto di vista," 62.

25. A. Rossi and G. Braghieri, "Un punto di riferimento per la città.

Edificio per uffici a Buenos Aires," *Lotus International,* no. 42 (1984): 27–36, with Santiago Calatrava, "Memoria tecnica:" 37–39.

26. See G. Polin, "Il Palazzo di Giustizia di Ferrara," *Casabella,* no. 479 (1982): 2ff.; idem, "Carlo Aymonino, Fausto Battimelli, Raffaele Panella. Centro direzionale Benelli a Pesaro," ibid., no. 497 (1983): 50–61. The recent competition project by Aymonino and collaborators for the IACP on the island of Giudecca in Venice was published in C. Magnani, "Il concorso dello IACP di Venezia per Campo di Marte alla Giudecca," ibid., no. 518 (1985): 4–21.

27. M. Scolari, "L'impegno tipologico," *Casabella,* nos. 509–510 (1985): 42–45.

28. Besides the writings cited in part one, chapter 4, note 26, see G. Caniggia and G. L. Maffei, *Il progetto nell'edilizia di base* (Venice, 1984) and idem, *Moderno non moderno. Il luogo e la continuità,* written with A. Boccardo, D. Corbara, and E. Lavagnino (Venice, 1984), a monograph on the work of Caniggia and his collaborators, written from the authors' point of view.

29. Besides the buildings at Trinità dei Pellegrini and the competition project for the Biblioteca Nazionale of Rome already mentioned, Caniggia executed—with his father Emanuele—the elementary schools of Isola del Liri of 1958–1961, which demonstrate a precocious interest in Ridolfi's architecture,

and the Ospedale Civico in the same city, of 1960–63. He also built the Casa Franzi in Albido with A. Regazzoni in 1962–63 and designed the Car barracks of Viterbo with Romano Greco and G. Sterbini in 1962.

30. The designers were: C. Caniggia, R. Greco, G. Imperato, in collaboration with the S. Brusa Pasqué group, and with F. Boracci Giardi, E. Cabianca, U. Roccatelli, and M. Vinciguerra.

31. See Caniggia and Maffei, *Moderno non moderno,* 13–14; idem, *Il progetto,* 24–27.

32. Idem, *Moderno non moderno,* 77ff.

33. For the competition project for Bologna, Caniggia collaborated with A. Boccardo, A. Ciriello, G. Conti, D. Corbara, L. Fanelli, E. Lavagnino, G. L. Maffei, P. Leoni, and M. Barabino. Regarding the competition for the station in Bologna, see M. Zardini, ed., "Il concorso per il nodo ferroviario di Bologna," *Casabella,* no. 497 (1983): 12–23, with notes by Tomás Maldonado, Pier Luigi Cervellati, and Bernardo Secchi, and an interview with Carlo Aymonino. This competition, which began with a decidedly flawed announcement, led to a series of oversized projects in which the theme of urban reweaving at least emerged as a problem.

34. Among the many attempts to elevate the professional climate in various Italian centers—such as the works of Luca Canali, Oswald

Zoeggeler, Mauro Saito, Francesco Cervellini, Rosa, and Saieva—one ought to note that of Pasquale Culotta and Giuseppe Leone, which resulted from their contact with the difficult realities of Sicilian life: see, for example, in spite of its schematic quality, the residential complex built in Cefalú. See P.-A. Croset, "Complesso residenziale a Cefalú," *Casabella*, no. 504 (1984): 54–63. On the other hand, we find the research projects of Renzo Piano rather perplexing, for, among other things, the "Meccan" emphasis placed on the Pompidou Center at Beaubourg in Paris (Piano & Rogers Studio, 1971–77). See, however, M. Dini, *Renzo Piano. Progetti e architetture 1964–1983* (Milan, 1983).

Chapter 13

1. On *Roma interrotta*, see part one, chapter 10 of this volume (bibliography in note 11). Also see F. Dal Co, ed., *10 immagini per Venezia* (Rome, 1980).

2. See the collection *Terza Mostra Internazionale di Architettura. Progetto Venezia*, 2 vols. (Milan, 1985).

3. See M. Tafuri, *Venezia e il Rinascimento* (Turin, 1985).

4. P. Portoghesi, "L'offerta progettuale," *Terza Mostra Internazionale*, 1:10.

5. See *Rinascita*, no. 31 (1985), in which Rossi responds to the criticisms of C. De Seta and V. Gregotti; Gregotti's answer can be found in issue no. 35 of the same review.

Chapter 14

1. See Portoghesi, *Dopo l'architettura moderna*; idem, "La fine del proibizionismo," in *La Presenza del Passato*, 9–14; idem, *Postmodern* (Milan, 1982); idem, *L'angelo della storia* (Rome-Bari, 1982); idem, *I nuovi architetti italiani* (Rome-Bari, 1985).

2. For a correct interpretation of Pevsner's historiographical construction, see M. Manieri Elia, "Il complesso d'Enea. Nikolaus Pevsner e la storiografia della 'continuità,'" *Casabella*, no. 423 (1977): 60–68. Also see M. L. Scalvini and M. G. Sandri, *L'immagine storiografica dell'architettura contemporanea da Platz a Giedion* (Rome, 1984), 73–97.

3. See J.-F. Lyotard, "Ripetizione, complessità, anamnesi," *Casabella*, no. 517 (1985): 44–45.

4. On Portoghesi's recent architecture, see G. Priori, *Simpatia delle cose. Oggetti e arredamenti progettati da Paolo Portoghesi* (Rome, 1982); idem, *L'architettura ritrovata. Opere recenti di Paolo Portoghesi* (Rome, 1985); idem, ed., *Paolo Portoghesi* (Bologna, 1985); *Paolo Portoghesi. Opere* (Modena, 1985), exhibition catalogue, with an essay by Claudio D'Amato.

5. See Portoghesi, *I nuovi architetti italiani*, passim.

6. Ibid., p. xi.

7. See F. Nietzsche, *Cosí parlò Zarathustra*, translation and appendices by M. Montinari, with an introductory note by G. Colli, 6th

ed., vol. 2 (Milan, 1981), 265–266 .

8. K. Löwith, *Nietzsches Philosophie der ewigen Wiederkehr des Gleichen* (Stuttgart, 1956); Italian trans. *Nietzsche e l'eterno ritorno*, 2nd ed. (Rome-Bari, 1985), 74 and 223.

9. Nietzsche, *Cosí parlò Zarathustra*, 2 : 266.

Chapter 15

1. F. Furet, *L'atelier de l'histoire* (Paris, 1982); Italian trans. (Milan, 1985), 51–65.

2. G. Teyssot, "Frammenti per un discorso funebre. L'architettura come lavoro di lutto," *Lotus International*, no. 38 (1983): 5–17.

3. M. Cacciari, "Nihilismo e progetto," *Casabella*, no. 483 (1982): 50–51. See also, idem, "Eupalinos o l'Architettura," *Nuova Corrente*, nos. 76–77 (1978): 422–42, an essay-review of M. Tafuri and F. Dal Co, *Architettura contemporanea* (Milan, 1976); idem, "Progetto," *Laboratorio Politico*, no. 2 (1981): 88–119; idem, "Adolf Loos e il suo angelo," in A. Loos, *Das Andere* (Milan, 1981), 9–34.

4. Cacciari, "Nihilismo," p. 51.

5. See Tafuri, *Progetto e utopia*.

6. M. Heidegger, "Costruire, abitare, pensare," *Lotus International*, no. 9 (1975): 38–43.

7. See J. Rykwert, "Chi ha chiuso la porta e gettato via la chiave?" *Casabella*, no. 484 (1982): 48–49; G. Vattimo, "Abitare viene prima di construire," ibid., no. 485: 48–49; F. Rella, "I sentieri del possibile,"
ibid., no. 486: 48–49; M. Cacciari, "Nihilismo e progetto. Risposta alle risposte," ibid., no. 489 (1983): 46–47. Vattimo has recently returned to problems near those at the center of that debate: see G. Vattimo, "Identità, differenza, confusione," ibid., no. 519 (1985): 42–43.

8. M. Scolari, "Ciò che si perde," *Casabella*, no. 493 (1983): 38.

Bibliographical Appendix

As mentioned in the preface, this bibliography includes only texts published between 1981 and the present (as well as a few texts previously omitted). For the preceding bibliography, see the notes on the text. We have tried to include, besides the few historical writings, texts that are at least representative of particular mentalities. Be forewarned, however, that the mounds of paper on the artificial platform of Italian debate consist mainly of hagiographical writings, useful only in caressing the "skin of the spirit" of various architects. This phenomenon, however, is not limited to the Italian situation; it is, therefore, susceptible to analysis and interpretation once its symptomatic value is recognized.

A. General Discussions of Recent Italian Architecture

Benevolo, L. *L'ultimo capitolo dell'architettura moderna*. Rome-Bari: 1985. Helpful, though Italian experiments are treated in the context of a comprehensive reading. This volume is useful less as a historical analysis, than as a tool to understand the changes in the working prospectives of a precise professional *tendenza*.

Belluzzi, A., and C. Conforti. *Architettura italiana 1944–1984*. Rome-Bari: 1985. An appreciable effort of documentation, though adhering too closely to the formula of a "guide" and barely historicized. The annotated bibliography on 195–201 is very useful, especially in its selection of architecture reviews.

De Seta, C. *Architetti italiani nel Novecento*. Rome-Bari, 1982. This gathers texts already published by the author, on architecture of the early twentieth century and the Fascist era, as well as articles on Albini, Gardella, Nervi, Rogers, and Benevolo, useful as introductions to various themes.

Dieci anni di architettura italiana 1970–1980. *Aura*, no. 1 (1983). This is a collection of interviews with architects and critics, with an introductory essay by B. Gravagnuolo, "Dal declino degli anni Settanta," 9–25. *Aura*, no. 2 (1984), features ample documentation divided according to *tendenza*.

Portoghesi, P. *I nuovi architetti italiani. Le luci del paradiso perduto.* Edited by Giovanna Massobrio. Rome-Bari: 1985. Though this work is to be criticized for its promotional character, it furnishes an ample graphic record of the younger generation's production.

Portoghesi, P. *Annali dell'architettura italiana contemporanea.* Edited by Maristella Casciato and Giorgio Muratore. Rome, 1985.

Cohen, J. L. *La coupure entre architectes et intellectuels, ou les enseignements de l'italophilie.* Paris: 1984. (*In extenso/1*, Recherches à l'École d'Architecture Paris-Villemin). An original and precise inquiry into the relations between French and Italian architectural cultures, which allows the author to trace a remarkably concise history of ideas.

Dal Co, F. *Architecttura italiana, 1960–1980,* 227–48. Vol. 4 of *Italia moderna 1960–1980. La difficile democrazia.* Milan: 1985.

Moschini, F. "L'architettura degli anni Ottanta." *Anni Ottanta,* exhibition catalogue, 354–81. Milan, 1985.

A reconsideration of the fifties can be found in *Controspazio* (n.s.) 14, nos. 1–2 (1983), with articles by

A. Greco, "I segni degli anni '50": 79–80; L. Menozzi, "Bildungsroman": 86–90; C. Barucci, "La pubblicistica di architettura dal 1945 al 1955:" 91–93; the issue also contains a series of interviews. Another reading of Italian "neorealism," set in the context of international *tendenze* of a similar vein can be found in the essay by M. Tafuri, "Architettura e realismo." In *L'avventura delle idee nell'architettura 1750–1980,* edited by V. Magnago Lampugnani, 123–36. Milan: 1985 (German original: Berlin, 1984).

See also the intelligent monographic issue of *Controspazio* 16, nos. 1–2 (1985), edited by Clementina Barucci and Antonella Greco, *Italia: verso nuove architetture. Problemi, tendenze, ricerche.*

On the younger Roman and Sicilian architects, see G. Polin. "Progettare per costruire: alcuni giovani architetti romani." *Casabella* 48, no. 501, special issue (1984): 18–33. Also see P. Culotta. "Giovani architetti siciliani." Ibid. 46, no. 515 (1985): 18–29.

B. The Architecture of Individual Cities and Regional Situations: Guides and Summaries

Gabetti, R. *Architettura, Industria, Piemonte negli ultimi cinquant'anni / G. Avigdor. Edilizia industriale e paesaggio.* Turin, 1977. This is a very articulate and well-documented volume, also useful as a source of analyses of other regional situations.

On Torino, see the excellent documentation in A. Magnaghi, M. Monge, L. Re. *Guida all'architettura moderna di Torino*. Turin: 1982. On Rome, see P. O. Rossi. *Roma. Guida all'architettura moderna 1909–1984*. Rome-Bari: 1984. (In collaboration with I. Gatti.) This volume contains detailed documentation but is lacking from a bibliographical point of view.

Regarding the controversy surrounding the programs for the future of the Imperial Forums, see the collection *Roma: continuità dell'antico. I Fori Imperiali nel progetto della città*. Milan: 1981. (This includes texts by A. La Regina, F. Coarelli, R. Nicolini, C. Aymonino, and R. Quinto.) Also see *Roma archeologia e progetto*. (catalogue) Rome: 1983. I. Insolera and F. Perego. *Archeologia e città. Storia moderna dei Fori di Roma*. Rome-Bari: 1983. For critical summaries of the broader debate, see C. Pavolini. "Fori Imperiali: le ragioni dell'archeologia." *Parametro* 16, no. 138 (1985): 43–49. Also see the articles by G. Rosa, R. Secchi, A. Melucco Vaccaro, M. Letizia Conforto and G. Martines, A. Carandini, E. Tortorici, R. Nicolini, C. Aymonino, A. Terranova, and A. Sayeva, ibid., no. 139 (1985).

See also *Controspazio* 15, special issue, no. 4, dedicated to *Roma: i problemi di una metropoli. La nuova architettura*, with a summary and documentation for projects and executions, and with a chronology of the Commune's administrative acts pertaining to the city and to architecture between 1976 and 1984.

Finally, see the essay by M. Manieri Elia, "La cultura della palazzina." *Italia moderna. Immagini e storia di un'identità nazionale*. Vol. 3, *Guerra, dopoguerra, ricostruzione, decollo*, 327–42. Milan: 1983. This includes a historical analysis of a specific building experiment in Rome.

Regarding Milan, see the essay by various authors, "I progetti e il piano per Milano." *Casabella* 48, no. 508 (1984): 18–29. On the prospects for Venice, see the monographic issue of *Rassegna*, no. 22 (1985).

On Bologna, see V. Quilici and A. Sichenze. *Costruttori di architetture. Bologna 1960–1980*. Rome: 1985. The authors analyze in depth the building policies and planning techniques adopted; the text also contains interviews with the protagonists.

C. Analyses of the Debate on Urban Planning

It is impossible to give an account here of the considerable mass of publications on the theme, though it is relevant because of its general coordinates and its relation to the differentiation from and recombination with other disciplines concerning the physical aspect of the city and countryside. We will limit ourselves, therefore, to texts and essays particularly illustrative of new directions.

Cervellati, P. L. *La città postindustriale*. Bologna, 1984. This essay examines the misunderstandings of the traditional "master plan" and the tragic degradation that industrialization and urban sprawl have inflicted on the ecosystem, in order to propose a careful recovery of urban "vacuums," historical structures, and suburban areas.

Secchi, B. *Il racconto urbanistico. La politica della casa e del territorio in Italia.* Turin: 1984. This text seriously attempts a stringent analysis of the history of urbanism as a discipline in Italy, and offers suggestions emerging more from the orientation of the analyses themselves then from subjectively elaborated, miraculous solutions.

Secchi, B. "Il piano." *Urbanistica,* no. 78 (1985): 2–5. This editorial introduced the first issue of the new series of the review. The issue is itself important, because it documents not only the preliminary design for the PRG for Bologna, but also the so-called "Progetto Milano."

Secchi, B. "La crisi dei vecchi strumenti urbanistici: l'esistente come patrimonio." *Italia moderna,* vol. 4: 189–204.

Romano, M. *L'urbanistica in Italia nel periodo dello sviluppo: 1940–1980.* Padua: 1985.

On the Bologna plan, also see G. Mattioli, R. Matulli, R. Scannavini, and P. Capponcelli, eds. *Bologna, una città per gli anni '90. Il progetto del nuovo piano regolatore generale.* Venice, 1985.

Casabella contains a particularly interesting debate on the theme. See, for example: P. Ceccarelli. "Dopo l'ideologia del planning." *Casabella* 47, nos. 487–488: 68–71.

B. Secchi. "Piani della terza generazione." Ibid. 49, no. 516 (1985): 14–15; Idem. "La ricostruzione della città." Ibid., no. 517: 22–23. G. Campos Venuti. "Ancora sui piani della terza generazione." Ibid., no. 518: 22–23.

Another summary can be found in G. Piccinato. "Le teorie dell'urbanistica italiana." *Urbanistica,* nos. 76–77 (1984): 28ff. The same issue of *Urbanistica* contains another example of the "*piano progetto,*" the new master plan of the Commune of Sassuolo. Regarding this also see A. Manfredini. "Sassuolo oltre Sassuolo." *Parametro* 16, no. 138 (1985): 60. Also see the preliminary scheme for the regulatory plan of Florence in *Urbanistica,* no. 81 (1985): 46–75.

On the preceding urban experiment in Florence, see M. Zoppi. *Firenze e l'urbanistica: la ricerca del piano.* Rome, 1983.

On the urban problems of Naples, see C. De Seta. *Dopo il terremoto la ricostruzione.* Rome-Bari, 1983. This contains an ample bibliography in the notes. Also see G. Cosenza, ed. "Il caso Napoli." *Casabella* 47, nos. 487–488 (1983): 30–43.

D. Monographs and Essays on Individual Architects

This is the area favored by commentators on architecture, even though distinctions are made between analyses that in some way attempt to insert various individuals into a historical context and merely occasional writings. One ought to note, however, that particular discussions rarely manage to overcome historiographical poverty, in spite of the prophetic, dignified, or decidedly hermetic tones assumed. We provide, however, a list of the most important works.

Asnago and Vender

Airoldi, R. "Documenti di architettura: Asnago e Vender." *Casabella* 46, no. 478 (1982): 42–47.

Aulenti

Croset, P.-A. "Aménagement intérieur del Museo d'Orsay." *Casabella* 46, no. 482 (1982): 48–61.

Croset, P.-A. and S. Milesi. "Gae Aulenti, Piero Castiglioni, Italo Rota. Il nuovo allestimento del Museo Nazionale d'Arte Moderna nel Centre Georges Pompidou." *Casabella* 49, no. 515 (1985): 54–59, with an interview of Dominique Bozo, "Ritorno al Museo": 60–63.

Aulenti, G. "Il progetto per il museo di Orsay: l'architettura come integrazione delle scelte." *Urbanistica*, no. 81 (1985): 30–34.

Aymonino

Conforti, C. *Il Gallaratese di Aymonino e Rossi, 1967–1972.* Rome: 1981. A good microhistorical analysis, with ample original documentation.

Polin, G. "Il Palazzo di Giustizia di Ferrara." *Casabella* 46, no. 479 (1982): 2ff.

Polin, G. "Carlo Aymonino,

Fausto Battimelli, Raffaele Panella. Centro direzionale Benelli a Pesaro." *Casabella* 46, no. 497 (1983): 50–61.

Aymonino, C. "Ferrara. Rehabilitación de la Iglesia y Convento del Gesú." *Periferia*, no. 1 (1984): 22–29.

Baldessari

Fagone, F. *Baldessari. Progetti e scenografie.* Milan: 1982.

BBPR

Piva, A., ed. *BBPR a Milano.* Exhibition catalogue. Milan: 1982.

Bega

Zironi, S. *Melchiorre Bega architetto.* Milan: 1983.

Caccia Dominioni

Polin, G. "Un architetto milanese tra regionalismo e sperimentazione: Luigi Caccia Dominioni." *Casabella* 46, no. 508 (1984): 40–51.

Canella

Suzuki, K. *Guido Canella.* Bologna: 1983. With an introduction by A. Christofellis.

Fiori, L., and S. Bondi, eds. *Guido Canella, Centro Civico di Pieve Emanuele.* With an introductory essay by M. De Micheli. Milan: 1984.

Savi, V., ed. *Guido Canella. Opere recenti.* Exhibition catalogue. Modena: 1984.

Caniggia

Caniggia, G., and G. L. Maffei. *Moderno, non moderno. Il luogo e la continuità.* Venice: 1984.

Daneri
Patrone, P. D. *Daneri.* With an introduction by E. D. Bona. Genoa: 1982. An extremely balanced and complete monograph.

De Finetti
Cappellato, G, and M. Macchietto. "Giuseppe De Finetti: inquieto maestro del nostro tempo." *Parametro*, no. 126 (1984): 16–55. The result of careful archival research.

Fiorentino
Fiorentino, M. *La casa.* Rome: 1985.

Gabetti and Isola
Cellini, F., and C. D'Amato. *Gabetti e Isola. Progetti e architettura 1950–1985.* Milan: 1985. A good comprehensive reading of the work of these two architects from Turin.

Gardella
Samonà, A. *Ignazio Gardella e il professionismo italiano.* Rome: 1981.

Porta, M., ed., *L'architettura di Ignazio Gardella.* Milan: 1985.

Grassi
Iacometti, G., ed., *Giorgio Grassi. Progetti e disegni 1965–1980.* Mantua: 1982.

Moschini, F. ed. *Giorgio Grassi. Progetti 1960–1980.* Florence: 1984.

Lahuerta, J. J. *Arquitectura de Giorgio Grassi.* Barcelona: 1985.

Grassi, G. "Scena fissa. Progetto per il teatro romano di Sagunto." *Lotus International*, no. 46 (1985): 7–21.

GRAU
Anselmi, A. *Occasioni d'architettura.* Rome: 1980.

Portoghesi, P. "Sulle fertili ceneri dell'ideologia. I cimiteri di Alessandro Anselmi." *Lotus International*, no. 38 (1983): 18–29.

Portoghesi, P. *Roberto Mariotti (G. R. A. U.), S. Gregorio Magno 1981–1984: la ricostruzione con il blu cobalto.* Presentation by F. Moschini. Rome: 1985.

Eroli, P. *Racconti di architettura. Progetti e pitture dal 1981 al 1984.* Presentation by F. Moschini. Rome: 1985.

Gregotti
Lovero, P. "La generazione dello Z. E. N. Evora, Vitoria, Palermo: tre quartieri a confronto." *Lotus International*, no. 36 (1982): 27–45.

Tafuri, M. *Vittorio Gregotti. Progetti e architetture.* Milan: 1982.

Polin, G. "Gregotti Associati. Nuovi uffici Bossi a Cameri." *Casabella* 47, no. 493 (1983): 2–9.

Brandolini, S., and P.-A. Croset. "Gregotti associati, G 14 Progettazione. Studio GPI. Cadorna-Pagano: un progetto per il centro di Milano." *Casabella* 48, no. 513 (1984): 52–63.

Gregotti, V. "La fabbrica universitaria. Dipartimenti dell'Università di Palermo di Vittorio Gregotti e Gino Pollini." *Lotus International*, no. 45 (1985): 41–53.

Gresleri, Varnier
Gresleri, G. and S. Varnier.

Costruire l'architettura. With a preface by G. Samonà and an essay by A. Cornoldi. Milan, 1981.

Marescotti

Ciucci, G. "Il 'manuale' nella cultura europea." Also see M. Casciato. "Quando Francoforte era sul Naviglio." These two essays, on 11–13 and 13–16 respectively, are part of the preface to the new edition of I. Diotallevi and F. Marescotti. *Il problema sociale, costruttivo ed economico dell'abitazione.* Rome, 1984. This volume also contains an introductory essay by Marescotti.

Mattioni

Alfonsi, G., and G. Zucconi, eds. *Luigi Mattioni. Architetto della ricostruzione.* Milan: 1985. This is a very balanced monograph examining the work of an important Milanese professional who has managed to remain outside the postwar debates of architectural culture. It was used as a *test* for an impartial evaluation of the culture of the "age of reconstruction."

Mollino

Brino, G. *Carlo Mollino. Architettura come autobiografia.* Milan: 1985.

Morandi

Boaga, G., ed. *Riccardo Morandi.* Bologna: 1984.

Muratori

Cataldi, G. ed. *Saverio Muratori architetto (1913–1973). Il pensiero e l'opera.* Exhibition catalogue. Florence, 1984.

The monographic issue of the review *Storia Architettura 7,* nos. 1–2 (1984), dedicated to Saverio Muratori, with writings by L. Quaroni, P. Maretto, G. Caniggia, S. Bollati, G. Cataldi, G. Marinucci, and G. Sermonti, and useful list of selected criticism by L. Marcucci.

Natalini

Polin, G. "Sede di una banca ad Alzate Brianza." *Casabella* 46, no. 486 (1982): 2ff.

Minardi, B. "Edificio a doppia maniera. Involucro tradizionale e contenuto sofisticato." *Lotus International* no. 37 (1983): 52–60.

Natalini, A. "Edificio con rivestimento in pietra. Sede della Cassa Rurale e Artigiana di Alzate Brianza, Como." *Lotus International,* no. 40 (1983): 4–18.

Savi, V. "Storia di un progetto. Adolfo Natalini e una sua architettura." *Lotus International,* no. 40 (1983): 19–21.

Natalini, A. *Figure di pietra.* Milan: 1984.

Nervi

Ramazzotti, L., ed. *Nervi oggi.* Proceedings from the convention in Ancona. Rome: 1983.

Nizzoli

Gravagnuolo, B., ed. *Gli studi Nizzoli. Architettura e design 1948–1983.* Milan: 1983.

Pagliara

Progetti, storie, racconti di Nicola Pagliara architetto. Naples: 1981.

Passarelli

Lenci, S. *Lucio Passarelli e lo studio Passarelli*. Bari: 1983.

Pellegrin

"Luigi Pellegrin: pensieri, progetti, opere 1973–1984." An interview of the author by Renato Pedio. In *L'architettura—cronache e storia* 31, nos. 358–359 (1985): 562–614.

Piano

Dini, M. *Renzo Piano. Progetti e architetture 1964-1983*. Milan: 1983.

Piccinato

De Sessa, C. *Luigi Piccinato architetto*. Bari, 1985. A work, however, that is unreliable from a scholary point of view.

Polesello

Gianugo Polesello. Progetti di architettura. With an introduction by P. Grandinetti. Rome, 1983.

Portoghesi

Priori, G. *L'architettura ritrovata. Opere recenti di Paolo Portoghesi*. Rome, 1985.

Priori, G. *Paolo Portoghesi*. Bologna, 1985.

Paolo Portoghesi. Opere. Exhibition catalogue, with an essay by Claudio D'Amato. Modena: 1985.

Purini and Thermes

Dal Co, F. "Franco Purini e Laura Thermes. 65 abitazioni a Napoli." *Casabella* 47, no. 494 (1983): 2–11.

Accasto, G. "Le cose nella casa. Considerazioni su un'architettura

di Franco Purini e Laura Thermes." *Lotus International*, no. 40 (1983): 74–79. This article is followed by one by F. Purini, "Casa del farmacista di Gibellina (Sicilia): un cantiere nel sud" on 80, and photos of the project and its execution on 81–89.

Purini, F., L. Thermes, with D. Modigliani. "La grande modanatura. Progetto per il centro civico di Castelforte, Latina." *Lotus International*, no. 43 (1984): 101–8

Quaroni

Terranova, A., ed., with P. Ciovra, P. Micalizzi, and M. L. Neri. *Ludovico Quaroni. Architetture per cinquant'anni*. Rome-Reggio Calabria, 1985. This contains a complete bibliography and a list of works.

Ricci

Nardi, A., ed. *Leonardo Ricci*. Pistoia: 1984.

Ridolfi and Frankl

Polin, G. "Nuovo palazzo per uffici del Comune di Terni." *Casabella* 47, no. 489 (1983): 48–61.

Cosentino, N. "Mario Ridolfi. Casa Luccioni a Terni, 1977–79." *Controspazio* 14, special issue, nos. 1–2 (1983): 63–69.

Cellini, F. "Su Mario Ridolfi. Geometria e costruzione della pianta centrale." *Lotus International* no. 37 (1983): 15–24.

D'Amato, C. "Il ciclo delle Marmore." *Lotus International*, no. 37 (1983): 25–33.

Benevolo, L. "Ricordo di Mario Ridolfi." *Casabella* 48, no. 508 (1984): 30.

Rogers, E. N.

De Seta, C. "Introduzione," 9–14, and L. Belgiojoso, "Testimonianza per Ernesto Rogers," 15–19. In E. N. Rogers. *Elementi del fenomeno architettonico*. Ed. C. De Seta. Naples: 1981. Rogers' later writings are gathered in Idem, *Esperienza dell'architettura*. Turin: 1958. And in *Editoriali di architettura*. Turin: 1968. (See also BBPR.)

Rossi

Braghieri, G., ed. *Aldo Rossi*. Bologna: 1981.

Aldo Rossi and 21 works. *A + U* special issue. Tokyo: 1982.

Johnson, E. J. "What Remains of Man—Aldo Rossi's Modena Cemetery." *Journal of the Society of Architectural Historians* 41, no. 1 (1982):. 38–54.

Savi, V. and M. Lupano, eds. *Aldo Rossi. Opere recenti*. Exhibition catalogue. Modena: 1983.

Savi, V. "Il cimitero aldorossiano. Traccia di racconto critico." *Lotus International*, no. 38 (1984): 30–43.

The project for the Carlo Felice Theater of Genoa by A. Rossi, I. Gardella, and F. Reinhart was published in *Casabella* 48, no. 502 (1984): 52ff.

This issue also contains a presentation by P. -A. Croset and G. Polin, and a critical essay by Gae Aulenti. The project was also published in *Lotus International*, no. 2 (1984): 12–25.

The project for the office building in Buenos Aires by A. Rossi and G. Braghieri (with the collaboration of M. Osks, G. Ciocca and M. Scheurer) can be found in *Lotus International*, no. 2: 26–39.

See also H. Piñon. "La lógica de la memoria." Idem. *Arquitectura de las neovanguardias*, 79–116. Barcelona: 1984. This essay is as disappointing as the entire volume, whose very title is unacceptable.

Samonà

"Il Teatro a doppia sala di Sciacca." *Casabella* 47, no. 480 (1982): 48–61.

Savioli

Brunetti, F. *Leonardo Savioli architetto*. Bari: 1982.

Scarpa

Rudi, A., ed. *Carlo Scarpa. Frammenti 1926–1978*. Monographic issue of *Rassegna*, no. 7 (1981).

Magagnato, L., ed. *Carlo Scarpa a Castelvecchio*. Milan, 1982. This contains essays by S. Marinelli, M. Dalai Emiliani, A. Rudi, and L. Magagnato.

Rudi, A., and V. Rossetto, eds. *La Sede Centrale della Banca Popolare di Verona*. Verona, 1983.

Marcianò, A. F., ed. *Carlo Scarpa*. Bologna: 1984.

Crippa, M. A. *Scarpa. Il pensiero, il disegno, i progetti*. Milano, 1984. This is a rather disappointing monograph.

Dal Co, F., and G. Mazzariol. *Carlo Scarpa. Opera completa.* Milan: 1984. This contains essays by G. Mazzariol and F. Barbieri, F. Dal Co, and M. Tafuri, a catalogue edited by S. Polano, various reports, a bibliography, and complete lists of works.

Semerani and Tamaro
Rosa, G., ed. *Semerani + Tamaro. La città e i progetti.* Rome, 1983. This includes a letter from M. Tafuri.

Superstudio
Pettena, G., ed. *Superstudio 1966–1982. Storia, figure, architettura.* Exhibition catalogue. Milan: 1982.

Valle
Polin, G. "Nuove abitazioni popolari a Venezia." *Casabella* 46, no. 478 (1982): 50–61.

Croset, P.-A. "Centro direzionale a Pordenone." *Casabella* 47, no. 495 (1983): 50–61.

Marpillero, S. "Grattacielo a metà. Gino Valle: uffici della Banca Commerciale Italiana a Manhattan." *Lotus International*, no. 37 (1983): 96–119.

Croset, P.-A., and G. Polin. "IBM Distribution Center a Basiano." *Casabella* 48, no. 500 (1984): 52–63.

Croset, P.-A. "Gino Valle. Edifico per uffici alla Défense a Parigi." *Casabella* 49, no. 519 (1985): 4–15; on 16–17, See "Una conversazione con Gino Valle."

Zacchiroli
König, G. K. *Enzo Zacchiroli. Il mestiere full-time.* Bari: 1980.

Zanuso
Brandolin, S., and G. Polin. "Studio Associato Marco Zanuso e Pietro Crescini. Un nuovo complesso teatrale a Milano." *Casabella* 48, no. 508 (1984): 4–15.

Zevi
Oppenheimer Dean, A. *Bruno Zevi on Modern Architecture.* New York: 1984. See the review by P. Polledri in *Design Book Review* (Summer 1985): 63–65.

E. Various Topics

On the work and ideas of Adriano Olivetti, and in relation to urban planning and architecture, see the volume by various authors, *L'immagine della comunità*, edited by M. Fabbri, A. Greco, L. Menozzi, and E. Valeriani, with an introduction by A. Quistelli and an anthology of writings. Rome: 1982. It discusses architecture and urban planning in Italy after the war.

On the competition for FIAT-Lingotto, see M. Zardini, ed. *Venti idee per il Lingotto.* Also see the essay by B. Secchi and interview with Mario Botta in *Casabella* 48, no. 502 (1984): 16–31, and the collection *Venti progetti per il futuro del Lingotto.* Milan: 1984.

On the architecture exhibition at the 1985 Venice Biennale, see *Terza Mostra Internazionale di Architettura. Progetto Venezia.* 2 vols. Milan:

1985. Regarding which, see F. Mancuso. "Biennale '85. Progetto Venezia." *Spazio e società*, nos. 31–32 (1985): 76–78.

A summary of the debate on typology can be found in the monographic issue of *Casabella* 49, nos. 509–510 (1985): 76–78.

On the competition for the Venice IACP on Giudecca, see C. Magnani. "Il concorso dello IACP di Venezia per Campo di Marte alla Giudecca." *Casabella* 49, no. 518 (1985): 4–21.

On the competition for the urban park of Bologna, see *Il Labirinto. Centotrentotto idee progettuali per il parco urbano del Porto Navile e della Manifattura Tabacchi.* 2 vols. Bologna: 1985.

Special attention has been paid, in recent years, to amassing archives of designs by contemporary Italian architects. These include the *Archivio del Progetto* at the University of Parma, which has collected the archives of, among others, Giuseppe Samonà, Ignazio Gardella, Carlo Aymonino, the STASS group, Pier Luigi Nervi, Gio Ponti, and Giuseppe De Finetti; the *Archivio Michelucci* at the Civic Museum of Pistoia; the *Archivio dell'Accademia di San Luca* in Rome, which preserves the designs of Mario De Renzi and Mario Ridolfi, as well as some by Pietro Aschieri and Giuseppe Capponi; the *Archivio Albini* at the Albini-Helg studio in Milan; and the *Archivio Piacentini* at the library of the Architecture School of the University of Florence.

Index

Aalto, Alvar Hugo Henrik, 8, 66
Achilli, Michele, 83, 89, 131–132
Agati, Luigi, 24
Albini, Franco, 3–4, 14, 22, 27–28,
    32, 38, 49–51, 65, 71, 82, 85–86
Albricci, Gianni, 32
Aldisio, Salvatore, 43, 62
Alexander, Christopher, 74
Ambasz, Emilio, 99
Andreani, Aldo, 57
Angelini-Dierna-Mortola-Orlandi,
    group, 118, 144
Anselmi, Alessandro, 160, 178
Antonelli, Alessandro, 57
Antonioni, Michelangelo, 58
Anversa, Maria Luisa, 84, 144
Aprile, Nello, 4
AR, group, 6–7
Architettura, group, 9, 38, 69, 172
Archizoom, group, 99
Argan, Giulio Carlo, 21–22, 54–55,
    71, 110
Ascione, Errico, 100
Asnago, Mario, 14
Asor Rosa, Alberto, 102
Astengo, Giovanni, 7, 22, 62, 97,
    101, 155
Astengo-Renacco, group, 32
Aulenti, Gae, 57–58, 90, 131, 133,
    135, 166–167, 180

Aymonino, Carlo, 17, 66–67, 69, 77,
    84, 89–90, 92–93, 119, 122–126,
    142, 144, 157, 160–162, 170, 172,
    180–181, 187

Bakema, Jacob, B. 68, 70, 119
Balestrini, Nanni, 90
Ballio Morpurgo, Vittorio, 81
Baltard, Victor, 57
Banfi, Antonio, 53
Banham, Reyner, 54, 58
Barabino, Carlo, 179
Barucci, Pietro, 81
Basile, Ernesto, 92
Battisti, Emilio, 144
Bega, Melchiorre, 68
Belgiojoso, Ludovico Barbiano di,
    22
Benevolo, Leonardo, 45, 60, 65–66,
    69–71, 88, 161
Benjamin, Walter, 125, 151, 190, 198
Berarducci, Francesco, 82
Berio, Luciano, 90
Bernasconi, Gianantonio, 35
Bianco, Mario, 7, 49–50
Bichara, Riccardo, 191
Bill, Max, 136
Blanchot, Maurice, 137
Blanco, Giorgio, 191
Blanqui, Louis-Auguste, 190

Bloc, André, 79
Bloch, Ernst, 114
Bocchi, Renato, 173
Böcklin, Arnold, 136
Bohigas, Oriol, 127
Bonatz, Paul, 60
Boselli, Serena, 32
Bottoni, Piero, 14–15
BPR, group, 4–5, 14, 28, 32, 38,
    51–54, 56, 65, 86, 109, 196
Braghieri, Gianni, 179–180
Braque, Georges, 112
Brass, Tinto, 90
Brigidini, Daniele, 89, 131–132
Brinkman, Michiel, 125
Brion, G., 113–114
Brivio, Peppo, 90
Bruschi, Arnaldo, 69
Buonarroti, Michelangelo, 79

Caccia-Dominioni, Luigi, 67, 86
Cacciari, Massimo, 114, 197–201
Cafiero, Vittorio, 69
Calcaprina, Cino, 4
Calia, E., 24
Calini, Leo, 69, 82
Campos-Venuti, Giuseppe, 69, 83,
    152, 155, 157
Canella, Guido, 56–57, 77, 79,
    89–90, 131–133, 135, 164, 170,
    174–175, 186
Caniggia, Gianfranco, 59, 61,
    181–182, 196
Cantàfora, Arduino, 145
Cappai, Igino, 130
Cardelli, Aldo, 4, 11
Caré, Arrigo, 11
Castore, group, 144
Ceccarelli, Paolo, 77
Cederna, Antonio, 44
Cellini, Francesco, 186, 192
Ceradini, Giulio, 11
Cervellati, Pier Luigi, 156
Chiarini, Carlo, 17, 173

Chiatante, Paola, 178
Christofellis, Alessandro, 175
CIAM, group, 6
Cicconcelli, Ciro, 46–47, 108
Cicconcelli, group, 46
Ciocca, Gaetano, 180
Clemente, Fernando, 155, 157
Cobelli, Giancarlo, 40
Colli, Giorgio, 192
Conte, Carlo, 36
Coprat Associates, 179
Cosentino, Nicoletta, 192
Cosenza, Luigi, 37
Cremona, Luigi, 173
Crotti, Sergio, 163
Cundari, Gianfranco, 191

Dal Co, Francesco, 30
Dall'Olio, Claudio, 21, 68
Daneri, group, 47
Daneri, Luigi Carlo, 33
Dardi, Costantino, 89, 93, 122, 142,
    186
Da Rios, Giovanni, 133
De Carlo, Adolfo, 36
De Carlo, Giancarlo, 22, 40, 58, 72,
    75–76, 89, 92, 119–121, 126, 153
De Chirico, Giorgio, 101, 136
De Feo, Vittorio, 81, 94, 100–101,
    174, 186
De Finetti, Giuseppe, 5, 57
De Gasperi, Alcide, 24
Del Debbio, Enrico, 48
Deleuze, Gilles, 189
Della Rocca, Aldo, 6
Della Volpe, Galvano, 100
De Lucia, Vezio, 165
De Renzi, Mario, 6, 33
De Rossi, Baldo, 83, 101
Derrida, Jacques, 196
De Sanctis, Francesco, 8
Di Cagno, Nico, 85
Dierna, Salvatore, 118, 144
Diotallevi, Irenio, 13–14

Doglio, Carlo, 40
D'Olivo, Marcello, 21, 74, 79
Dorso, Guido, 8
Drocco, Guido, 175
Duchamp, Marcel, 5, 99, 191
Dudok, Willem Marinus, 57, 66

Eberstadt, Rudolph, 63
Eco, Umberto, 89–90
Ehn, Karl, 125
Einaudi, Luigi, 15, 21

Fabbri, Gianni, 172–173
Fagiolo, Marcello, 50
Fahrenkamp, Emil, 60
Fariello, Francesco, 60
Farina, Paolo, 130
Fellini, Federico, 58, 122
Feltrinelli, Giangiacomo, 89
Figini, Luigi, 14, 32, 35–36, 86
Finsterlin, Hermann, 79
Fiocchi, Annibale, 35–36, 39
Fiorentino, Mario, 4, 11, 17, 19, 32,
    78, 82–84, 119, 123–126, 144, 173
Fiorese, Giorgio, 175
Fiori, Leonardo, 36
Fioroni, Alessandro, 82
Forbat, Fred, 10
Fornaroli, Antonio, 68
Fortini, Franco, 75, 94
Foschini, Arnaldo, 16, 33
Fossati, Paolo, 38
Frankl, Wolfgang, 19, 87–88
Frassinelli, Giampiero, 177
Freud, Sigmund, 190, 196
Furet, François, 197

Gabetti, Roberto, 3, 30, 54–57,
    129–131, 135, 166–167, 174–175,
    192, 196
Gadda, Carlo Emilio, 85, 137
Garcia La Fuente, M. Clara, 175
Gardella, Ignazio, 4, 14, 22, 27, 32,
    36, 38, 53–54, 58, 65, 85–86, 113,
    179, 196

Gaudì, Antoni, 132
Gehlen, Arnold, 189, 192
Gellner, Edoardo, 21
Ghidini, L., 14
Giacometti, Alberto, 5
Giordani, Pier Luigi, 77, 157
Giura Longo, Raffaele, 65
Giurgola, Romaldo, 93
Goethe, Johann Wolfgang von, 141
Gori, group, 47
Gorio, Federico, 17, 24, 45, 83, 123
Grandi, Maurizio, 14
Grassi, Giorgio, 50, 100, 136,
    141–143, 173–175, 181
GRAU, group, 93–94, 100–101, 143,
    178
Gregotti, associates, 119, 125–126,
    131, 151, 167
Gregotti, Vittorio, 55–57, 89–91,
    115, 125–127, 129, 144, 161, 166,
    170–172, 175
Gropius, Walter, 21, 70–71
Grossi, Giuseppe, 174
Group '63, 99
Guerriero, Alessandro, 187
Guidi, Ignazio, 6

Heidegger, Martin, 189–190, 197,
    199–200
Helg, Franca, 71
Hilberseimer, Ludwig, 141
Hölderlin, Friedrich, 197

Insolera, Italo, 69, 92
Isola, Aimaro, 3, 30, 54–57, 129–131,
    135, 166–167, 174–175, 192, 196

Jacobsen, Arne, 70
Jencks, Charles, 189

Kafka, Franz, 101, 190
Kahn, Louis, 93, 100–101, 171, 177
Kiesler, Fredrick, 79
Klee, Paul, 93, 113–114, 190
Krier, Leon, 142

Labrouste, Henri, 57
Lacan, Jacques, 192
LaMalfa, Ugo, 75
Lambertucci, Alfredo, 68
Lang, Fritz, 87
Lanza, Maurizio, 17
La Pietra, Ugo, 99
Lazzari, Laura, 89
Le Corbusier, 10, 21, 47, 55, 66–67,
    70, 93, 116, 123, 177, 190
Léger, Ferdinand, 112
Lenci, Sergio, 17
Leo, Ludwig, 142
Leoncilli, Giancarlo, 187
Leoni, P., 185–187
Levi, Carlo, 23, 53
Levinas, Emmanuel, 189
Lévi–Strauss, Claude, 91
Libera, Adalberto, 33, 68–69
Libertini, Lucio, 75
Ligini, Cesare, 81
Lissitzky, L., 138
Loos, Adolf, 5, 136, 180, 190
Lorenzetti, Ambrogio, 62
Loris Rossi, Aldo, 166
Löwith, Karl, 192
Luccichenti, Amedeo, 26, 69
Luccichenti, Ugo, 26
Lugli, Piero Maria, 17, 24, 123
Lukács, György, 56
Lynch, Kevin, 76, 91
Lyotard, Jean-François, 149, 191

Macchi Cassia, Cesare, 144
Mackay, D., 127
Mafai, Mario, 94
Magistretti, Vico, 67, 89, 122
Magnani, Carlo, 173
Mainardis, Piero, 130
Malagricci, Domenico, 87
Malara, Empio, 164
Maldonado, Tomás, 172
Malevich, C., 101, 190
Malpeli, Cherubino, 6

Mamino, Lorenzo, 175
Mangiarotti, Angelo, 67
Manieri-De Feo, group, 94
Manieri-Elia, Mario, 69, 160
Manieri-Nicoletti, group, 65
Manzone, Antonino, 74
Marcenaro, Caterina, 50
Marconi, Paolo, 59
Marescotti, Franco, 13–16
Maretto, Paolo, 155
Marino, Roberto, 78, 171
Marinucci, Guido, 81
Martellotti, Paolo, 143, 145
Martini, Arturo, 112
Martorell, J. M., 127
Mattioni, Luigi, 15, 68
Mazzarone, Rocco, 24
Melanesi, Italo, 173
Melnikov, Kostantin, 10, 132
Melograni, Carlo, 17, 65, 69
Melotti, Fausto, 5
Mendelsohn, Erich, 79
Mendini, Alessandro, 187
Meneghetti, Ludovico, 57, 89–90
Menichetti, Giancarlo, 17
Menna, Filiberto, 99
Messina, Bruno, 66, 115
Michelucci, Giovanni, 7, 9, 28–30,
    54, 78, 80, 196
Mies van der Rohe, Ludwig, 55,
    190
Minardi, Bruno, 174
Minoletti, Giulio, 4
Modigliani, D., 179
Mollino, Carlo, 21
Monaco, Vincenzo, 26, 69
Moncalvo, Enrico, 175
Mondrian, Piet, 113
Moneo, Rafael, 171
Monestiroli, Antonio, 174, 186
Monge, Mariolina, 175
Montale, Eugenio, 85
Montinari, Mazzino, 192
Montuori, Eugenio, 69, 82

Morabito, Giovanni, 186
Morandi, Giorgio, 137
Morandi, Riccardo, 82, 107
Moretti, Luigi, 26–27, 69, 81
Moroni, Piero, 69, 72, 85
Morselli, Alessandro, 164
Mozzoni, G., 14
Mumford, Lewis, 23, 30
Muratori, Saverio, 6, 12, 33, 60–62,
   100, 181, 196
Musmeci, Sergio, 36, 40
Muzio, Giovanni, 57, 91

Natalini, Adolfo, 142
Natalini, Fabrizio, 177–178
Nervi, Pier Luigi, 69, 74, 81, 114
Nicolin, Pier Luigi, 186
Nicolini, Renato, 160, 162
9999, group, 99
Nietzsche, Friedrich, 190, 197, 199
Nizzoli, associates, 108
Nizzoli, Marcello, 5, 35–36, 38

Oliveri, Mario, 36
Olivetti, Adriano, 7, 22–24, 30,
   35–40, 54, 75, 86, 108, 112, 130,
   166, 172
Osks, M., 180
Ottieri, Ottiero, 37

Paci, Enzo, 52
Pagano, Giuseppe, 4, 13, 33
Pagano, group, 9
Pagliara, Nicola, 145
Panella, Raffaele, 173
Panzarin, Francesco, 173
Panzieri, Raniero, 75
Pasolini, Pier Paolo, 115
Passarelli, Fausto, 80
Passarelli, Lucio, 80
Passarelli, Vincenzo, 80
Passi, Dario, 145
Pellegrin, Luigi, 46–47, 93, 108–109,
   166–167

Perilli, Achille, 90
Perniola, Mario, 189
Perret, Auguste, 57, 66
Persico, Edoardo, 4–5, 108
Perugini-Del Debbio, group, 48
Perugini, Giuseppe, 4
Perugini-Monteduro, group, 81
Pevsner, Nikolaus, 70, 191
Piacentini, Marcello, 63, 81
Piano, Renzo, 166
Picasso, Pablo, 91
Piccinato, Luigi, 6, 22, 25, 31, 36, 39,
   62
Pintori, Giovanni, 38
Piranesi, Giambattista, 100, 144
Pirrone, Gianni, 115
Pirzio Biroli, Roberto, 187, 191
Poelzig, Hans, 93, 116
Polesello, Gian Ugo, 91, 94, 173, 186
Polesello, group, 144
Pollini, Gino, 14, 32, 35–36, 67, 86
Pollock, Jackson, 79
Ponti, Gio, 32, 68
Porta, Marco, 144, 163, 166
Portoghesi, Paolo, 59, 79, 92, 157,
   160, 187, 189–192
Purini, Franco, 3, 91, 101, 126–127,
   143–145, 170, 178–179, 186
Püschel, Konrad, 10

Quaroni, Ludovico, 9, 11, 18, 22–25,
   36, 39–40, 44–47, 60, 62–65, 72–74,
   76–77, 82, 84–85, 88, 92–93, 101,
   115–118, 124, 143, 153, 160–161
Quaroni-Ridolfi, group, 10–12,
   17–18, 123, 173
Quistelli, Antonio, 74

Radiconcini, Silvio, 21
Raineri, Giorgio, 55, 130, 175
Raineri, Giuseppe, 55
Ranieri, E., 39
Ranzi, Maurizio, 160
Rauschenberg, Robert, 94

Rebecchini, Marcello, 144
Rebecchini, Salvatore, 44
Reinhart, Fabio, 179
Renacco, Nello, 32, 39
Renna, Agostino, 142
Restany, Pierre, 99
Ricci, Leonardo, 78–79, 186
Ridolfi, Mario, 3, 6, 10–13, 17–20, 25, 29–30, 36, 47, 56, 86–88, 101, 114, 123–124, 173, 196
Rinaldi, Giulio, 17
Rocchetto, Stefano, 173
Rogers, Ernesto Nathan, 3, 5, 9, 28, 51, 53, 55–58, 71, 88, 99, 113, 135
Ronconi, Luca, 133
Rosa-Cornoldi-Sajeva-Manlio Savi, group, 144
Rosenzweig, Franz, 190
Rosi, Francesco, 64
Rosselli, Alberto, 68
Rossi, Aldo, 3, 6, 56–57, 77, 91, 100, 123, 135–139, 141–145, 178–181, 187, 192, 196
Rota, Italo, 166–167
Ruffolo, Giorgio, 101
Rykwert, Joseph, 201

Sacripanti, Maurizio, 90, 92–94, 101, 160
Safdie, Moshe, 80
Salzano, Edoardo, 83
Samonà, Alberto, 92–93, 144
Samonà, Giuseppe, 21–22, 27–28, 31, 38, 56, 65–66, 72, 77, 88, 92–93, 101, 114–118, 144
Samonà-Piccinato, group, 31
Santi, Danilo, 98
Saraceno, Pasquale, 75
Sarfatti, Sandra, 133
Sartogo, Piero, 166
Savioli, Leonardo, 78–79, 98
Scarpa, Carlo, 3, 21–22, 38, 46, 51, 88, 111–114, 117, 192
Scasso, Fabio, 173

Schawinsky, Xanti, 38
Scheurer, M., 180
Schinkel, Karl Ludwig, 142
Scimemi, Gabriele, 82
Scolari, Massimo, 145, 180, 201
Scotellaro, Rocco, 53
Secchi, Bernardo, 152–154, 158
Semerani, Luciano, 91
Sereni, Emilio, 91
Sinisgalli, Leonardo, 38
Siza Vieira, Alvaro, 171
Smithson, Alison, 119
Smithson, Peter, 119
Sordina, Francesco, 172–173
Sottsass, Ettore, 99
Stancanelli, Giuseppe, 155
Stella, Franco, 174
Sterbini, Franco, 6
Stern, Robert, 189
Stirling, James, 122, 127, 144, 171
Stoppino, Giotto, 89–90
Storoni, Enzo, 63
Strum, group, 99
Stübben, Joseph, 63
Sullo, Fiorentino, 84
Superstudio, group, 99, 177
Sylos-Labini, Paolo, 75

Tadolini, Scipione, 6
Tamaro, Gigetta, 91
Tange, Kenzo, 76, 156, 165
Team X, 58, 119
Tedeschi, Enrico, 6
Tentori, Tullio, 24
Terragni, Giuseppe, 26, 127
Tessenow, Heinrich, 138
Testa, Virgilio, 81
Teyssot, Georges, 197
Thermes, Laura, 101, 143, 178–179
Togliatti, Palmiro, 24
Tönnies, Ferdinand, 30
Torricelli, Angelo, 175
Trincanato, Egle, 66
Troeltsch, Ernst, 21

Vaccaro, Giuseppe, 46
Valle, Gino, 67–68, 172
Valori, Michele, 17, 24, 55, 69, 123
Van den Broek, Johannes Hendrik, 70
Van de Velde, Henry, 116
Vattimo, Gianni, 189, 192, 197
Vender, Claudio, 14
Venezia, Francesco, 175–176, 178, 196
Veneziani, Guido, 67
Venturi, Robert, 81, 90, 101
Verga, Giovanni, 115
Viganò, Vittoriano, 67
Villa, Angelo, 173
Visconti, Luchino, 20
Vitellozzi, Annibale, 69, 81
Vitellozzi–Castellazzi, group, 65
Vittoria, Edoardo, 35, 69, 72, 163
Vittorini, Elio, 4, 40, 75–76
Vittorini, Marcello, 45, 83, 89, 101, 110

Weber, Max, 21
Weinbrenner, Friedrich, 141
Winckelmann, Johann Joachim, 141
Wittgenstein, Ludwig, 91, 170
Worringer, Wilhelm, 126
Wright, Frank Lloyd, 8, 21, 46, 70, 79, 108, 112–113

Zanotti-Bianco, Umberto, 44
Zanuso, Marco, 54, 67
Zevi, Bruno, 5, 8–9, 20–22, 36, 40, 57, 70–71, 79, 82, 100, 117
Zocca, Mario, 6
Zoeggler, Oswald, 192

organic arch: 9

analizing arch: symptoms, not actual works: 195

✓ Arch: 197 ("completed nihilism")

Art & Arch pose question, Don't answer it 200.